I0800455

IMAGES
of America

GLOBE

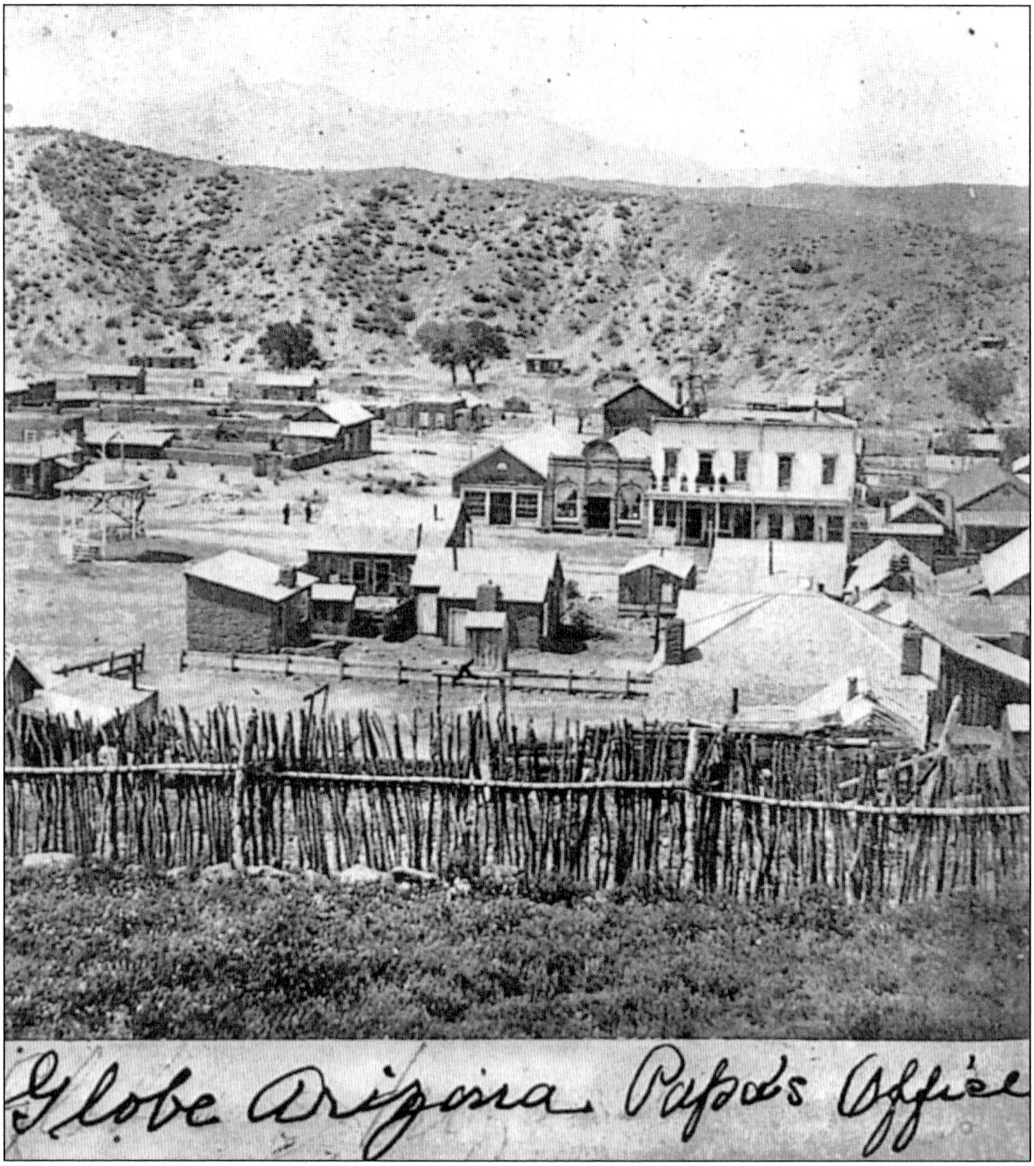

The town's original structures were located near Alice Gulch, the site of the first silver claims. Within a short time, the growth of "Globe City" extended for several blocks to the south. This 1882 view looks west across Broad Street to the Arizona Silver Belt building, the F. W. Westmeyer store, and the Pascoe Hotel.

ON THE COVER: Con Crowley had mining experience in Michigan and Colorado before coming to Globe in 1876. He worked in the local mines and prospected in his spare time. In 1899, he started several copper claims along Pinto Creek, west of Globe. These holdings became known as the Cactus Mine. The town of Crowley grew up around his crude log home along the creek. In 1910, the mining town was home to about 150 people, a post office, store, a number of neat white houses, and a school with 27 pupils taught by Myrtle MacGregor. The cover image shows workers at a headframe of the Cactus Mine in 1906. The mine and town were abandoned by the mid-1910s.

IMAGES
of America

GLOBE

Wilbur A. Haak and Lynn F. Haak
Gila County Historical Museum Archive

Arizona Historical Foundation

ARCADIA
PUBLISHING

ISBN 978-0-7385-4833-3

Published by Arcadia Publishing
Charleston, South Carolina

Printed in the United States of America

Library of Congress Catalog Card Number: 2007934176

For all general information contact Arcadia Publishing at:
Telephone 843-853-2070
Fax 843-853-0044
E-mail sales@arcadiapublishing.com
For customer service and orders:
Toll-Free 1-888-313-2665

Visit us on the Internet at www.arcadiapublishing.com

To pioneering miners and ranchers who, with their families, settled in southern Gila County from the 1870s to the present.
With our thanks—the Authors

Contents

Acknowledgments		6
Introduction		7
1.	First People: Hohokam, Salado, and Apache	9
2.	Globe: The "Queen City"	21
3.	Mining	39
4.	Buildings and Businesses	57
5.	Schools and Churches: The Four "Rs"	75
6.	Entertainment, Sports, and Diversions	87
7.	The People of Globe	105
8.	Law and Disorder	121
Bibliography		127

ACKNOWLEDGMENTS

Our thanks to the many people who made this book a reality: the board of directors of the Gila County Historical Society and Museum for allowing us the use of their library and photo-archives; C. M. and Suzanne Medlock and Paul R. Machula for editing for both historical accuracy and text; Historic Globe Mainstreet executive director Kip Culver for the introduction; and finally, Arizona Historical Foundation director Dr. Jack August for suggesting us as authors and foundation publications director, Jared Jackson, for making the project a delightful experience.

Unless otherwise indicated, all images in this book were provided courtesy of the Gila County Historical Society and Museum.

INTRODUCTION

Let me invite you to join me at the top of a hill. Not just any hill, but "G" hill, so named because of the enormous concrete letter "G" built on this steep Arizona slope above the community of Globe. This vantage point is a good place to take an overview of Globe and to read from the landscape the history that shaped it. From this point, one is impressed with the variety of lands sweeping in from all directions: canyons, mountains, desert, and tree-lined creeks and washes. In one direction you take in the canyons at the base of the forests of the Pinal Mountains. Here the ancient Salado settled before the Apache came to call this area home. From another direction, the bouldered, cragged hillsides give way to the slopes where the Old Dominion Mine once stood. There great wealth was pulled from this landscape. As the mine flourished, so did the city along Pinal Creek, and with both came the railroad along the same path. More neighborhoods, schools, and a variety of churches come into view. The historic commercial district is in the view beneath you from "G" hill, a medley of architectural styles and purposes. Most of the prominent landmarks that identified Globe a century ago are still there, giving Globe its defining character and authenticity.

What may not come across from the aforementioned bird's-eye view of Globe is its people. They may fade into mere dots on the landscape from this view. However, they are most important. Rugged, rough terrain requires the same characteristics in the individuals who dare to forge a home upon it. The human spirit has ever been and still is in Globe. Looking into this pictorial history, watch for the opportunities to see the faces as they appear. These are the people, a rich and varied mix of them, who came to Globe by birth or by some sagacious choice to find their lives.

It is my great pleasure to applaud the authors for their commitment to this compilation, and invite you to indulge in this glimpse of images of Globe.

—Kip Culver
Cobre Valley Center for the Arts
Historic Globe Main Street Program

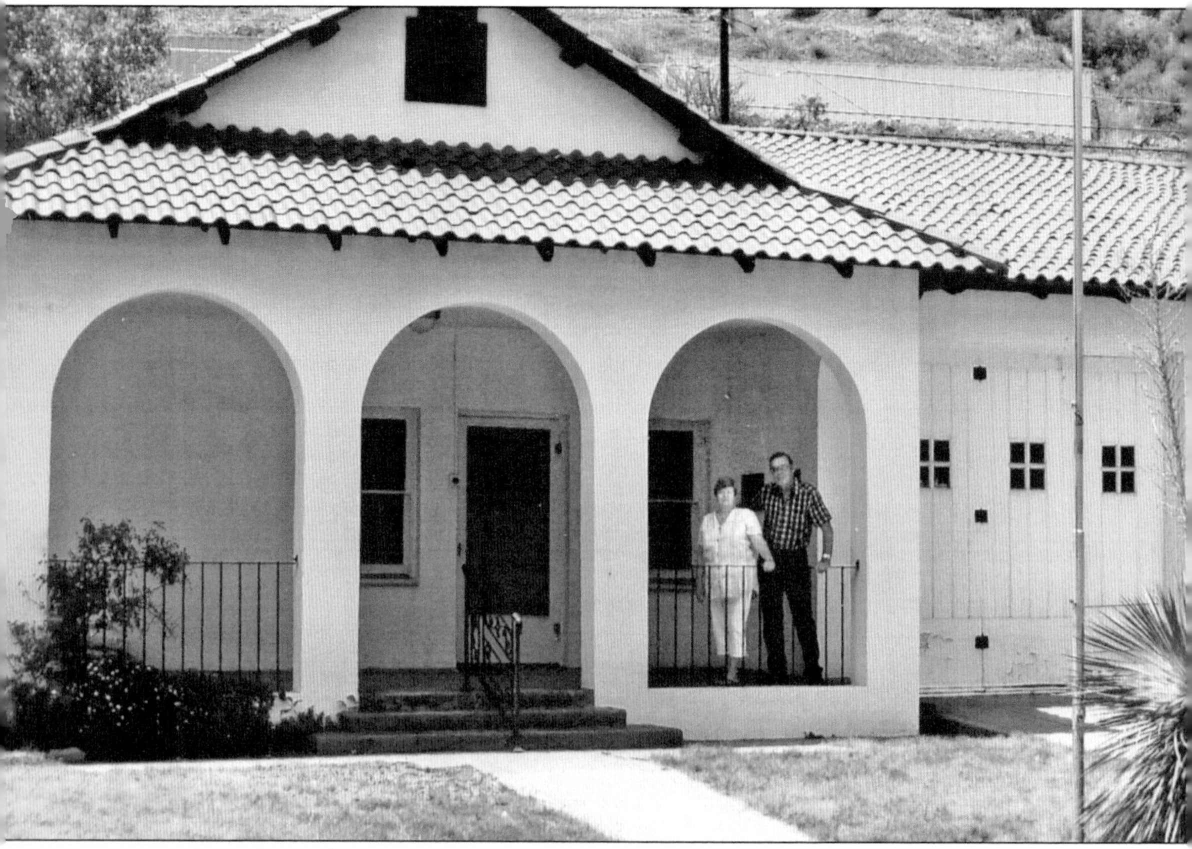

Pictured are the authors on the porch of the former Globe-Miami Mine Rescue Station. The Globe-Miami Mine Rescue and First Aid Association was organized in 1918. Its purpose was to provide uniform training and facilities, to render prompt and efficient service at the time of an injury, and to aid in fire prevention. The Mine Rescue Station opened in its attractive mission-style building the next year. The station closed in 1971, and in 1972, it was made available to the Gila County Archeological and Historical Society for use as a museum. The building was placed on the National Register of Historic Places in 1990.

One

First People
Hohokam, Salado, and Apache

Central Arizona's canal builders, called Hohokam, settled as far east as the Tonto Basin and Pinal Creek. Archeologists suggest they were in this area as early as 550 AD. They lived in pit houses and subsisted by irrigated farming, hunting, and gathering.

Starting in the 10th century, Anazasi and Mogollon people from northern and eastern societies migrated to the area. The melting pot society was formed by these peoples called Salado.

The Salado settled widely along the tributaries of the Salt River. In the Globe area, there were three major settlements—Gila, Pinal Pueblos, and Besh ba Gowah—plus hundreds of lesser sites. The Salado were farmers who grew squash, beans, corn, and cotton and obtained food, clothing, household items, and implements from desert plants and animals.

By the early 1400s, the Salado had gone elsewhere. Near the end of that century, people who called themselves "Indeh" wandered into the area. The Indeh were later given the name Apache, probably by the Spanish.

After many years of confrontation, a reservation was established at San Carlos in 1872. The Indian agency and an army camp were also located there. The Apaches, both willingly and by force, gradually settled on the reservation and learned a new, unfamiliar lifestyle.

For many years, newcomers passed through San Carlos on their way to Globe. By the late 1890s, the railroad ran through the town. About this time, the military camp was deactivated, and the reservation was opened to private enterprise. Traders and businessmen, some from Globe, opened a trading post, a hotel, and other establishments at San Carlos.

In the early years of the 20th century, a few Apache families moved to the Globe area. Clusters of Apache wickiups were located near Globe, in neighboring Miami and at Little Hollywood.

During the 1920s, construction started on Coolidge Dam in a box canyon on the Gila River. The town of San Carlos was destined to be covered by the water impounded behind the dam. By the end of the decade, the people of San Carlos were moved north a few miles to Rice. In 1930, the name of that town was changed to San Carlos.

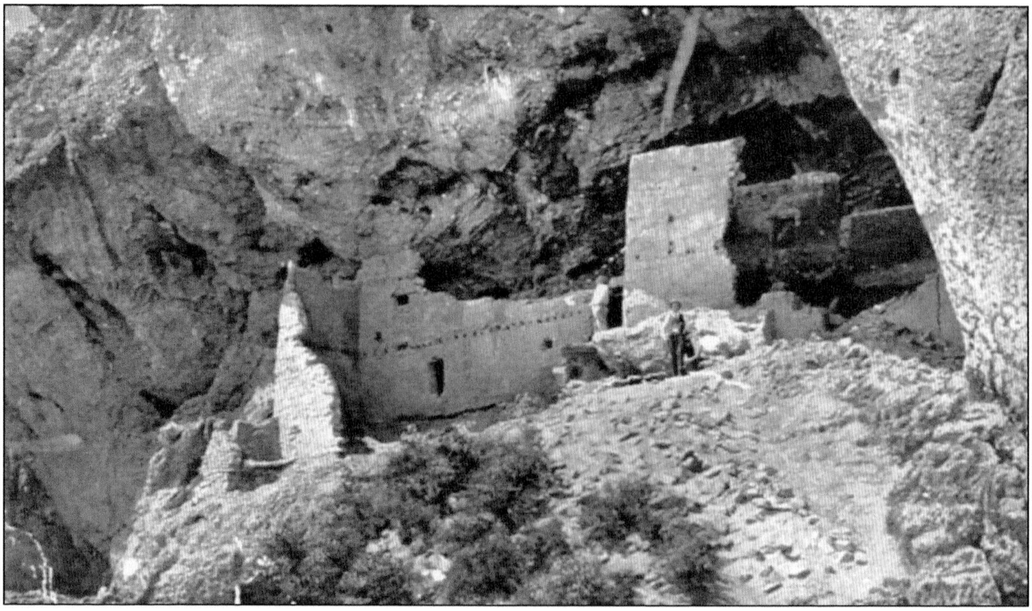

The Salado people lived in small compounds or villages in a wide area of east-central Arizona. Most of them were located near streams that provided ready access to water for crops and domestic use. The Tonto Cliff Dwellings (above) is a later structure, located here for defensive purposes. Although remote from their fields and water sources, cliff houses provided security and unimpaired views. Besh ba Gowah (below) was situated on a bank above Pinal Creek and consisted of over 200 rooms. Artifacts found here indicate the Salado traded locally, and as far away as the Pacific coast.

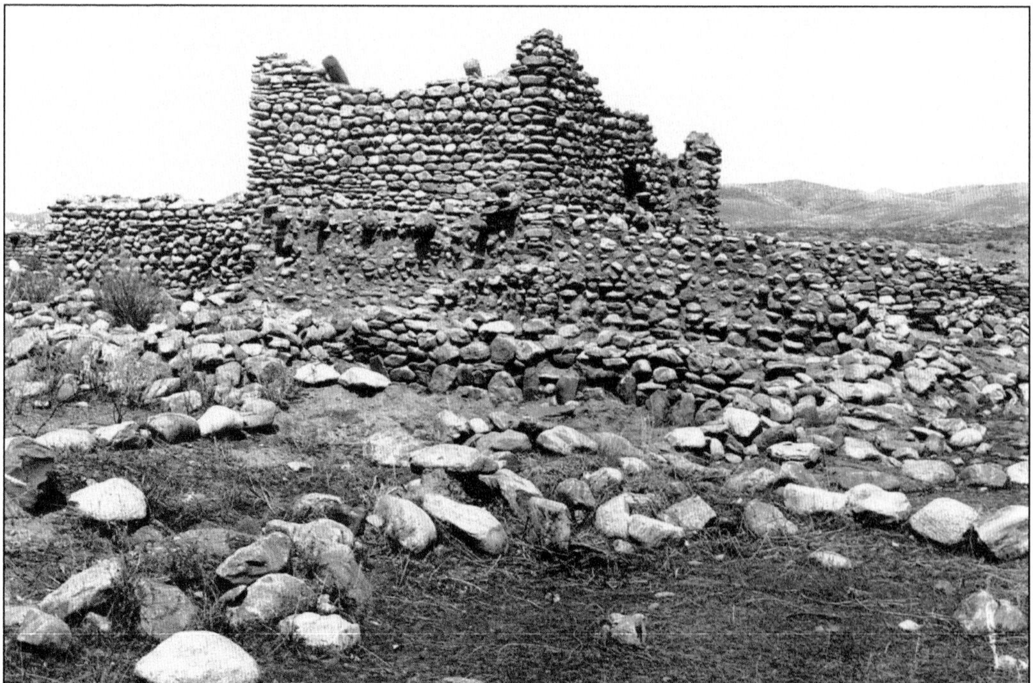

Adolph Bandelier made a cursory study of Besh ba Gowah in 1883. Some amateur work was done in the 1920s. Irene Vickrey came to Besh ba Gowah in 1935. Vickrey gave the ruin its name, an Apache phrase meaning "place of metal." For more than five years, Vickrey supervised the excavation, research, and artifact collection at the site. She died at age 35 in October 1940. She left behind extensive notes, a ruin that went virtually untouched for over 40 years, and many valuable artifacts.

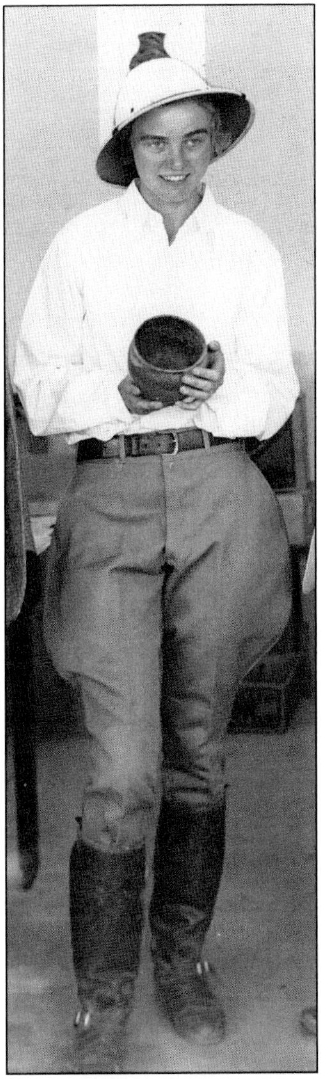

The crafts of the Salado were made from stones, bones, homegrown cotton, plant fibers, imported shells, beads, and clay. Best known is the Salado pottery, created primarily for domestic use, but also for ceremonial use and trade. Utilitarian unadorned redware was ubiquitous, but patterns from different areas developed into unique decorative colors and designs. The photograph illustrates examples of Gila, Roosevelt, and Pinto pieces.

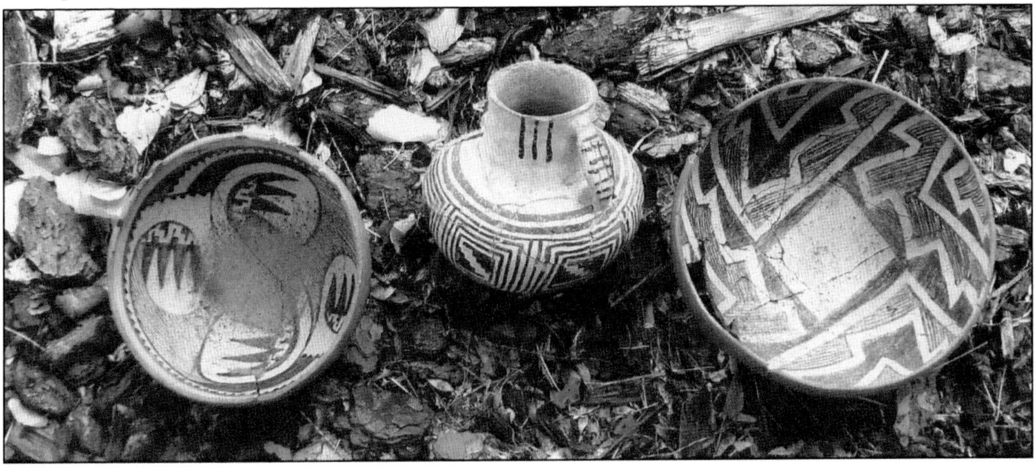

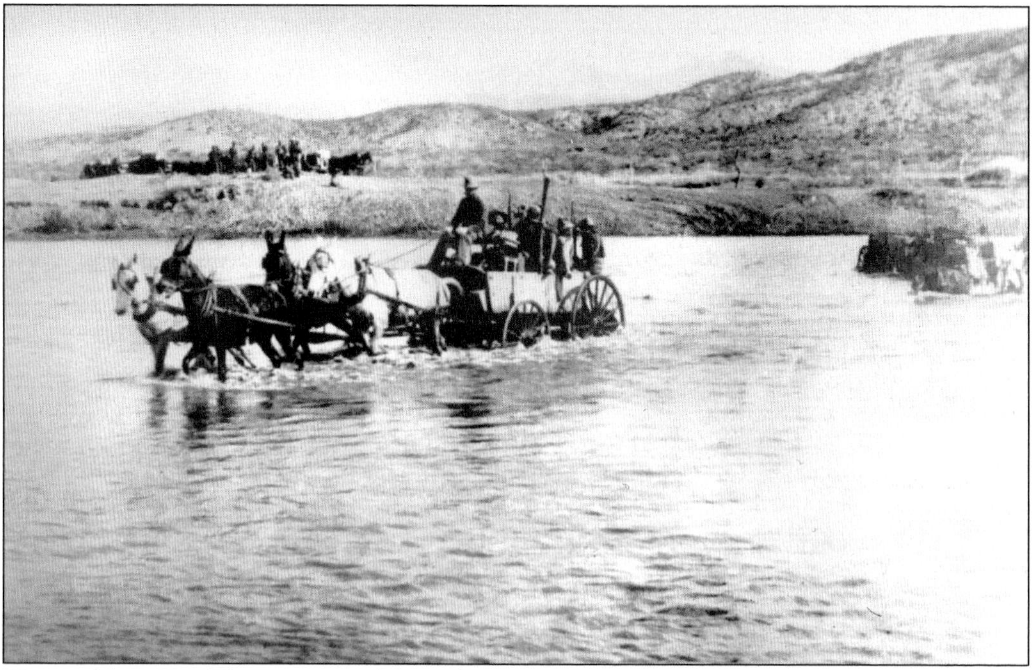

The road from Fort Thomas crossed the Gila River near San Carlos. Pictured are troops from the 5th Cavalry fording the river on their way to Camp San Carlos on the north bank.

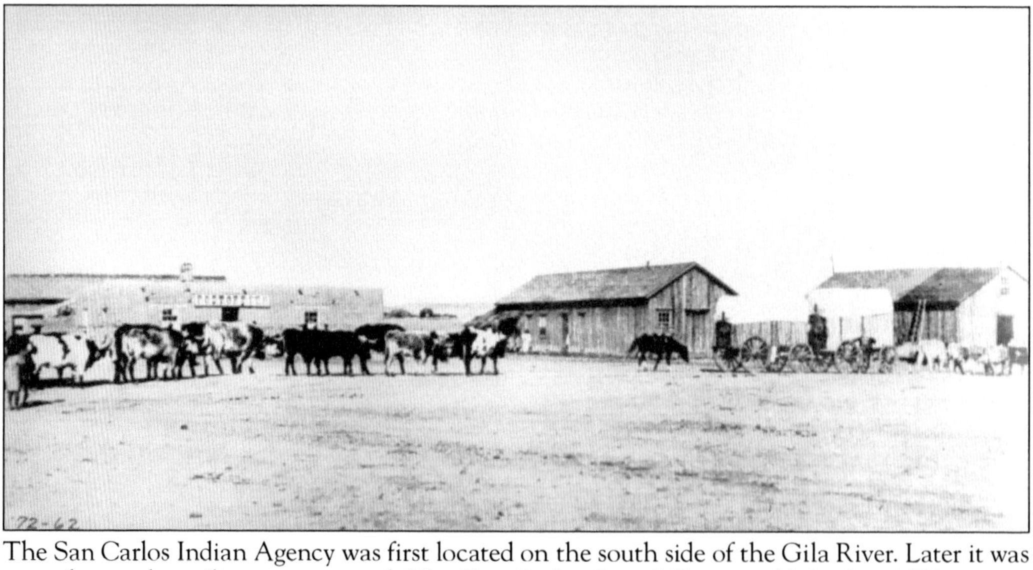

The San Carlos Indian Agency was first located on the south side of the Gila River. Later it was moved near the military compound. The San Carlos Post Office, established in 1875, is seen (left) in the photograph. Other agency buildings included the commissary, agency office, and living quarters.

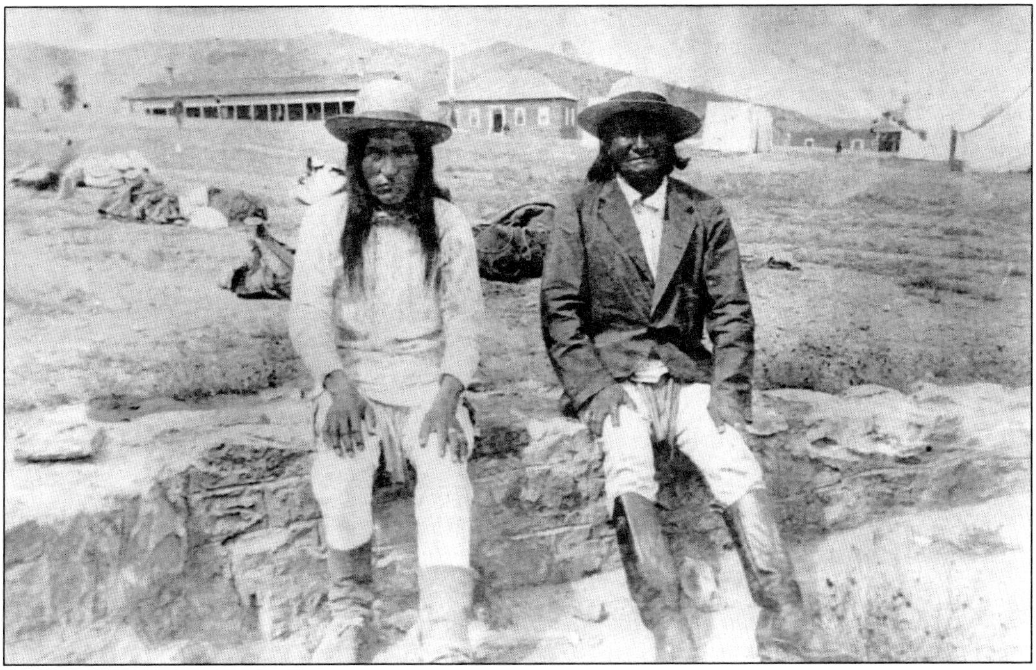

This photograph of Naiche (left) and Geronimo was probably taken after their final surrender in 1886. Naiche, the son of the great Apache chief Cochise, became an Apache leader after the death of his father in 1874. He later traveled extensively with Geronimo.

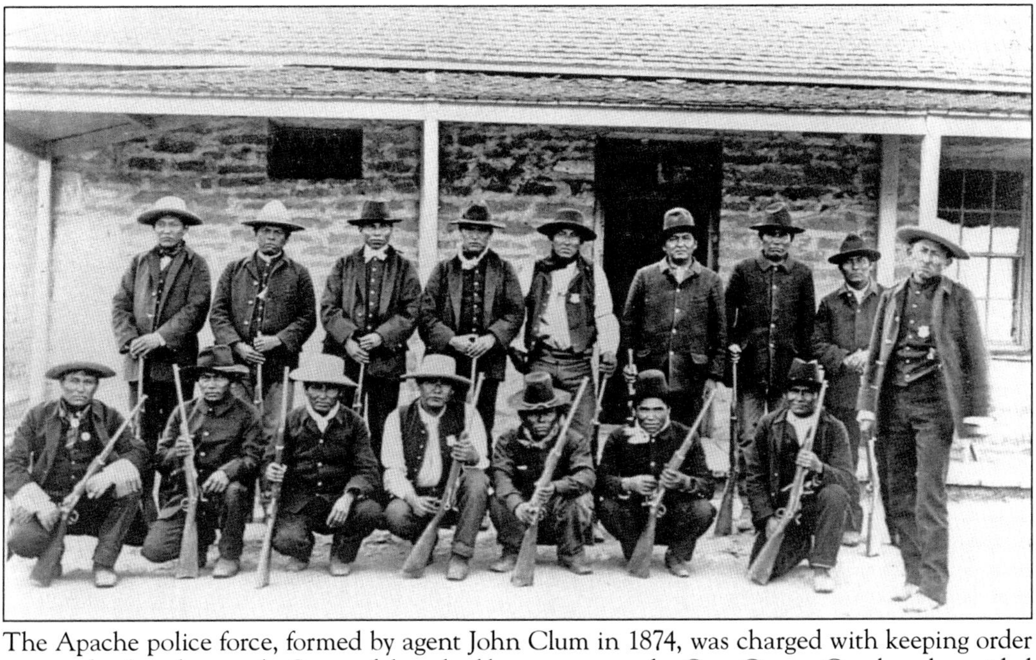

The Apache police force, formed by agent John Clum in 1874, was charged with keeping order among the Apache people. Some of them had been scouts under Gen. George Crook and provided experience. This photograph was taken around 1900 at the original San Carlos.

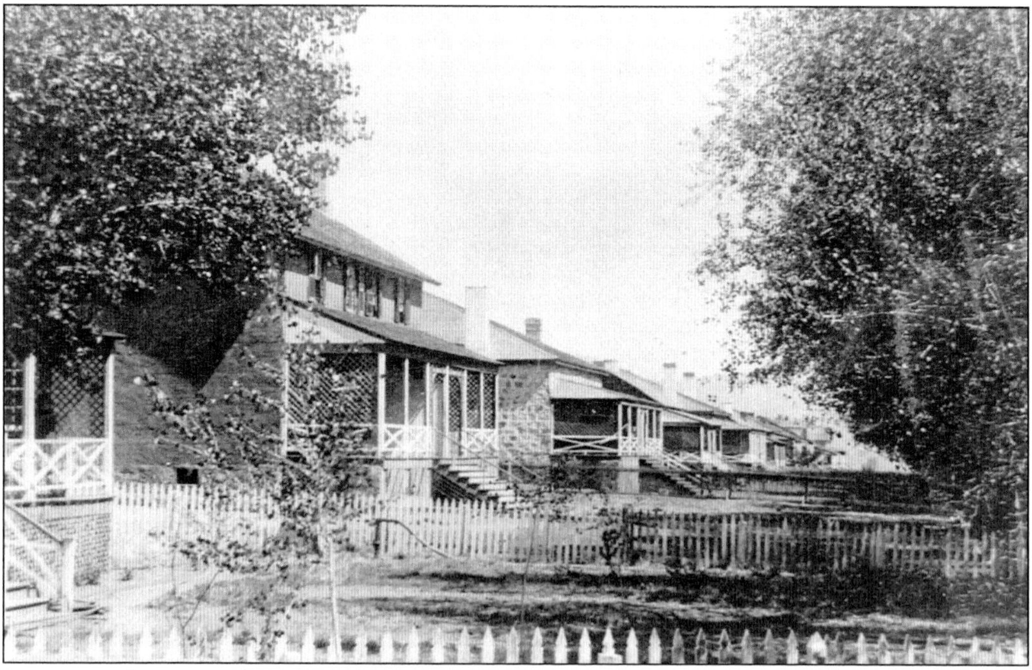

Living conditions in the enlisted men's quarters at Camp San Carlos were described as being inadequate and unsanitary. The officer's quarters, however, were "good and satisfactorily repaired," according to author Ray Brandes. As seen here, the officer's houses were large and attractive with enclosed porches and tidy, fenced yards.

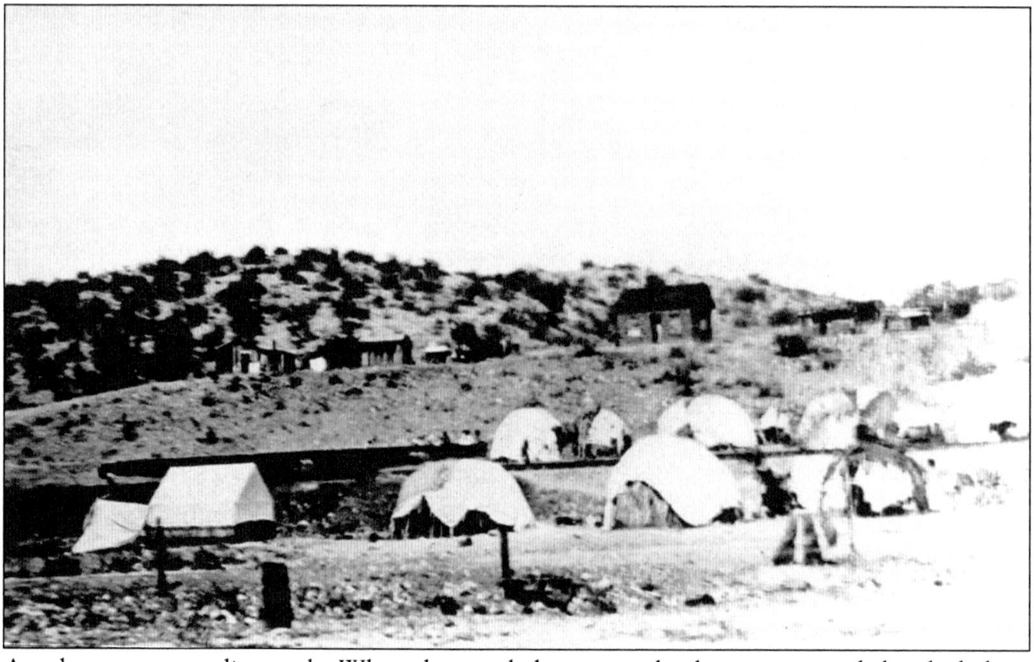

Apaches were nomadic people. When they settled temporarily, they put up crude brush shelters known as wickiups. On the reservation, many chose to live permanently in wickiups, which were substantially built and were usually covered with a tarpaulin or other heavy material.

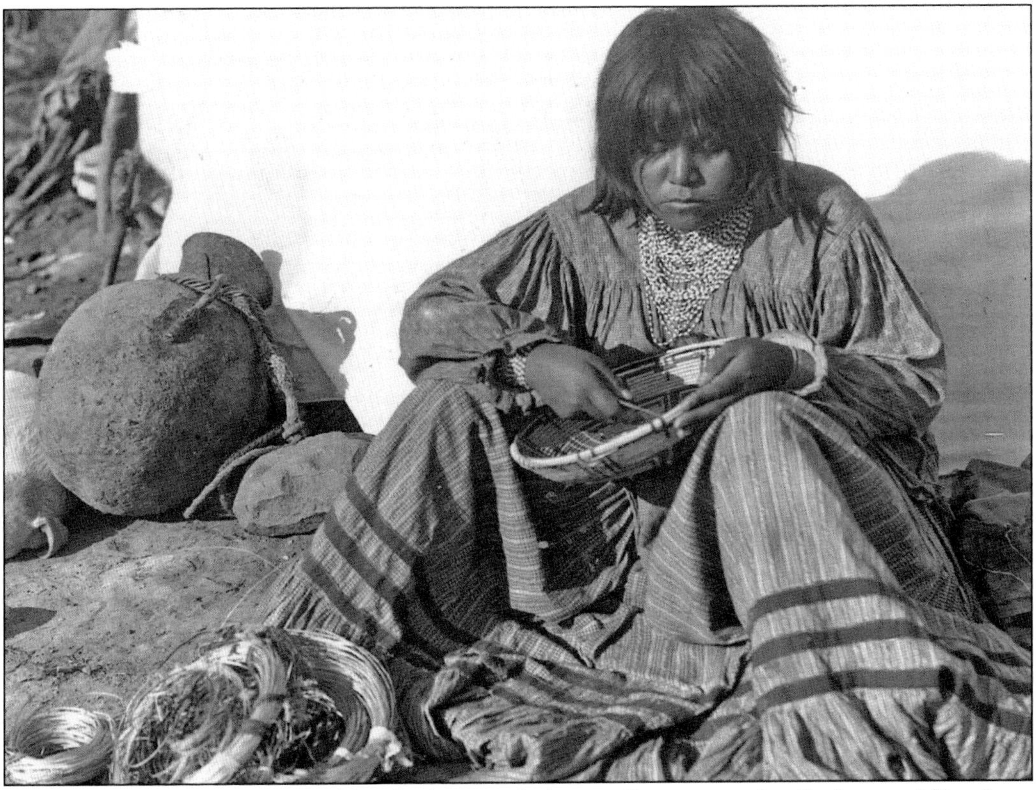

Apache women were weavers of fine baskets made from willow, yucca, devil's claw, and fiber from other desert plants. Initially they consisted of rather plain but useful objects such as trays, bowls, burden baskets, and storage. By the end of the 19th century, the women were producing baskets with intricate animal and geometric designs.

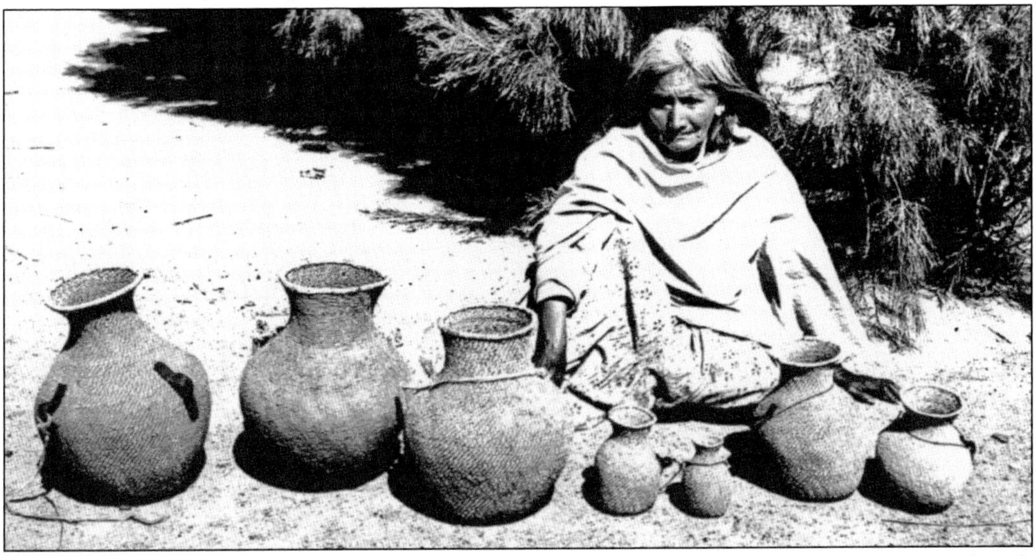

This Apache woman is admiring her handmade water jugs (or *tus*). The jugs are covered with creosote pitch inside and out to make them watertight. Each basket has flaps for attaching a carrying strap.

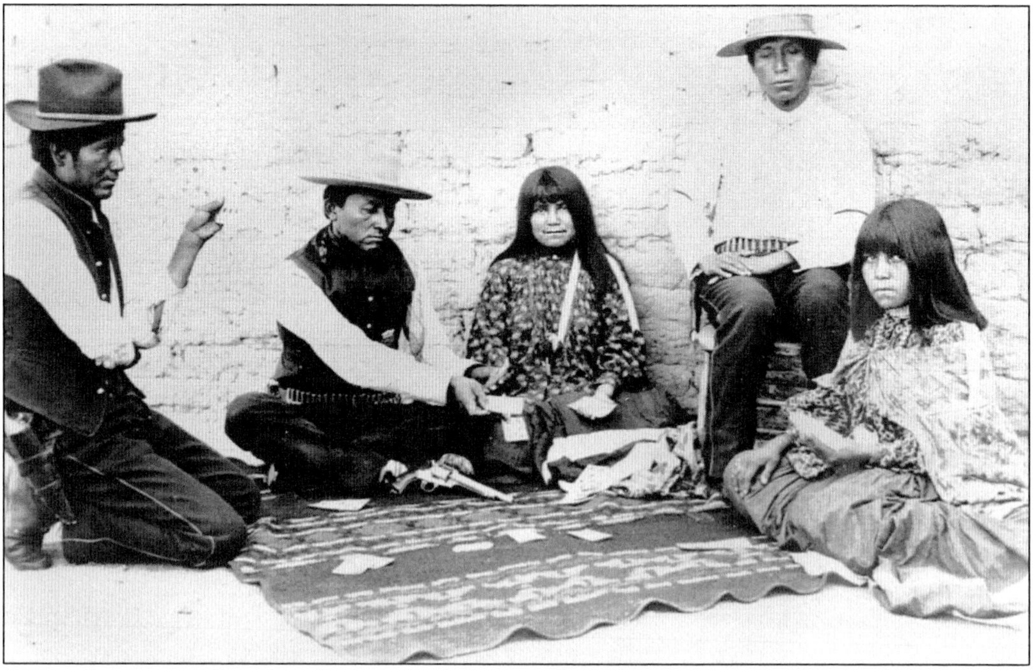

Pictured above are four Apache people playing cards and one observer. They probably learned this game from soldiers or traders. All three of the men are police officers, as evidenced by their firearms, ammunition belts, and badges.

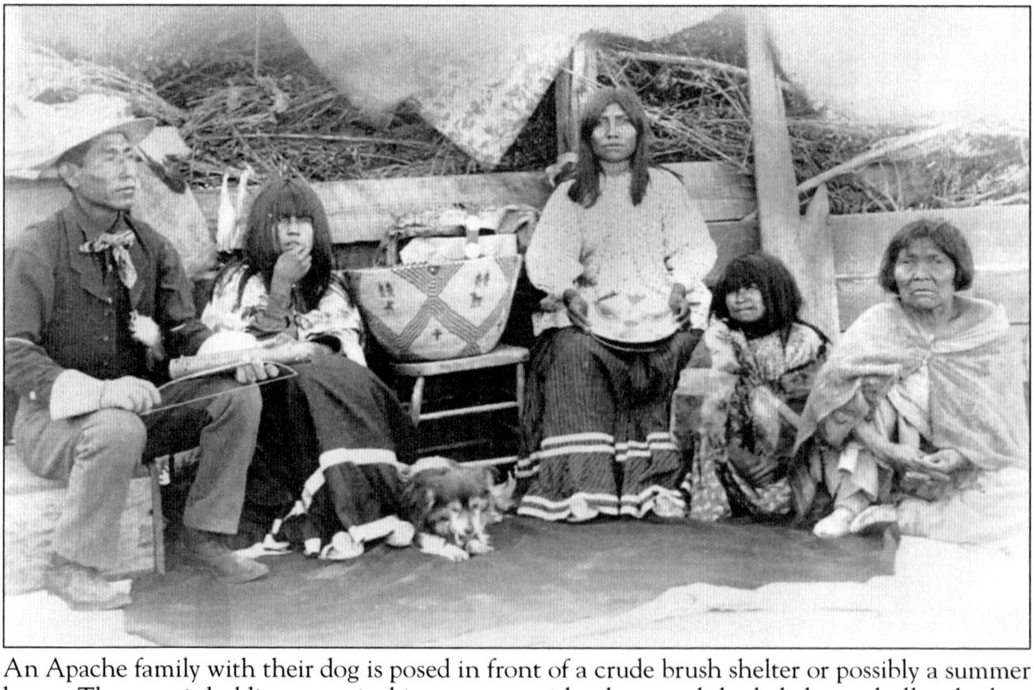

An Apache family with their dog is posed in front of a crude brush shelter or possibly a summer house. The man is holding a musical instrument with a bow, and the lady has a shallow basket. A large basket with a delicate design is displayed on the chair.

Once confined to the reservation, the women lost their traditional supply of tanned animal hides for clothing and footwear. The agency commissary began to issue bolts of cotton calico as a replacement and the simple, comfortable "camp dress" came into being.

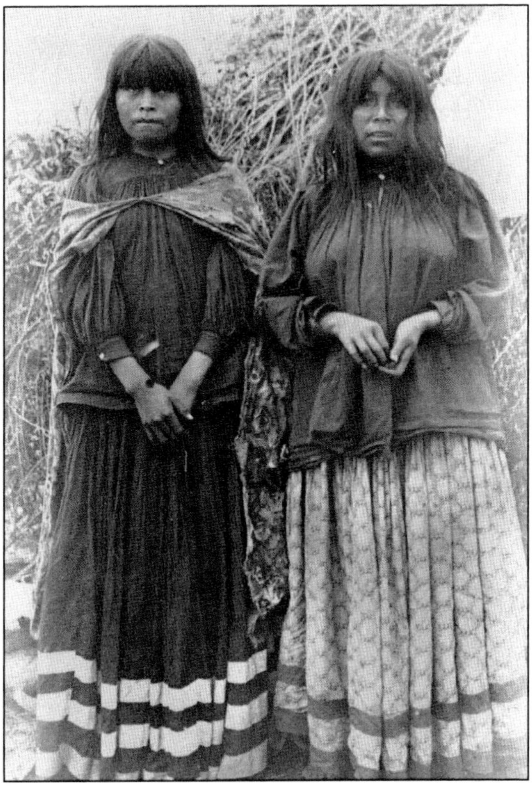

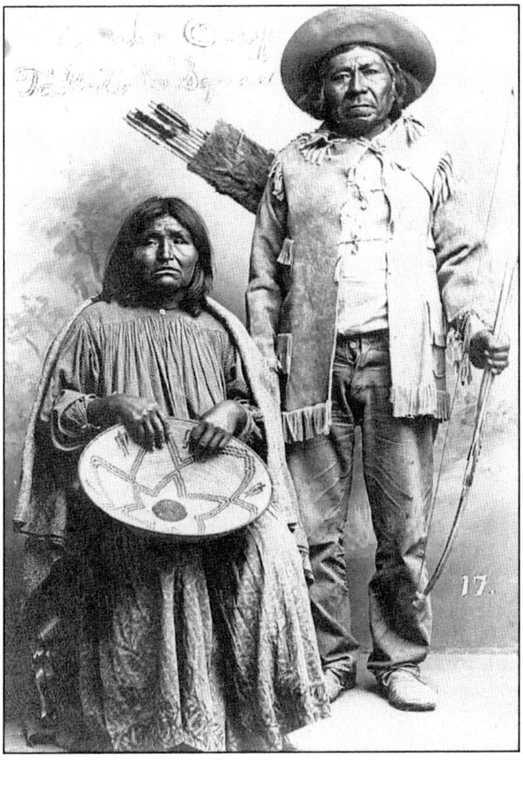

Talkalai became a scout under Gen. George Crook in the 1870s. After his scouting years, he joined agent John Clum's police force. He retired to Miami, Arizona, with his wife, May. On May 4, 1930, he was scheduled to be a guest at the dedication of Coolidge Dam, but he was not feeling well and never arrived. He died at home in Miami at well over 100 years of age.

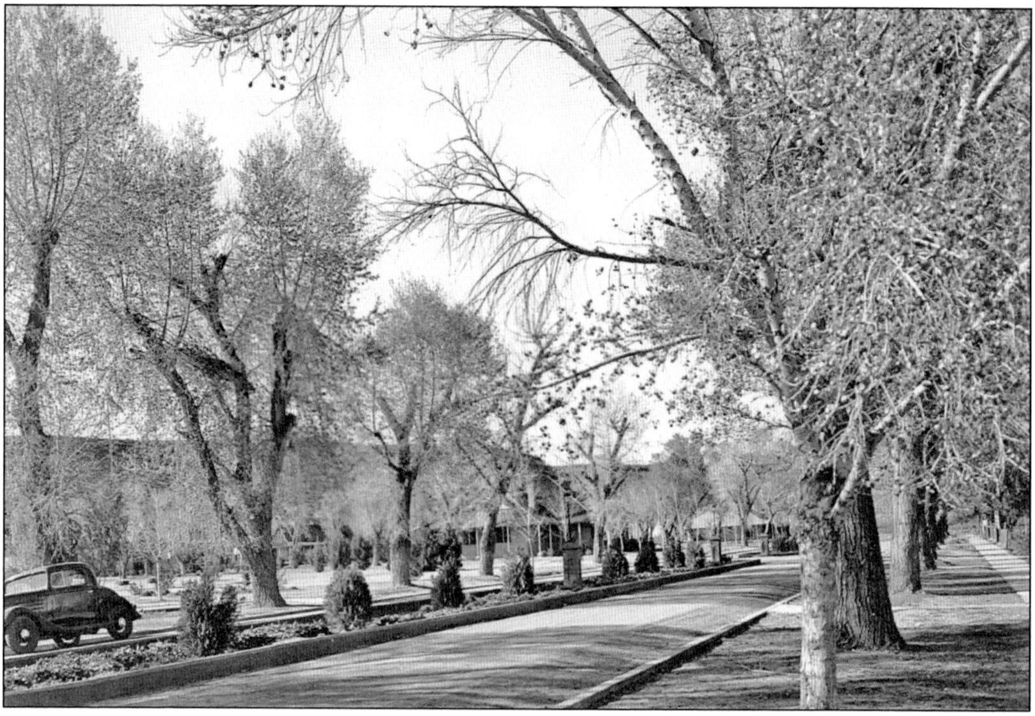

In 1930, the name of the town of Rice was changed to San Carlos. This tree-lined main street in the new San Carlos was home to the tribal headquarters, government housing, trading posts, the hospital, two churches, Rice Elementary School, and, at one time, a bowling alley.

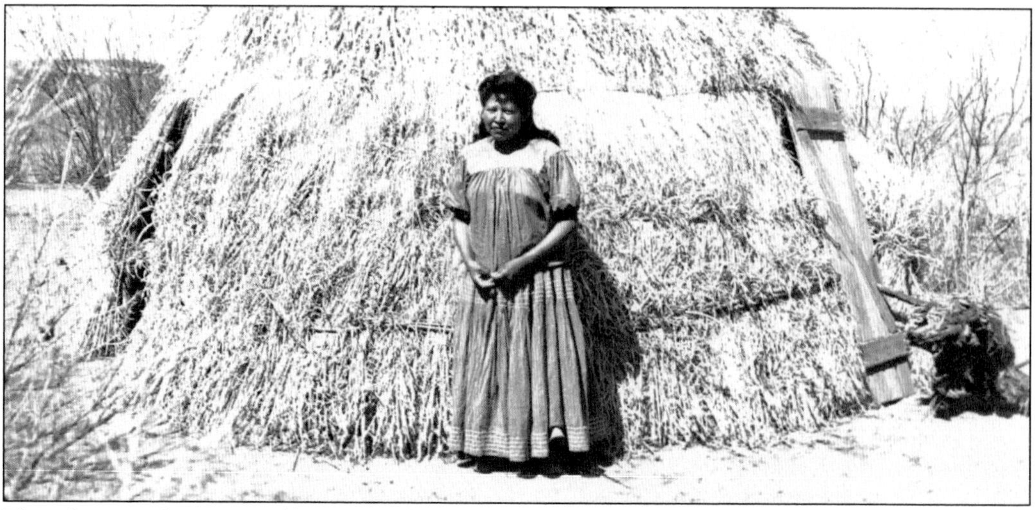

This photograph is an excellent example of an Apache wickiup. By 1960, nearly all of the wickiups in the San Carlos area had been replaced by wood-frame homes.

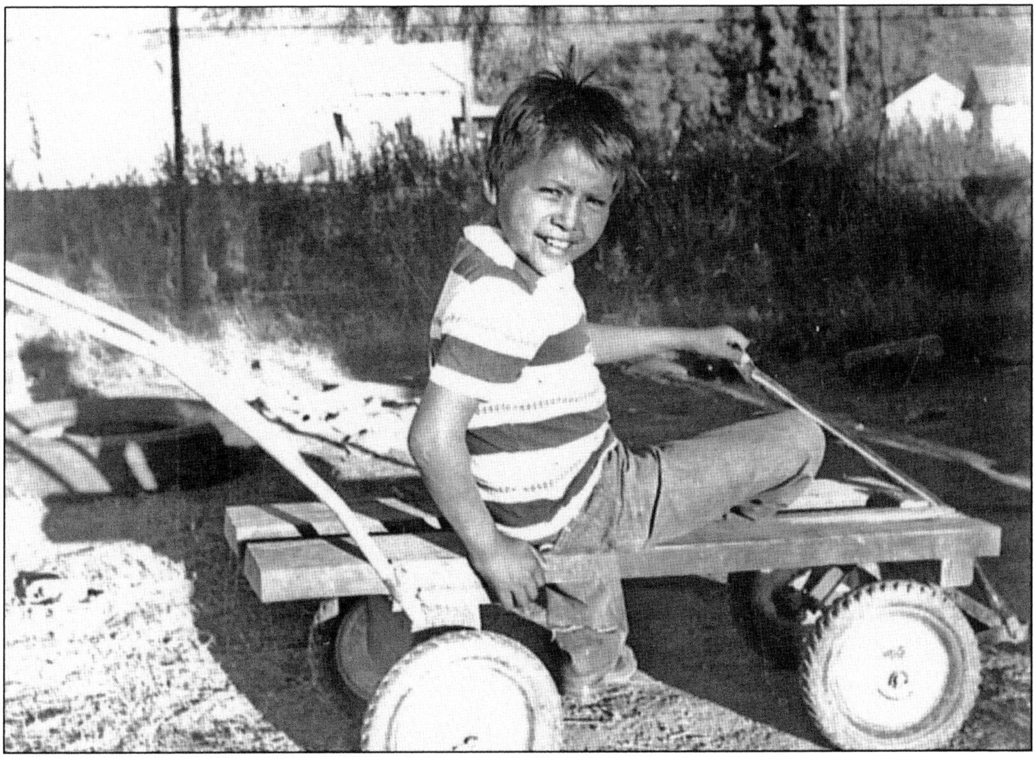

This young Apache lad seems extremely pleased with his new "woody" wagon.

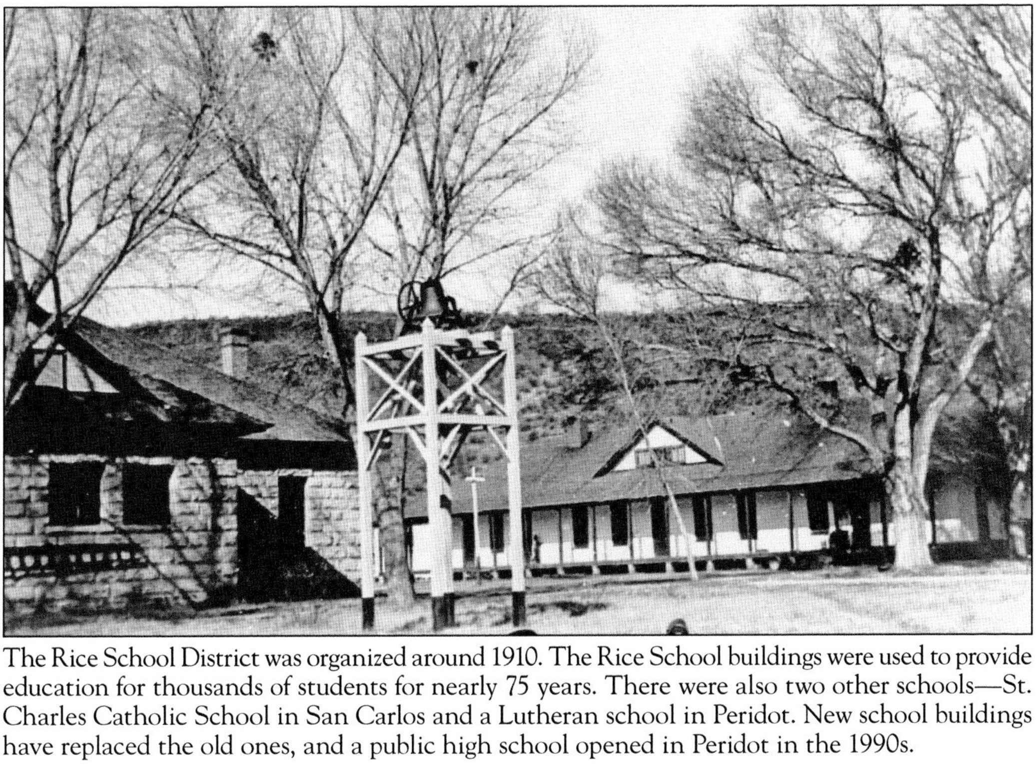

The Rice School District was organized around 1910. The Rice School buildings were used to provide education for thousands of students for nearly 75 years. There were also two other schools—St. Charles Catholic School in San Carlos and a Lutheran school in Peridot. New school buildings have replaced the old ones, and a public high school opened in Peridot in the 1990s.

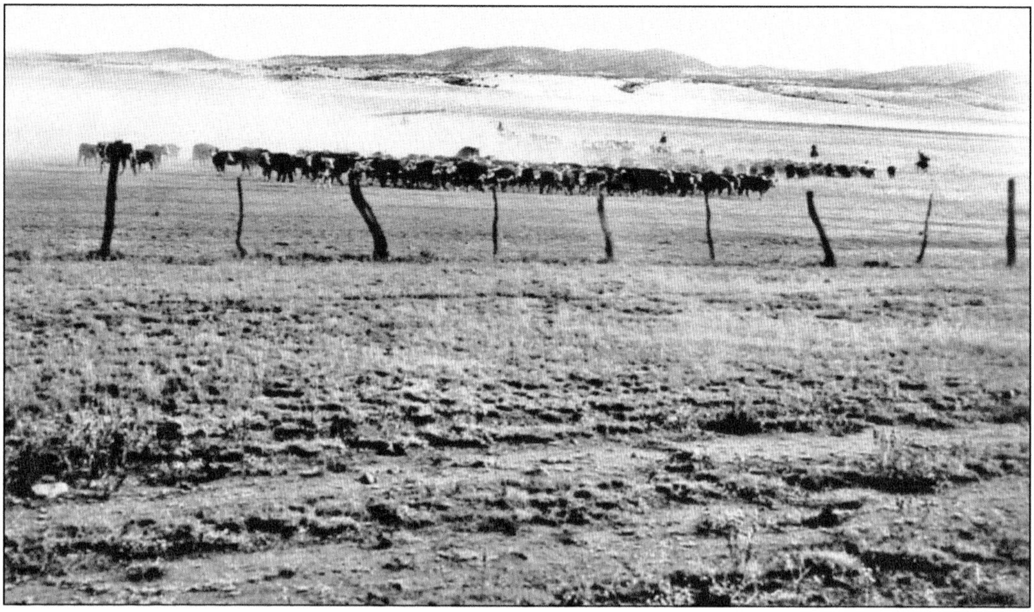

Cattle raising has long been part of life on the San Carlos Reservation. Initially, off-reservation ranchers had agreements to run cattle on Apache land. After the contracts were terminated in 1938, the tribe organized several cattle associations with ranch headquarters at scattered locations. Twice each year, Apache cowboys drove cattle to holding pens at Calva and San Carlos. Buyers came from many states to bid on well-fed Apache cattle.

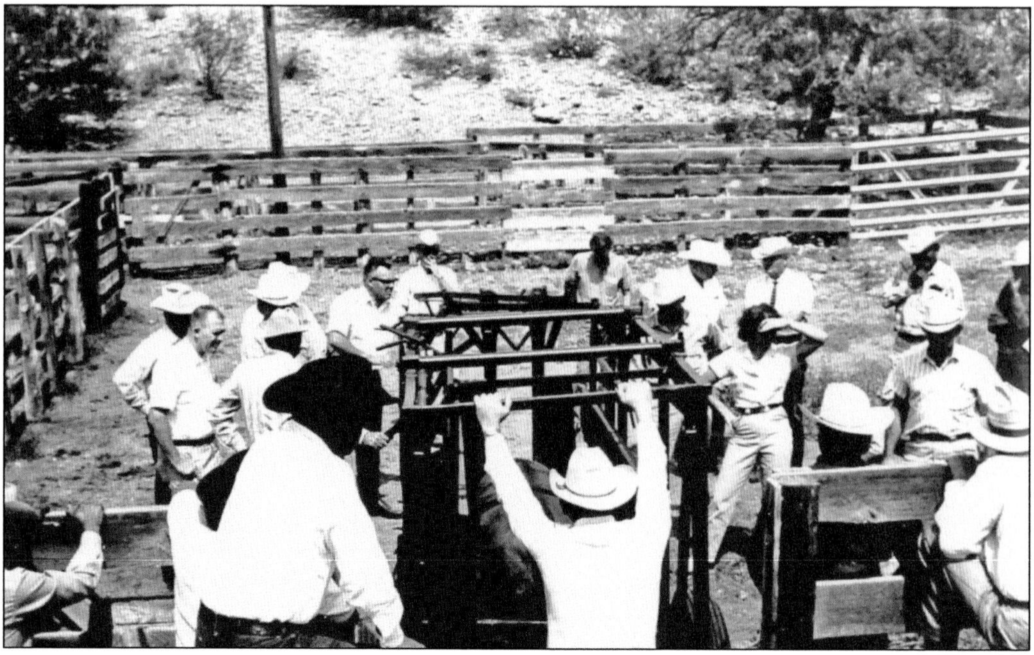

Two

GLOBE
THE "QUEEN CITY"

In 1910, the editor of the *Arizona Silver Belt* newspaper called Globe "the Queen City." This was a bit flattering, perhaps, but Globe was in its heyday. Business was thriving, several attractive new buildings stood tall on Broad Street, and the city's population was approaching 12,000 inhabitants. The past was exciting and the future full of promise.

Globe's first citizens were prospectors and miners who established a camp near Alice Gulch, the site of several silver claims. It was called Hammond's Camp until reports of the nearby discovery of a globe-like chunk of silver. The name Globe City was shortened to Globe in 1878.

Globe grew quickly. New businesses moved in seemingly every week. The post office was established in 1876, and the first edition of the newspaper was issued two years later. Cattle were grazing on the surrounding hills, and Globe became the place for shopping, shipping, and whiling away a payday weekend. By 1880, according to the Census takers' count, there were over 1,000 individuals. That same year, the Methodist church bell began calling people to worship. The next year, Globe was designated the seat of newly organized Gila County.

During the next 20 years, Globe continued to grow. However, the good times were interrupted seemingly every other year by recession, depression, mine layoffs, and disasters. In 1885, a fire destroyed the Pascoe Hotel and Arizona Silver Belt buildings and damaged several more. Nine years later, a second major fire left 39 homes and buildings in ruins. Flooding of Pinal Creek in 1890 resulted in the drowning of blacksmith William Middleton, and much damage was again done by floodwaters four years later. Six people died in Globe's worst flood in 1904.

On the brighter side, the community experienced a moderate "boom" in the early 1890s, brought on by expansion at the mine. Also, the Gila Valley Globe and Northern Railroad, after 20 years of waiting, finally arrived in Globe in December 1898.

The arrival of the railroad and a favorable economy brought on Globe's heyday. The first two decades of the 20th century brought new businesses and buildings, churches, schools, automobiles, and movies.

Meanwhile, two large copper mines were under development west of Globe. A sister city, called the "Wonder City of Miami" by the newspaper, was later founded six miles from Globe, the "Queen City."

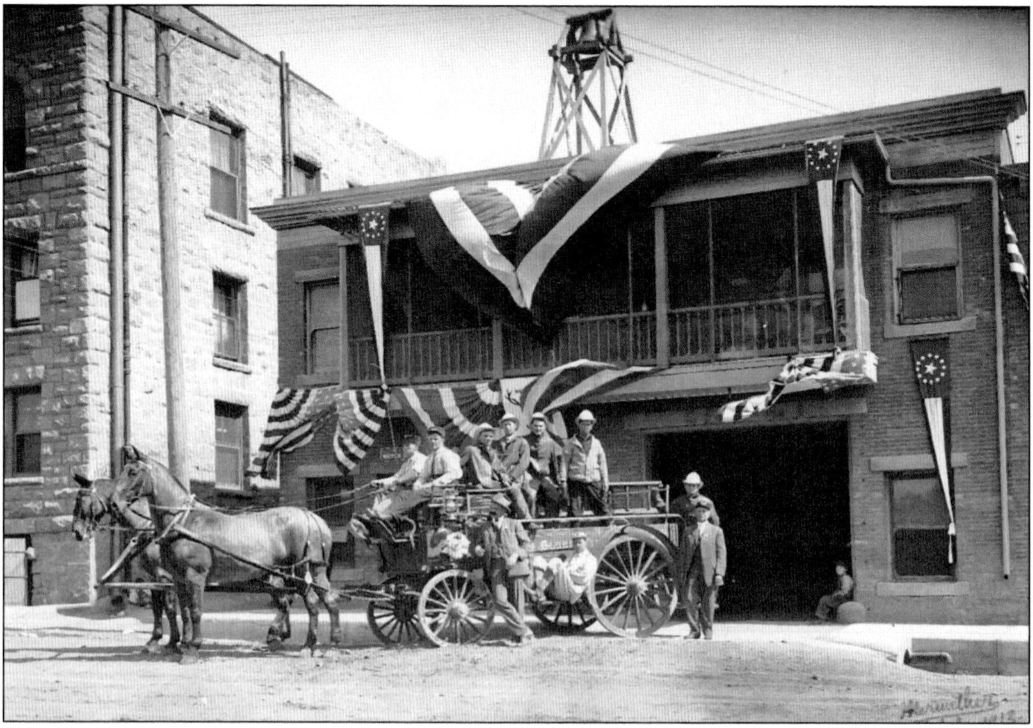

In the 19th century, very little could be done to put out a major fire. The sharply dressed volunteer fire department (below) shows off their brand new hand-pulled hose cart. The building on the left is the eight-sided hose house; it formerly served as a bandstand! Posed in front of the new fire station (above) is the recently purchased horse-drawn fire wagon. The balcony on the fire house was later screened and used as a sleeping porch.

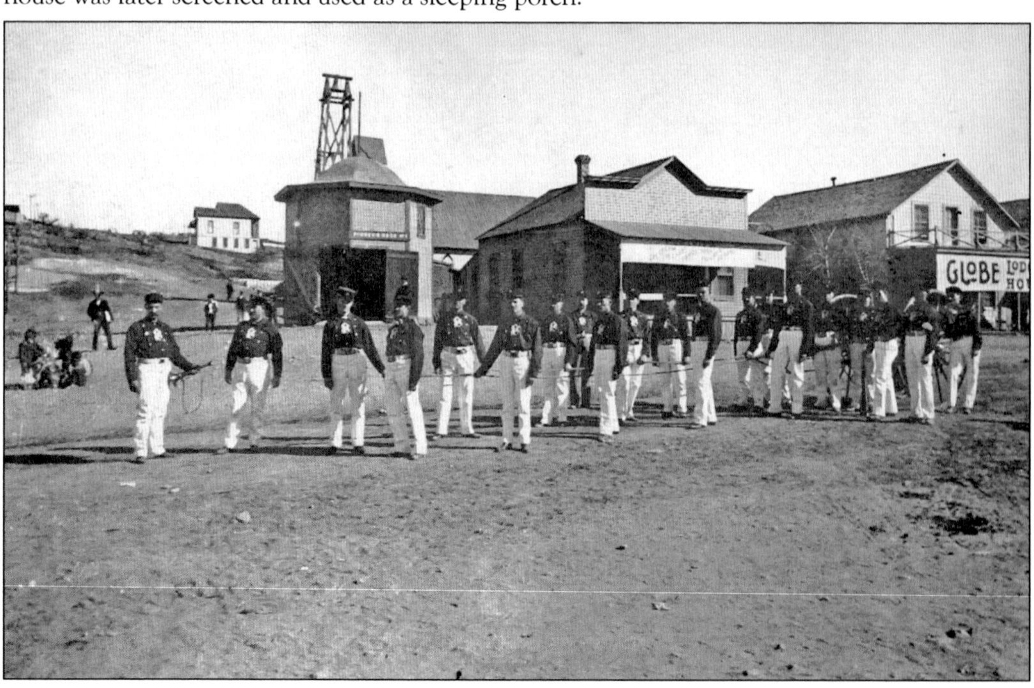

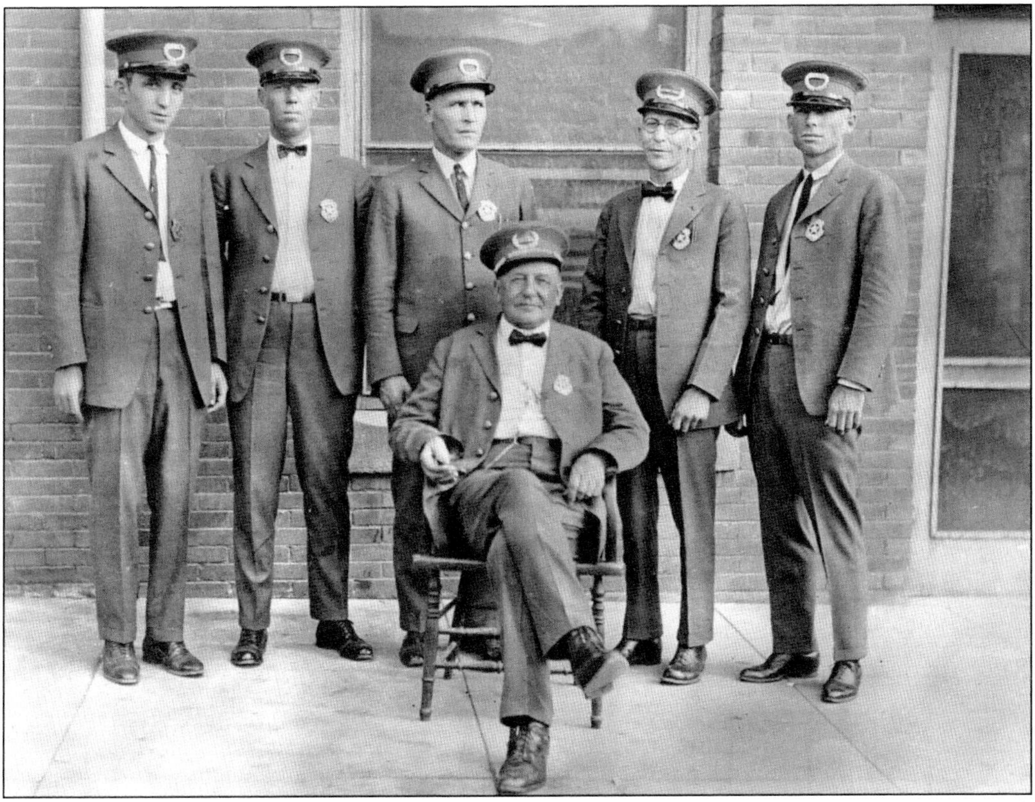

The men of the Globe Police Department, dressed in neat suits, white shirts, and ties, pose with the chief of police.

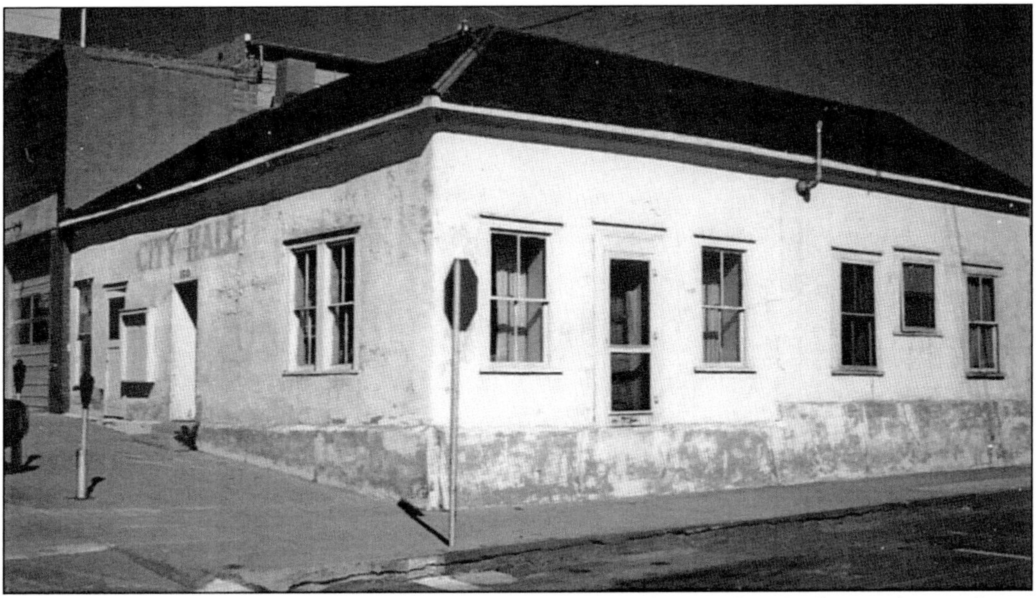

In the 1880s, this adobe building was the first hospital in Globe. After the hospital moved into bigger-and-better quarters, this building served as city hall for many years. In 1972, the building was razed to make room for the headquarters of the Globe Police Department.

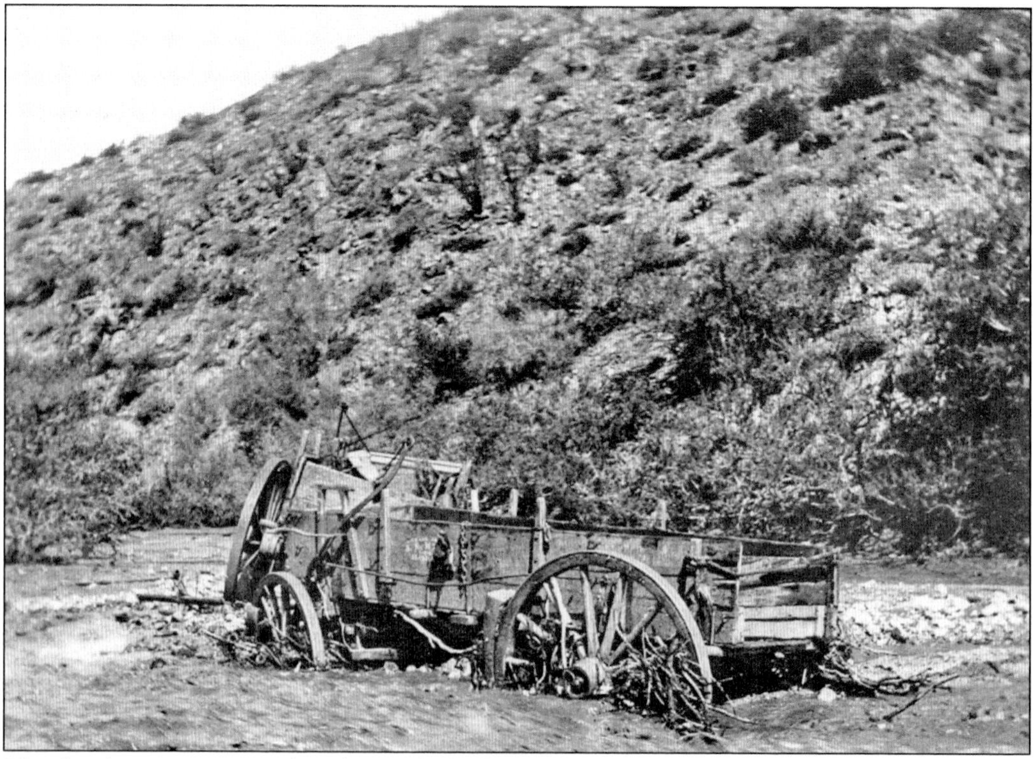

This freight wagon is mired in the mud of a flooded Pinal Creek. The driver apparently made it to shore, but a horse was injured and drowned.

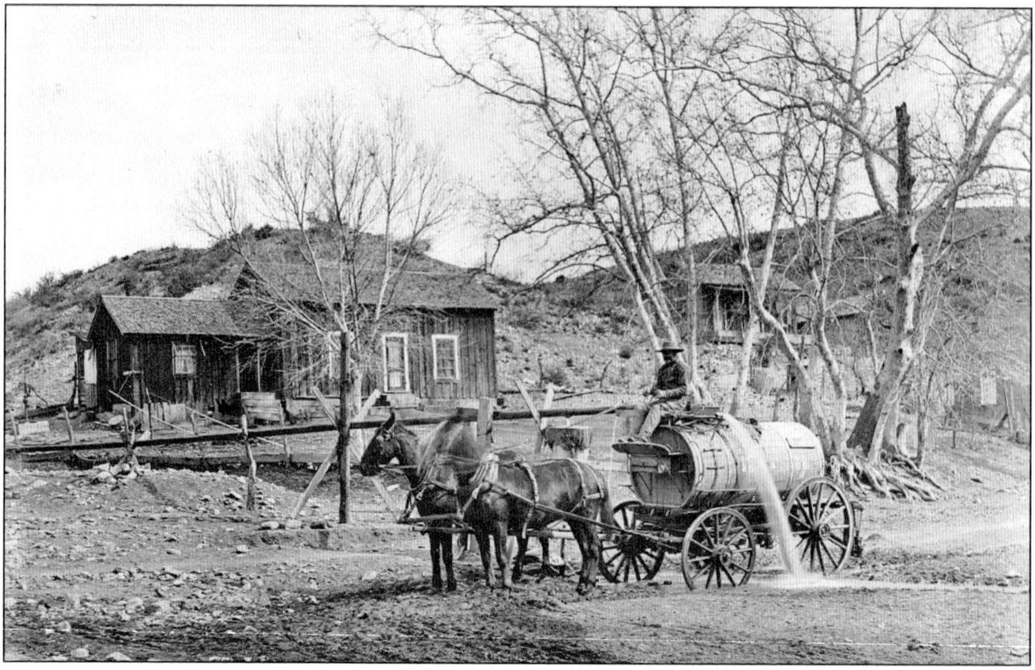

The man in the driver's seat seems oblivious of the fact that the water from the pipe is flowing over, not into, the water tank.

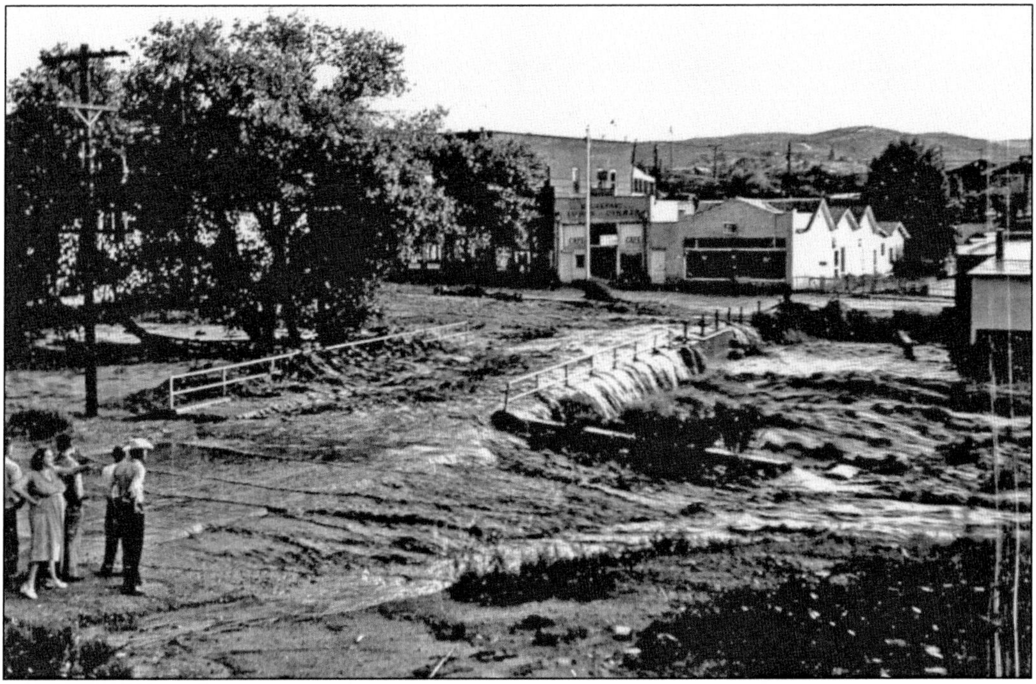

Flooding of Pinal Creek and its tributaries was an all too frequent occurrence. The 1954 flood did significant damage in Globe. The photograph above shows the water flowing over the vehicular bridge at Broad and Yuma Streets. The flood aftermath photograph below demonstrates the power of the 1954 flood. Four of the trucks pictured belonged to the Mountain States Telephone and Telegraph Company.

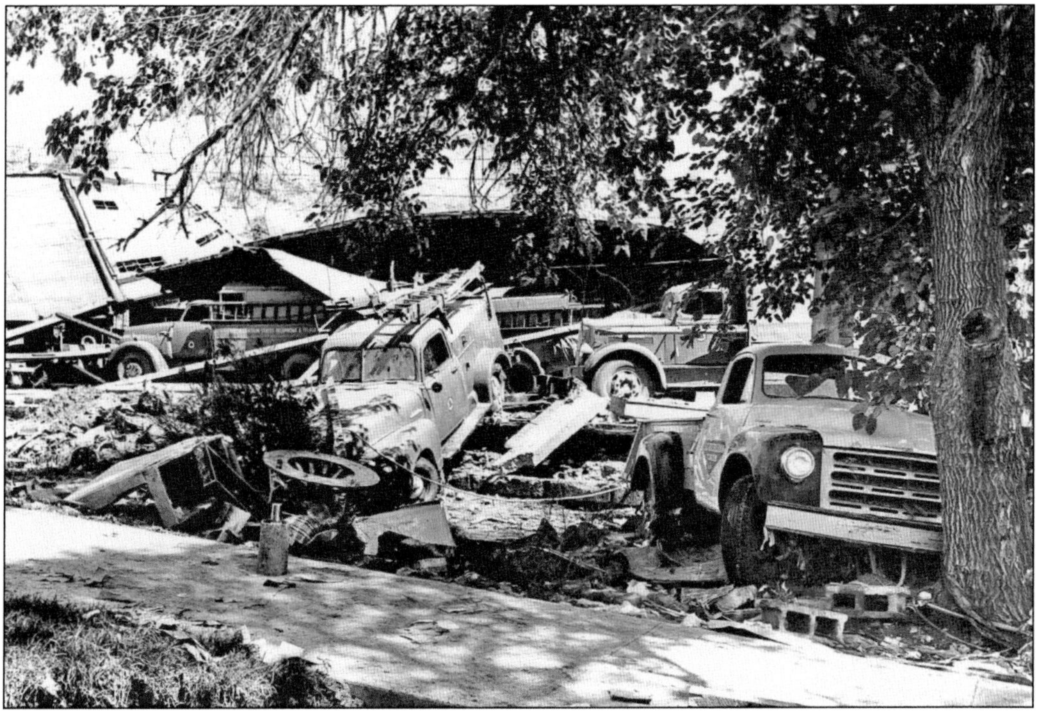

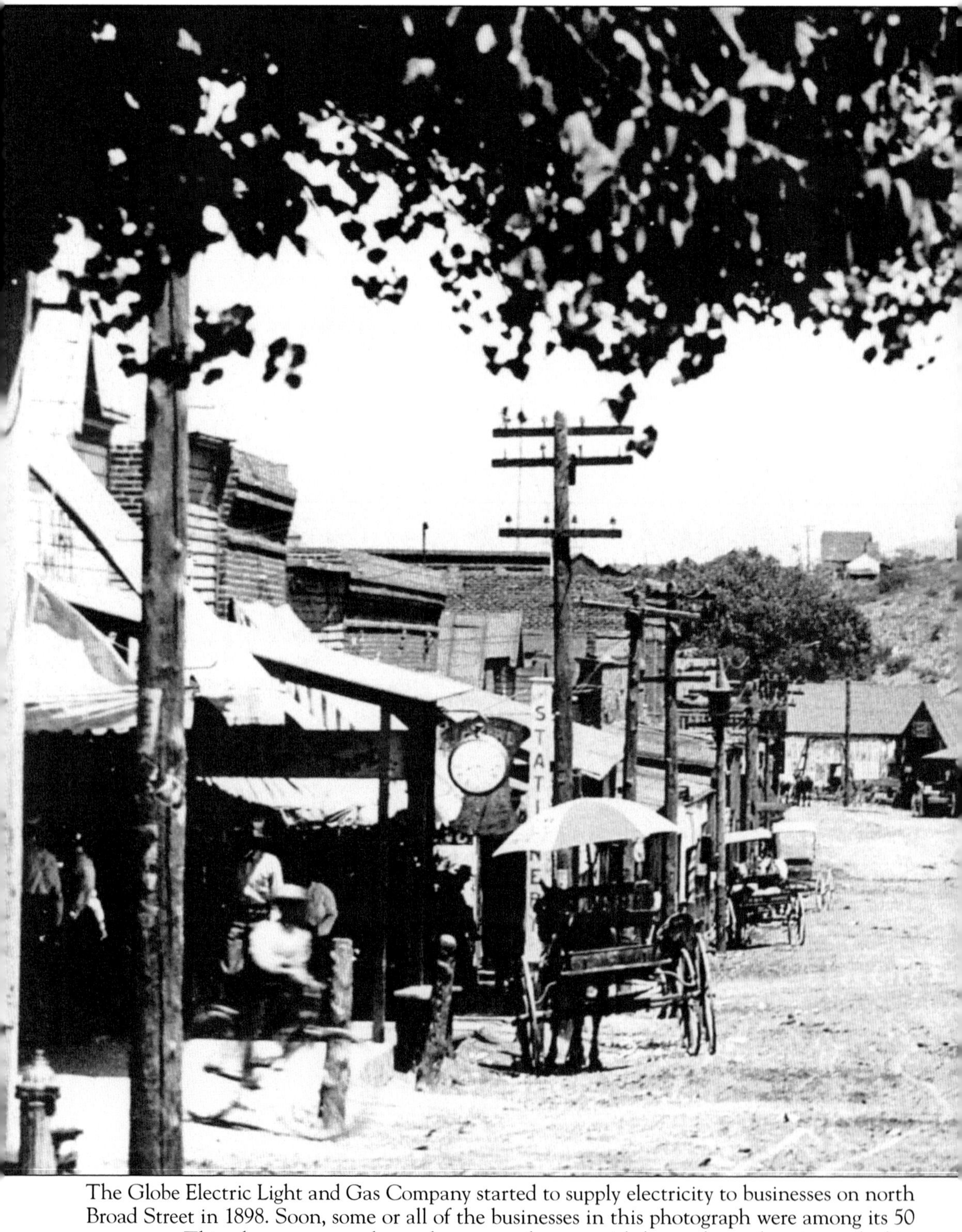

The Globe Electric Light and Gas Company started to supply electricity to businesses on north Broad Street in 1898. Soon, some or all of the businesses in this photograph were among its 50 customers. This pleasant scene shows the unpaved street with horse-drawn buggies parked in

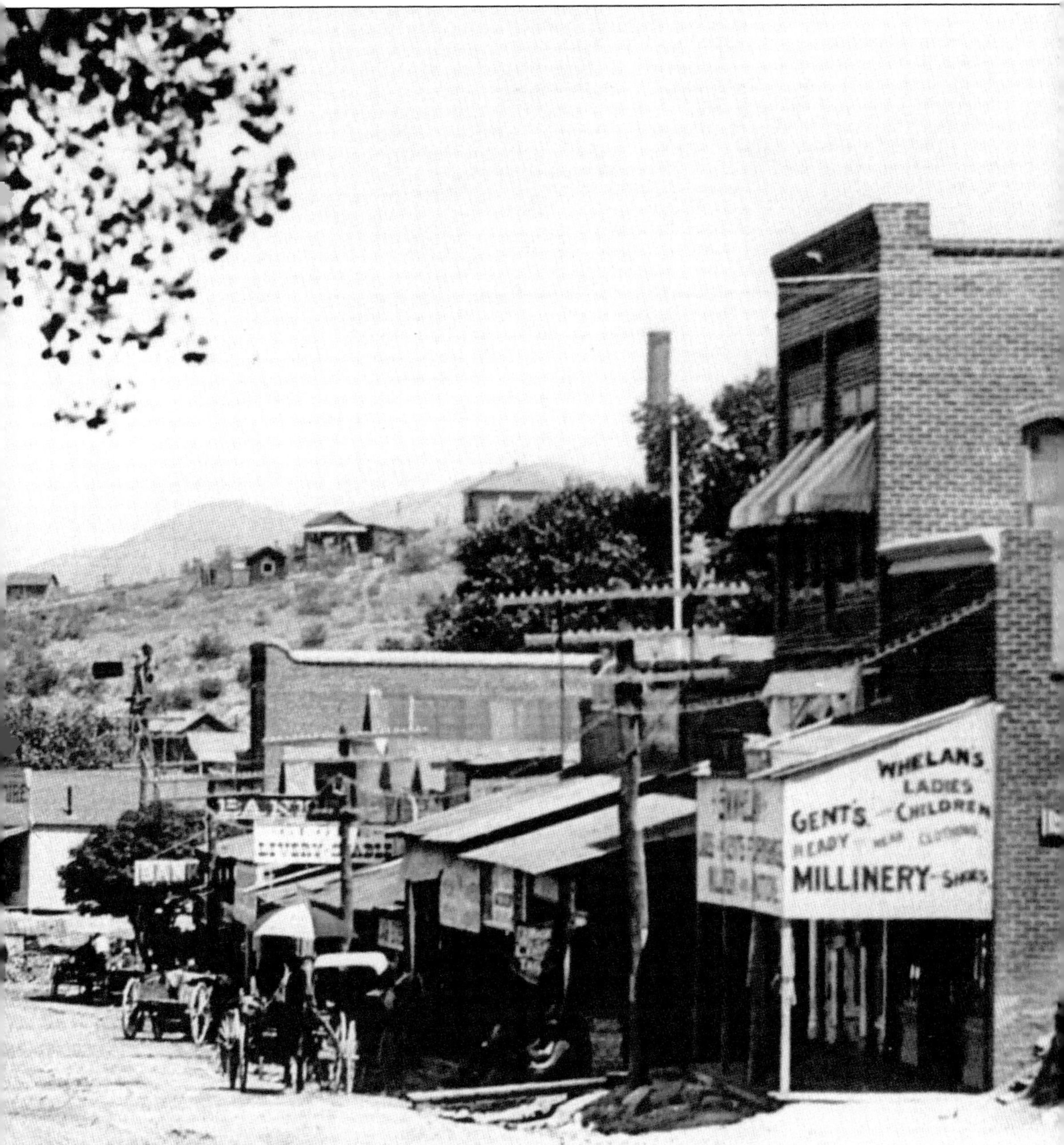

front of several places of business. On the right, Whelan's Store sold ladies', children's, and gents' clothing and accessories. Beyond the store are the Globe Livery Stable and a bank. Among the shops on the left is a stationer where the hanging clock is located.

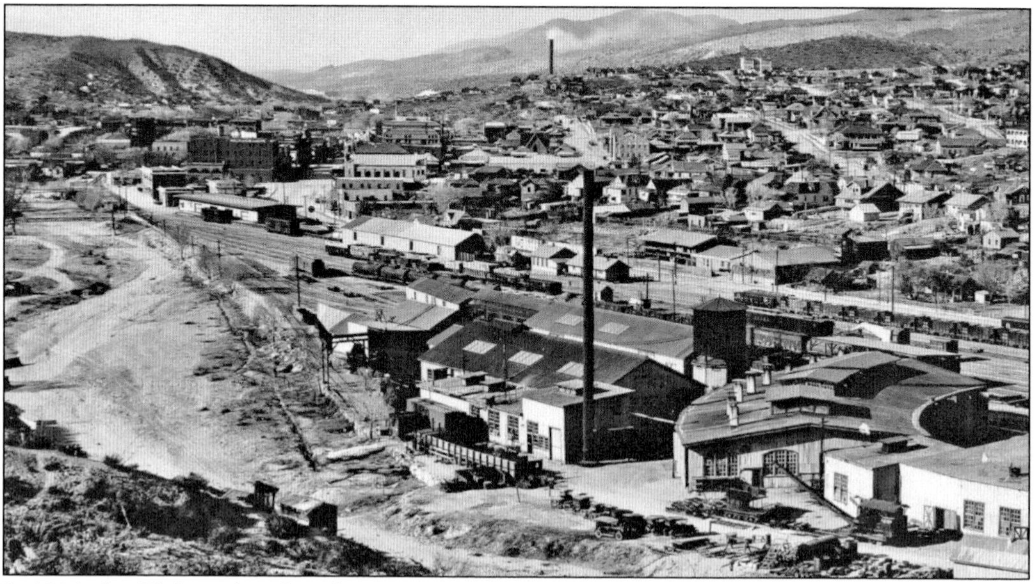

In 1924, the Globe railroad yard consisted of the roundhouse (right), the adjacent machine shop, warehouses beyond the tracks, and other buildings. The smokestack of the smelter at the Old Dominion Mine can be seen in the distance.

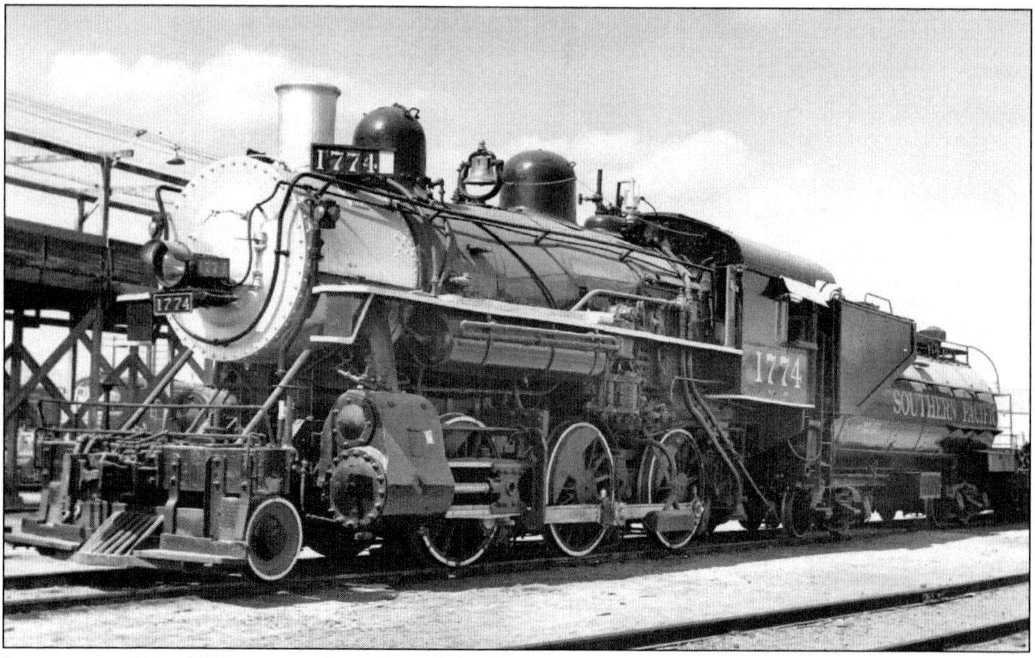

Locomotive No. 1774 operated on the Globe branch of the Southern Pacific Railroad for many years before it was retired to the scrap yard in Sacramento. The people of Globe loved the faithful old engine and petitioned Southern Pacific to return it to Globe. Since the mid-1950s, it has been displayed in a Globe city park.

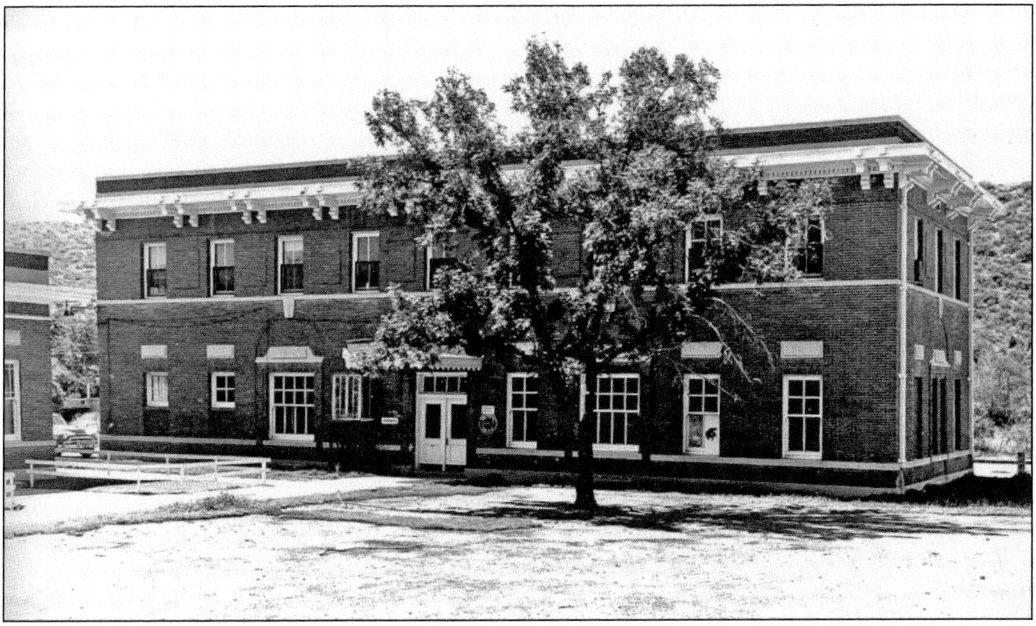

Globe's first railroad depot was a small wooden structure that soon proved to be inadequate. In 1916, a new two-story depot was built in downtown Globe. The next year, the adjacent restaurant and express office were added. After World War II, passenger usage dwindled, and the passenger train made its last run on December 31, 1953.

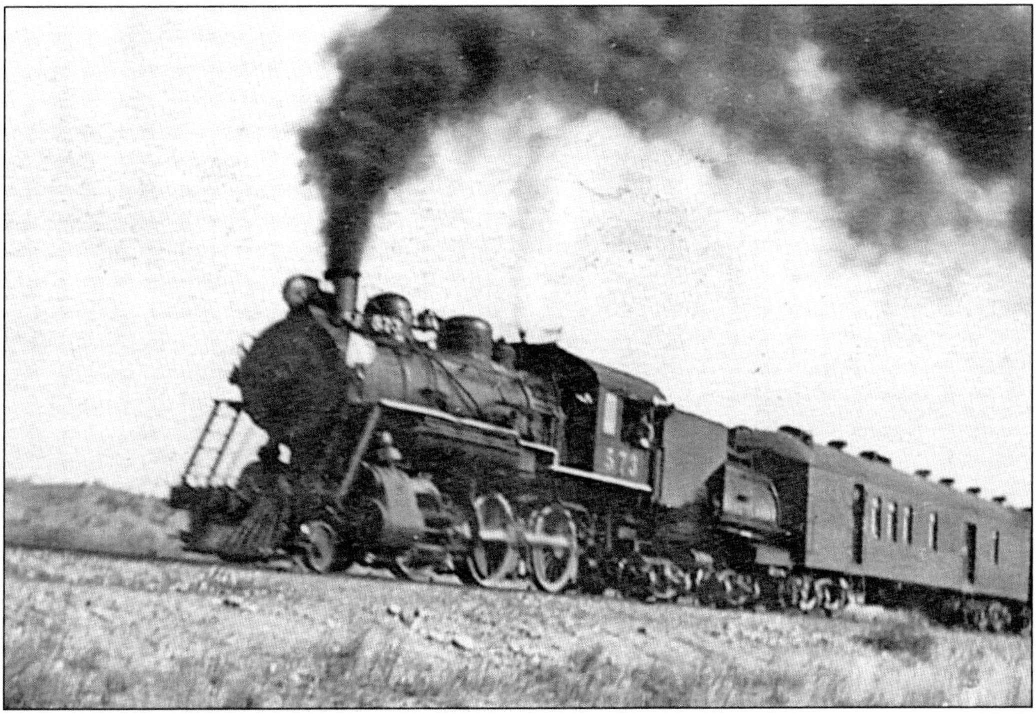

At Copper Hill, just a few miles north of Globe, several copper mines were operating in 1910. The Amster branch of the Gila Valley Globe and Northern Railroad was completed. It served the Arizona Commercial, Superior and Boston, and Arizona-Michigan mines for 20 years.

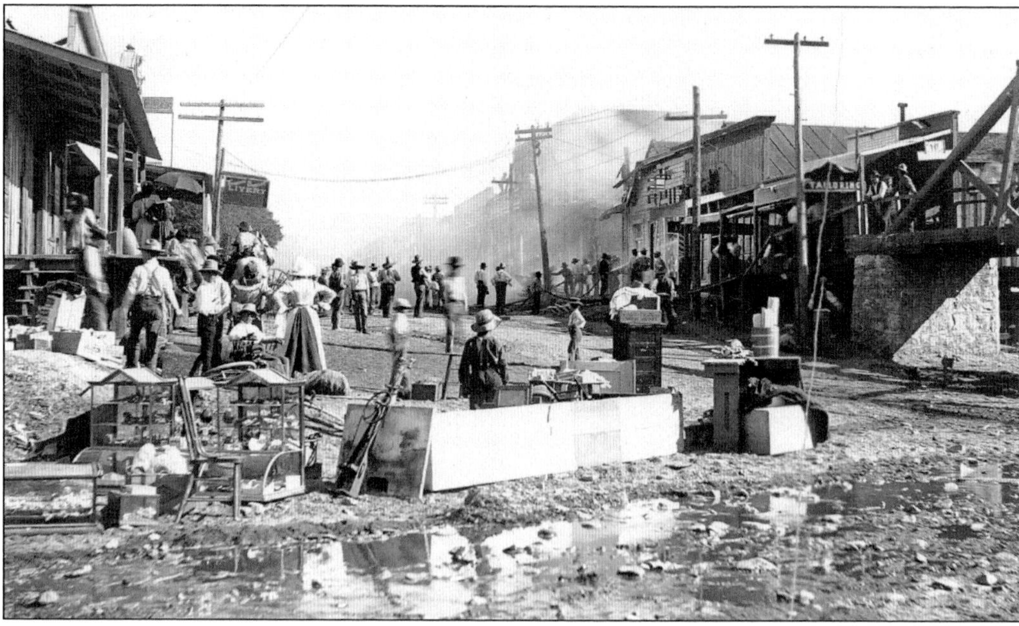

The fire of 1894 destroyed 39 structures on North Broad Street. The photograph above was taken during the fire. Many merchants moved items from their buildings in an attempt to save at least a part of their stock. After the fire (below), only adobe and concrete walls remained. Most of the merchants were soon back in business.

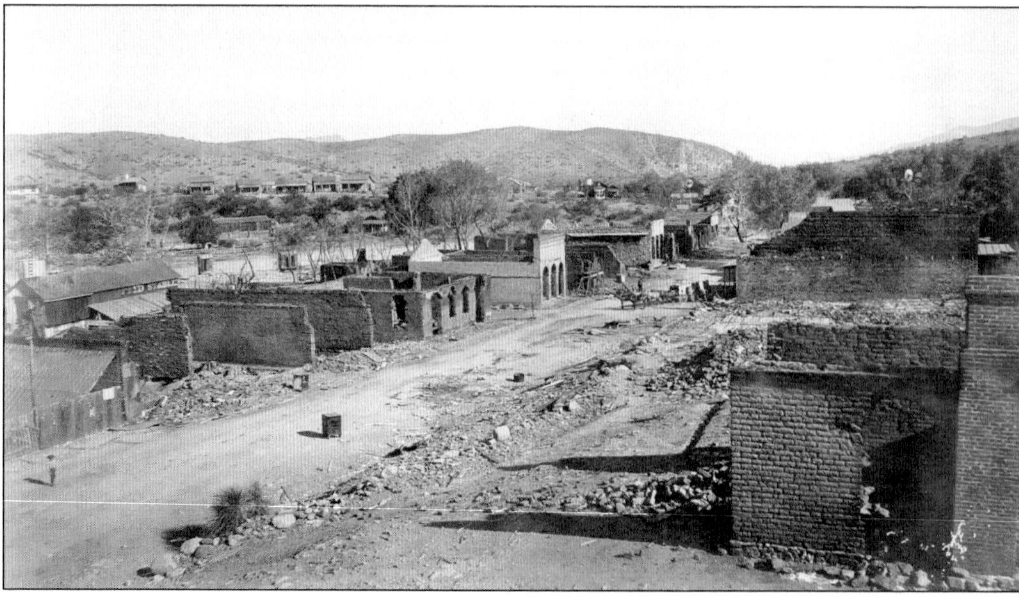

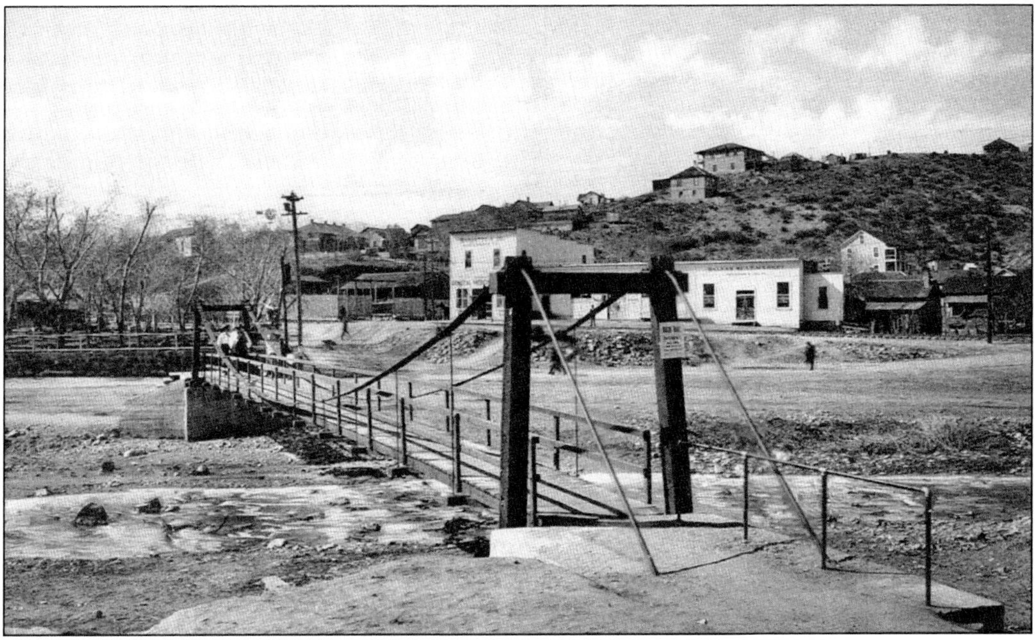

Kinney Park (above, far left) was located across Pinal Creek just a block from the business district. The park was a popular, shady spot for picnics, dances, holiday events, and other family or community gatherings. The creek had running water much of the time, so in 1910, a wooden suspension bridge was built to facilitate foot traffic to the park. A decade later, the bridge was replaced by a concrete balustrade bridge. Below, this bridge carried pedestrian traffic across the often-muddy North Broad Street.

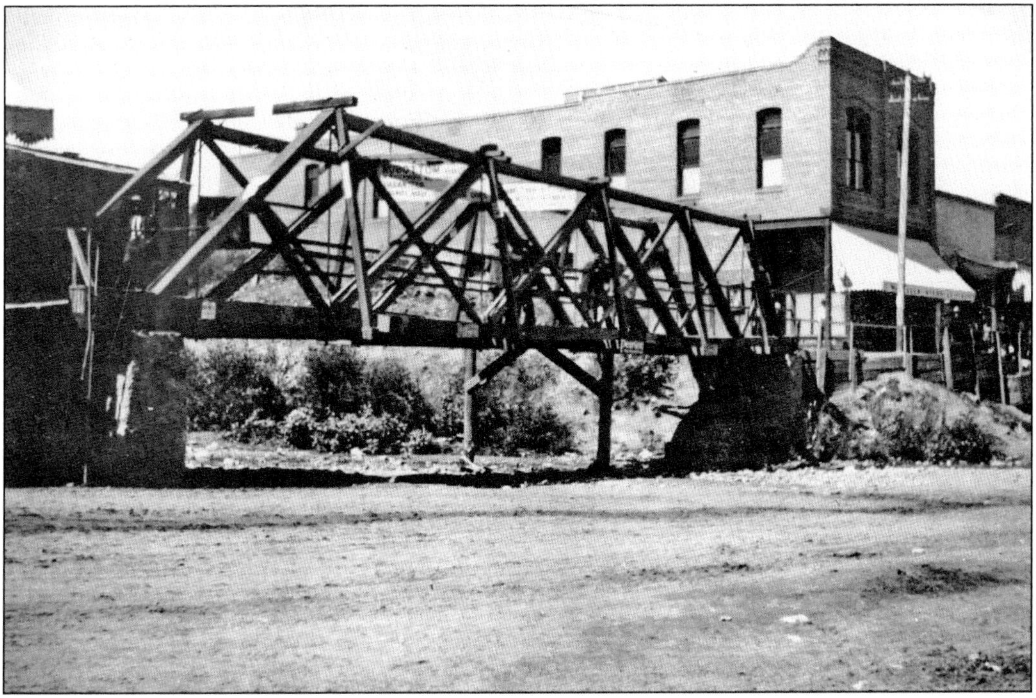

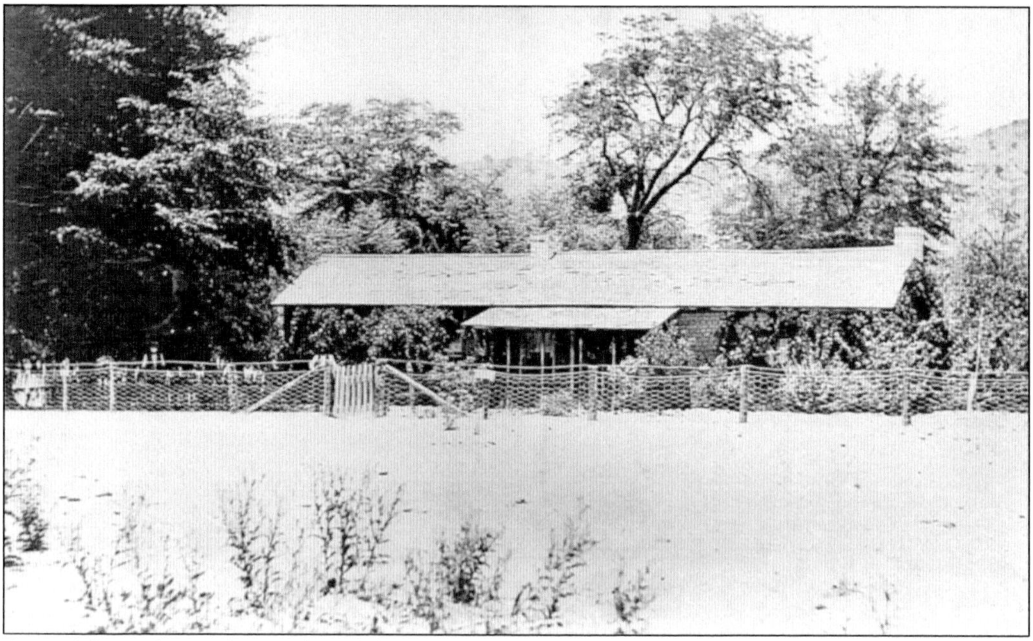

One of the early ranches in the Globe area was Pinal Ranch, established by Robert and Elizabeth Irion in 1878. After 1900, the ranch was best known for its fine apple orchards. The Irions and son Dudley Craig operated the ranch for 75 years. The 14-room adobe ranch house is now more than 125 years old.

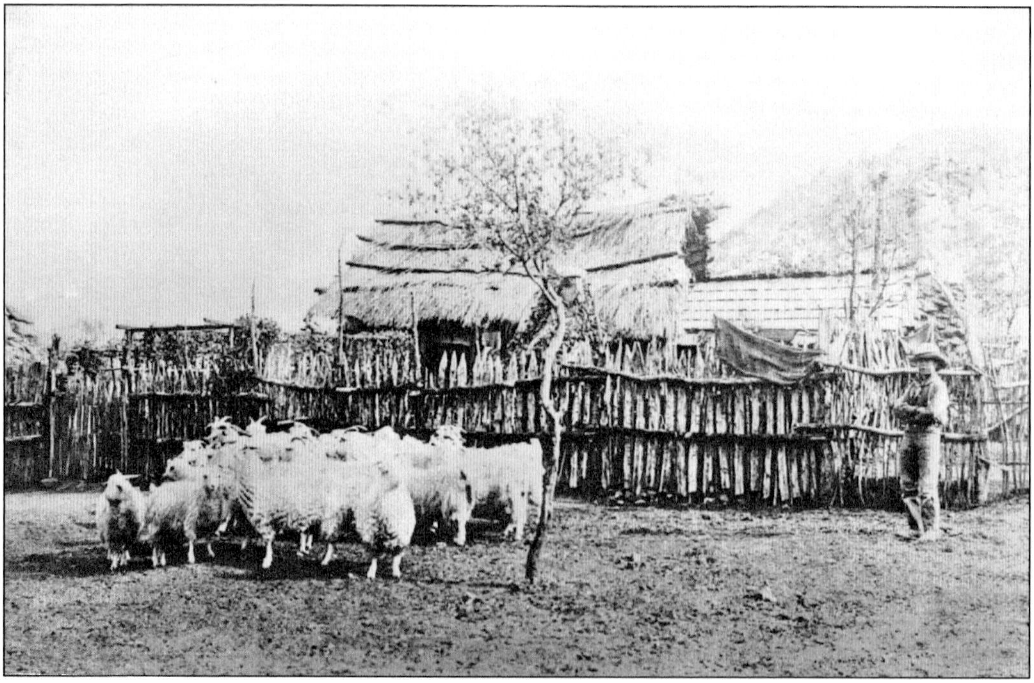

Widow Laura Bohme moved onto some mining claims west of Globe in 1892. In 1898, she married Phineas Clanton, and they raised cattle and goats, some of which are pictured near the ranch house.

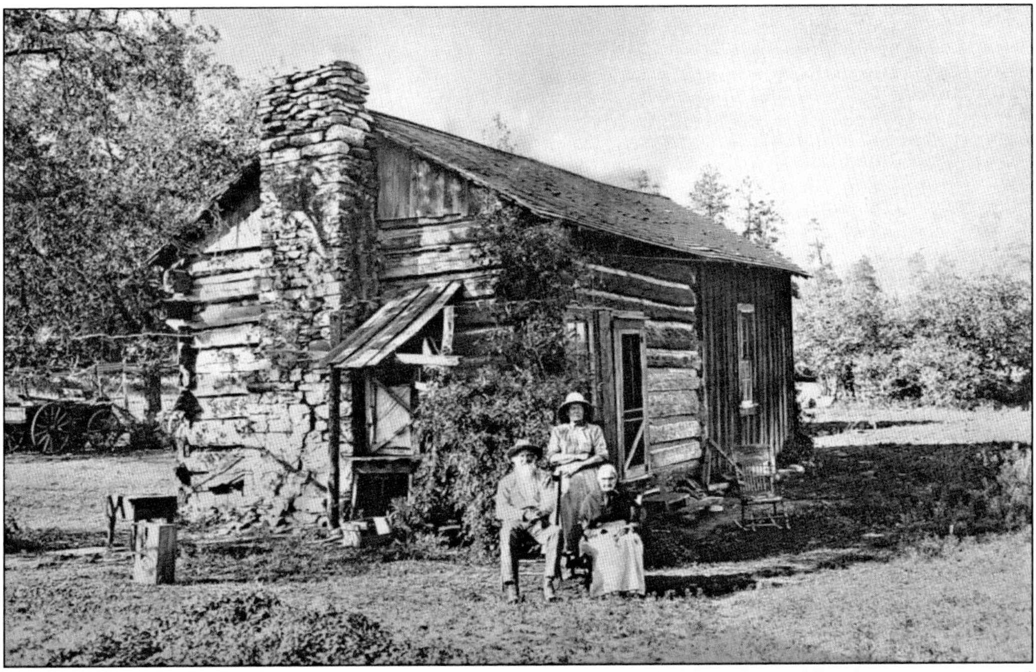

Globe was a place where a cowboy from the Bouquet Ranch (above) could ride into town and carouse for the weekend. If there was money left, he would stock up on Arbuckle's coffee and Copenhagen and be ready for work at daybreak on Monday.

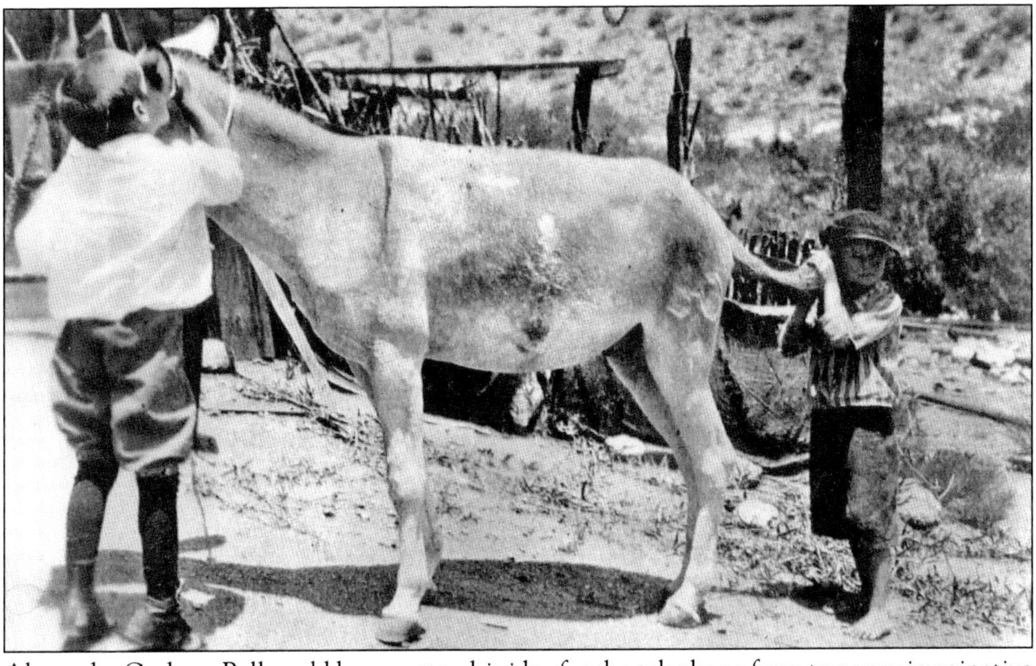

Alexander Graham Bell could have gotten his idea for the telephone from two very imaginative lads near Globe, Arizona. Here Bill Berry is sending a message to his friend Robb Ross.

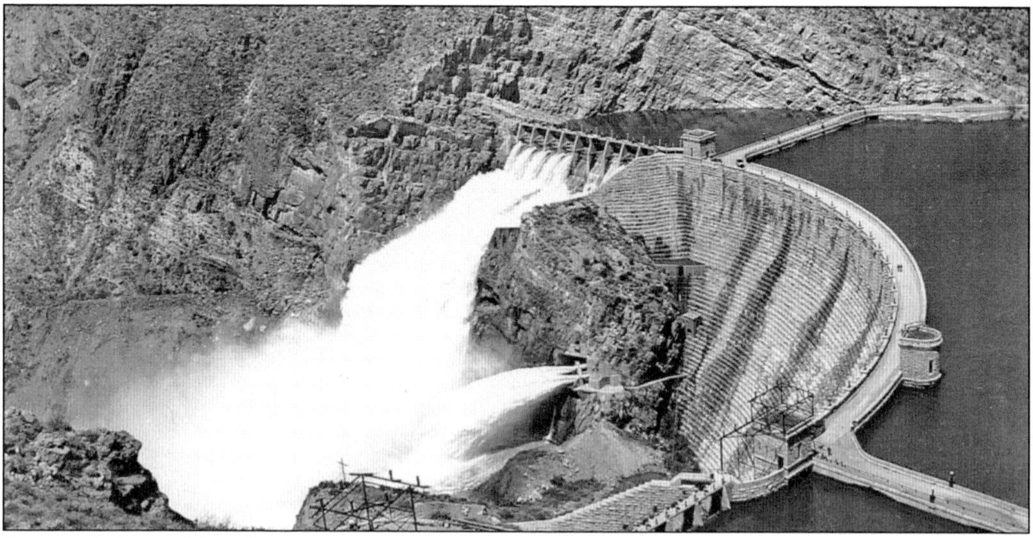

Roosevelt Dam (above) was constructed from 1904 to 1911 on the Salt River about 35 miles northwest of Globe. During the early construction phase, Globe was the shipping hub for supplies and equipment for the project. The dam supplied irrigation water and hydroelectric power to the cities of the Salt River Valley and has long been a favorite recreation site for Arizona residents and visitors alike. Theodore Roosevelt participated in the dedication of the dam on March 13, 1911. The town of Roosevelt (below) developed rapidly on a level area above the Salt River. Some of Globe's merchants established businesses there. On the left are a bakery, grocery store, drugstore, and the American Restaurant. The construction workers' camp is seen on the hill in the distance. When water in the reservoir began to rise, the buildings were either dismantled or moved to above the high water level.

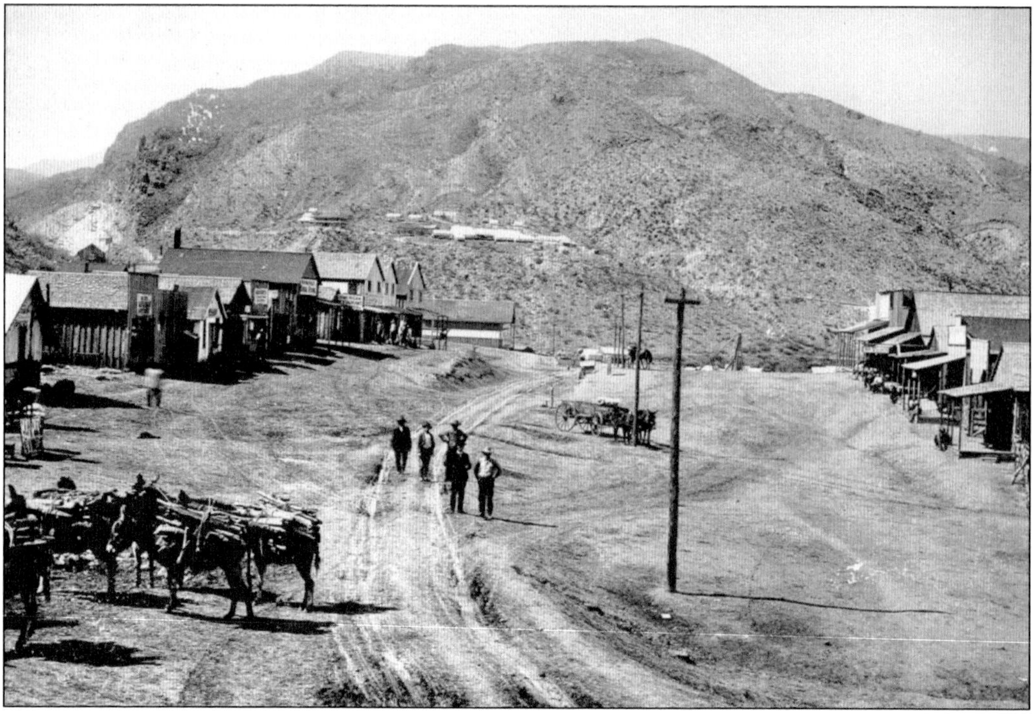

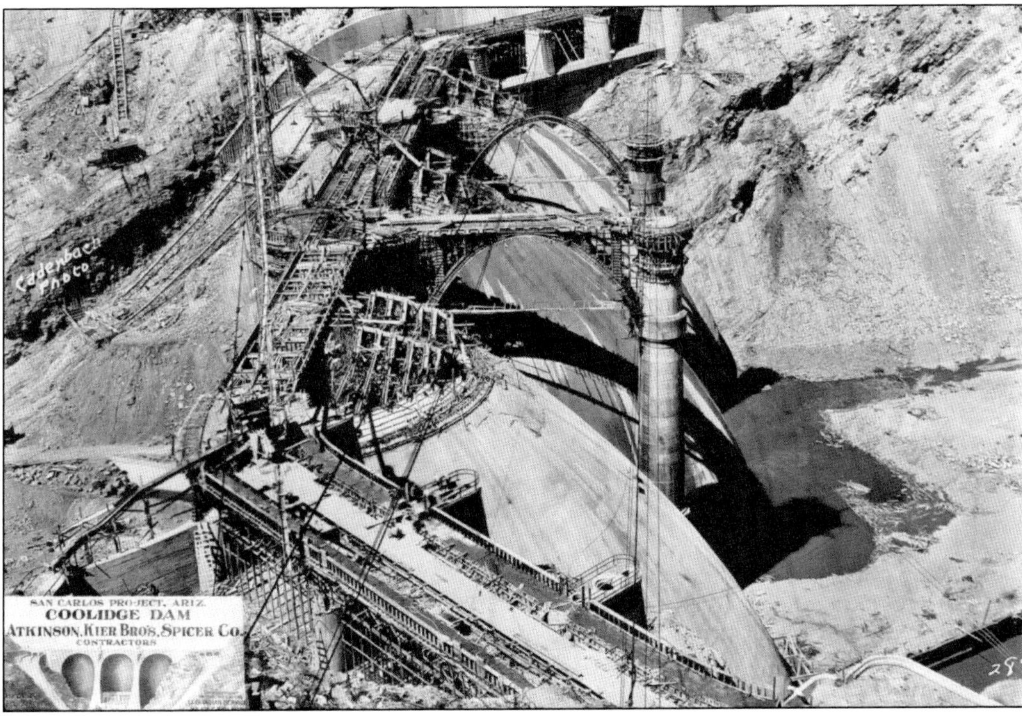

This is a contractor's photograph of the construction of Coolidge Dam on the Gila River almost 30 miles from Globe. The dam was dedicated in 1930, and Pres. Calvin Coolidge and Will Rogers were there to help in the celebration.

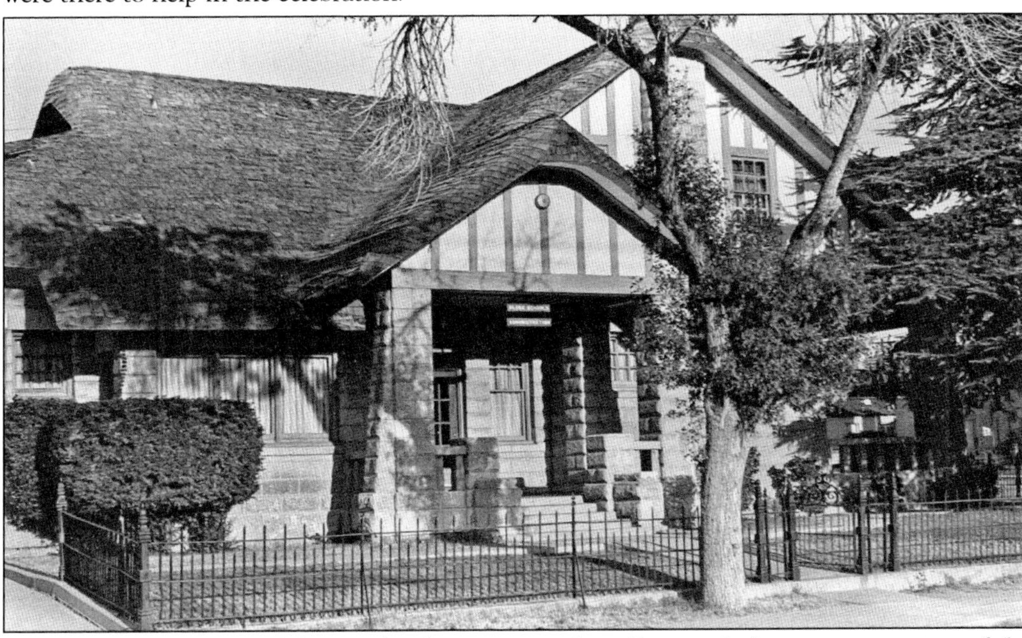

T. J. Long's first job in Globe was freighting materials to Roosevelt during construction of the dam. After the freighting ended, he was occupied in a variety of businesses, including a Dodge and Plymouth dealership. The unique Long home on Ash Street is now the administrative offices of the Globe School District.

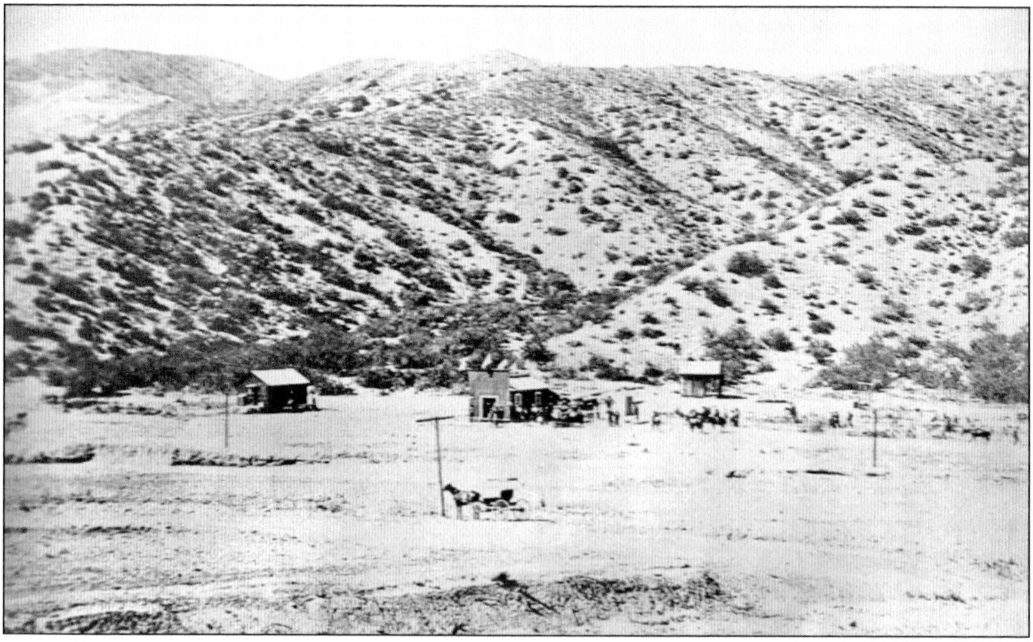
A small crowd is gathered at one of Miami's first structures, probably a land office, c. 1908.

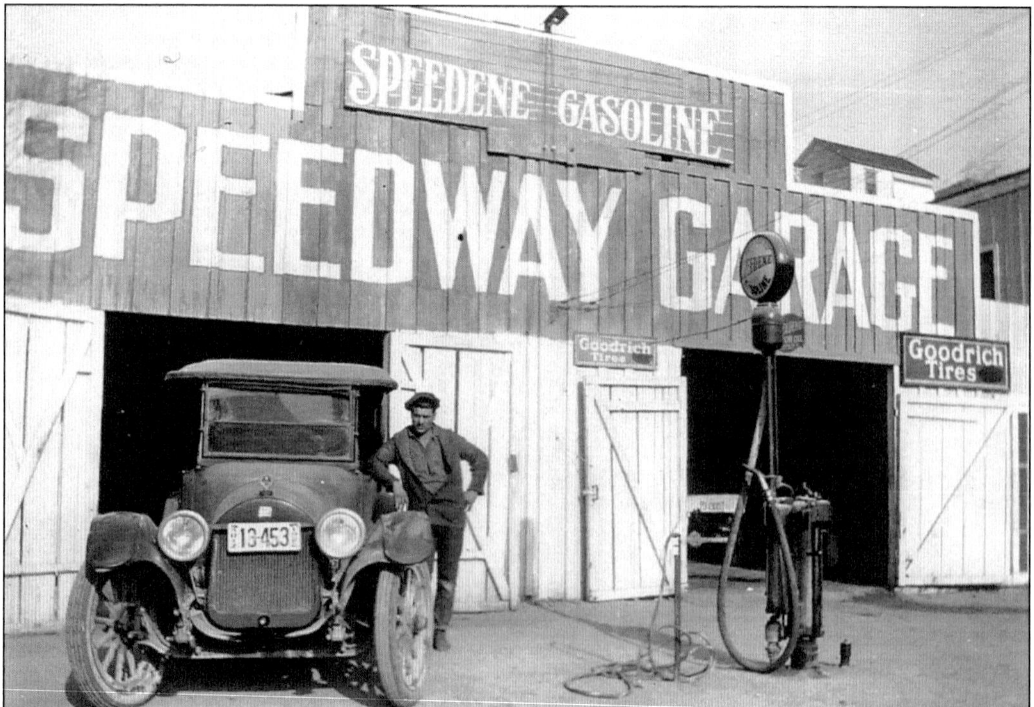

The Speedway Garage on Live Oak Street in Miami offered gasoline, oil, water, tires, and service to the drivers of Miami before 1920.

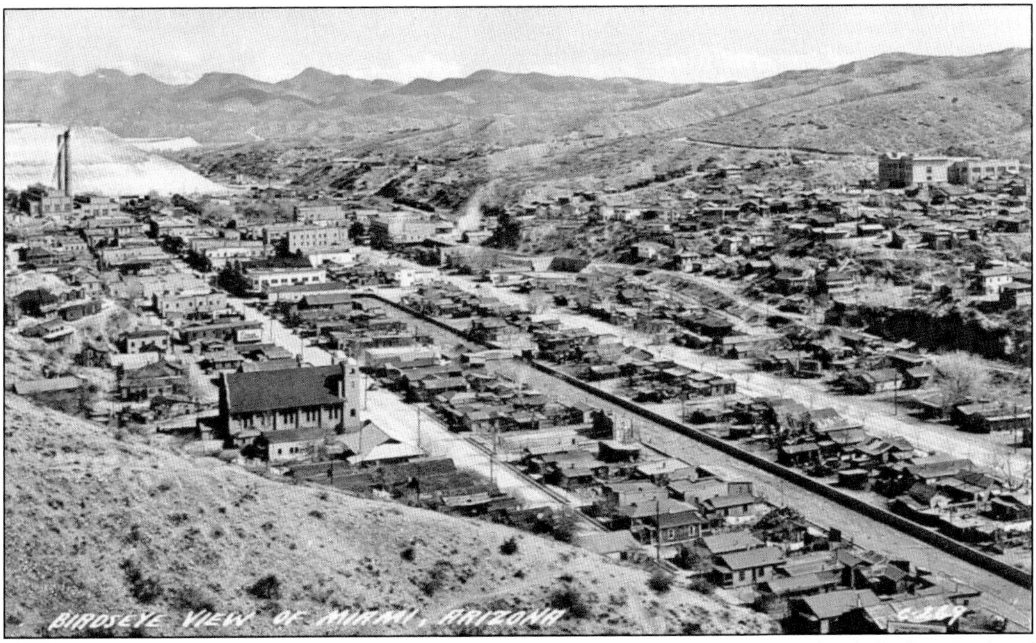

This 1953 view from a hillside shows the Miami business district and, on the left, Our Lady of the Blessed Sacrament Roman Catholic Church.

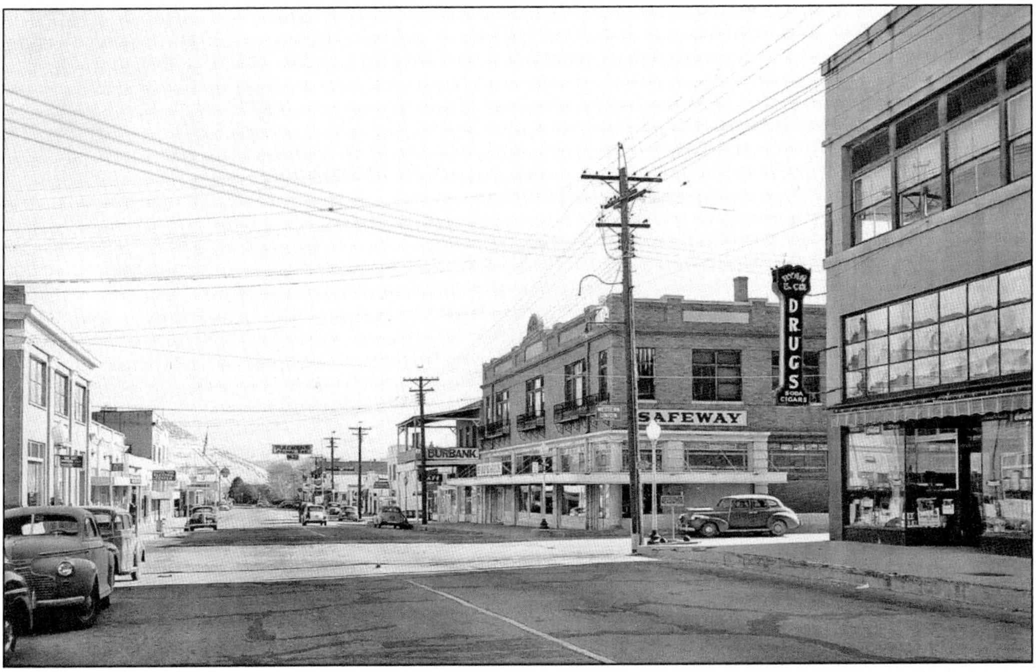

The new Safeway store shares space with Western Union in an attractive Live Oak Street building c. 1938.

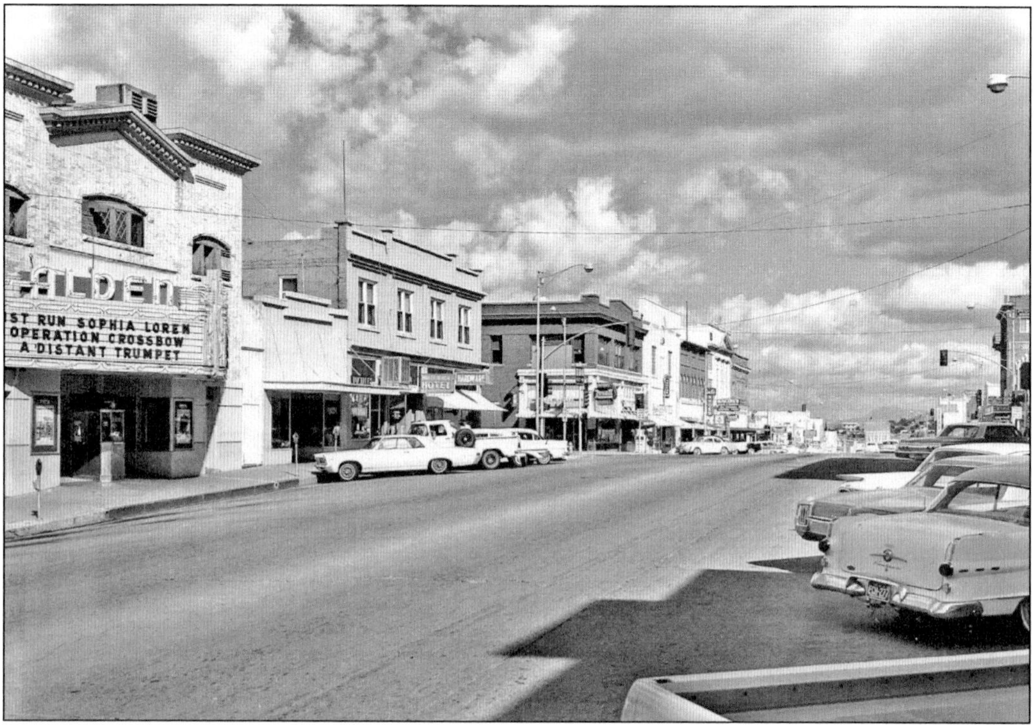

Independent photographer Bill Norman took many wonderful photographs featuring scenes in Globe, and some fantastic Arizona skies.

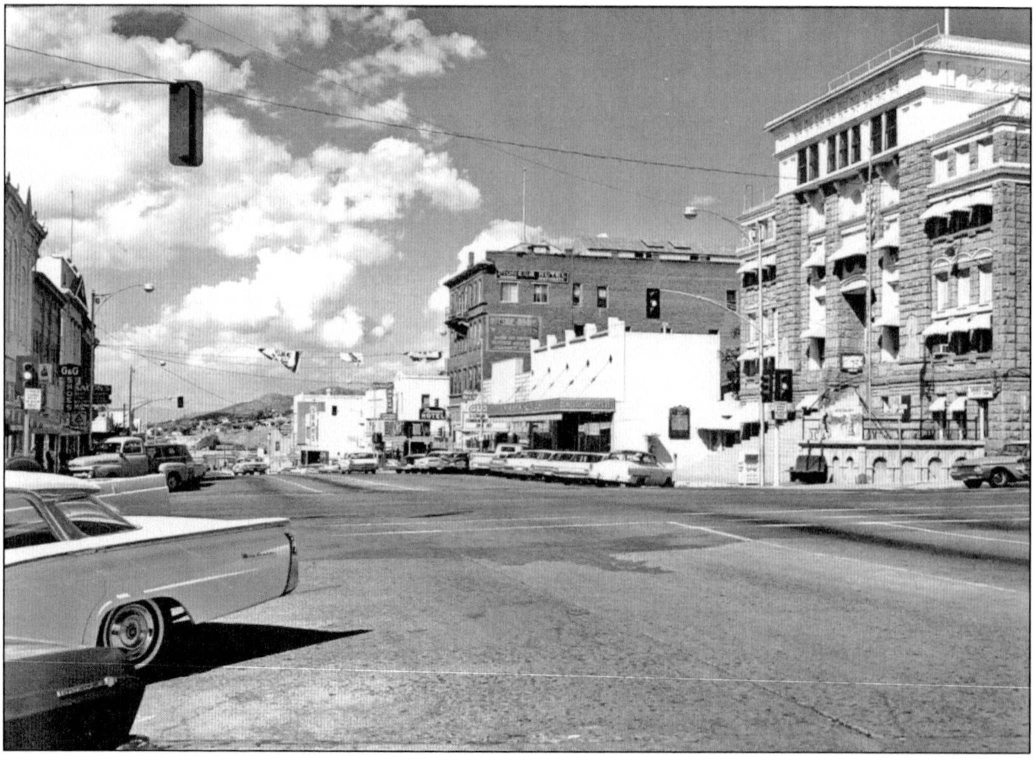

Three

Mining

"Some years ago a prospector was placing a location notice and heard a noise near him. On looking up, he saw a woman whom he described as 'the most beautiful he had ever seen.' The newcomer inquired of the prospector what he was doing. On learning that he too was marking a location, she informed him that she had already filed on the land. The prospector, surmising that the lady was unmarried, requested that he be allowed to have an interest in the property on agreeing to do a share of the location work. On this basis, a compromise was effected. The prospector proceeded to name the claim 'Ida May' after his newly made acquaintance, and going up a hillside located another claim he called 'Little Beauty.' Circumstances, however, did not shape events as fiction would have them, for Ida May married another, and the prospector, failing of an alliance with the most beautiful woman he had ever seen, wedded not at all." —Arizona Silver Belt, 1910

The Ida May and Little Beauty were two of many silver claims in the Globe area. The Stonewall Jackson at McMillenville and the Mac Morris at Richmond Basin were profitable mines. Other silver producers included the Irene, Miami, Rescue, and Pioneer mines. The silver veins "pinched out" by 1885.

Globe did not become a ghost town, as many other silver camps. Before 1880, several small copper mines were producing ore, and in 1882, two of them merged to become the Old Dominion Copper Company. For nearly 50 years, the Old Dominion Mine was the barometer of Globe's economy and well-being.

Lack of adequate transportation limited the development of the mine for 20 years. The arrival of the Gila Valley Globe and Northern Railroad in 1898 jump-started a huge expansion and modernization of the mine and ushered Globe into its boom years.

The Old Dominion Mine shut down in 1931. It produced 800 million pounds of copper, provided a comfortable living for thousands of miners and their families, and dictated the economy and growth of Globe as a city.

Meanwhile, two large mines near neighboring Miami began producing copper in the 1910s. Nearly 100 years later, they continue to provide work and wealth to the people of Globe and Miami.

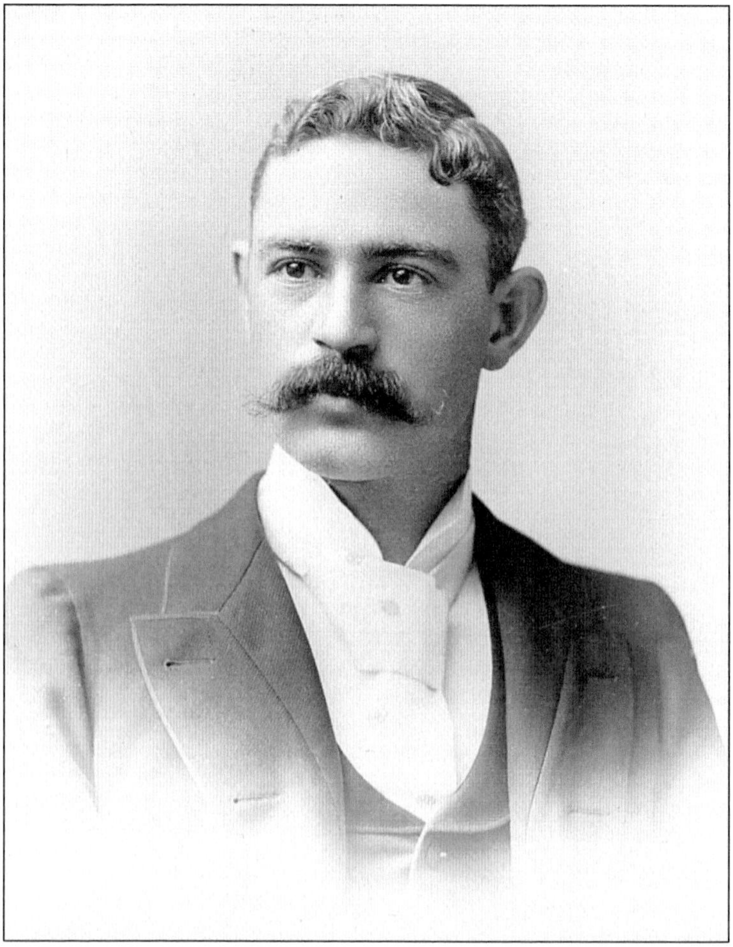

By the early 1880s, silver mining was coming to an end. Twenty years later, though, Valerius Y. Smith began to rework the famous Stonewall Jackson Mine at McMillenville. Smith and a few friends worked until 1916, when he died at age 49. With the boss gone, no one continued to work.

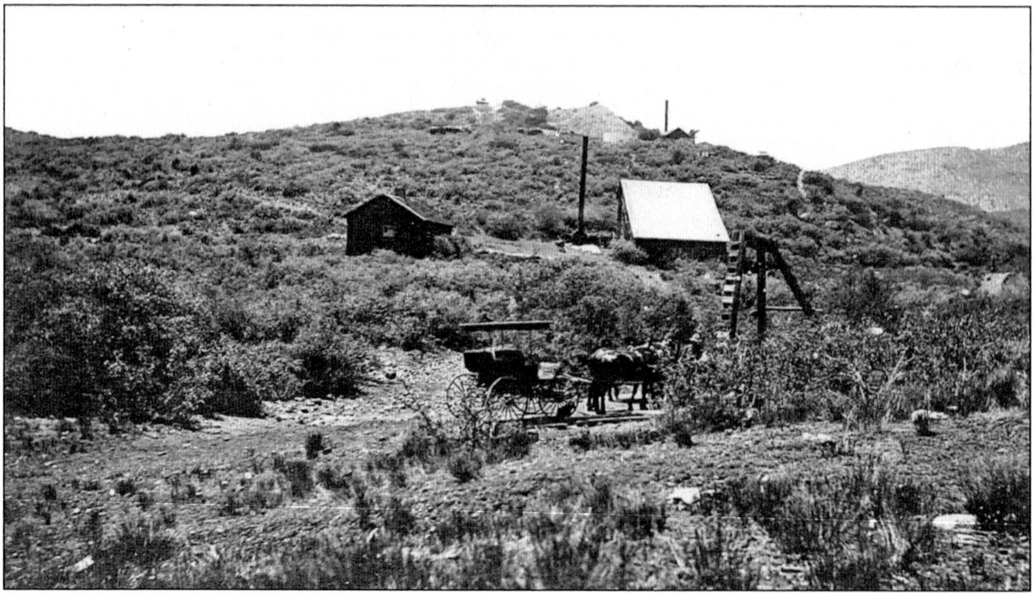

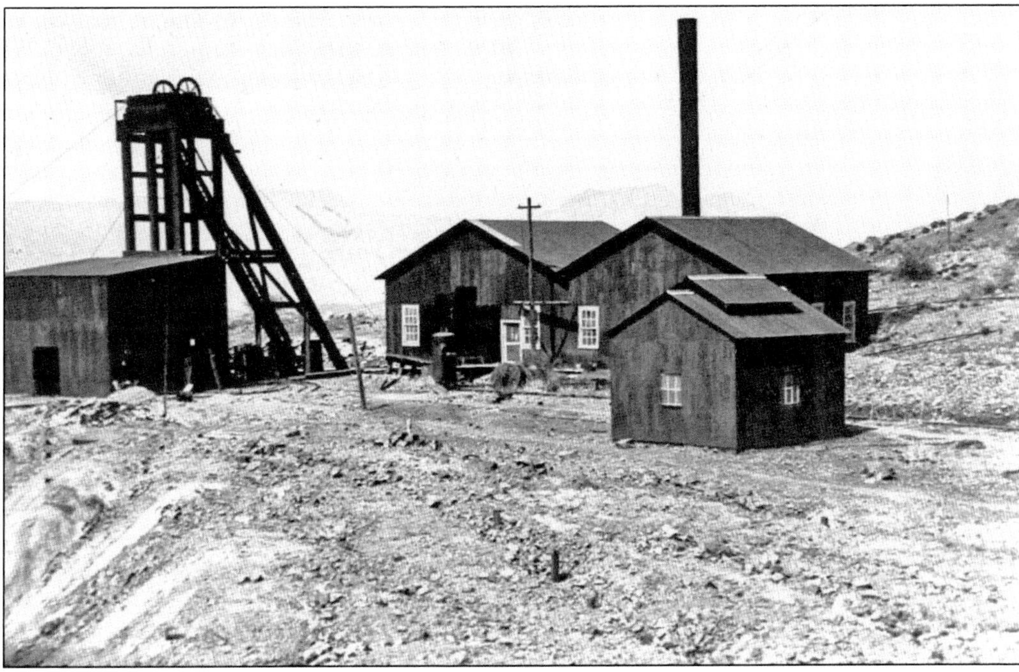

This 1914 photograph is of the headframe, hoist house, and other structures at the Old Dominion Mine. The larger "A" shaft, built in 1905, provided primary access to the mine.

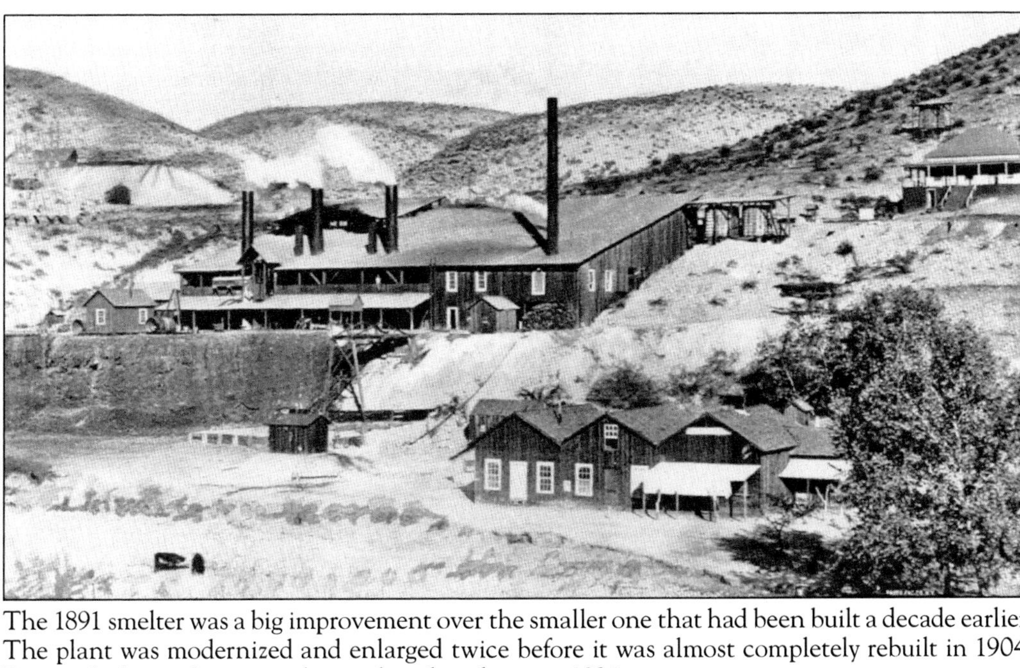

The 1891 smelter was a big improvement over the smaller one that had been built a decade earlier. The plant was modernized and enlarged twice before it was almost completely rebuilt in 1904. Due to declining business, the smelter shut down in 1924.

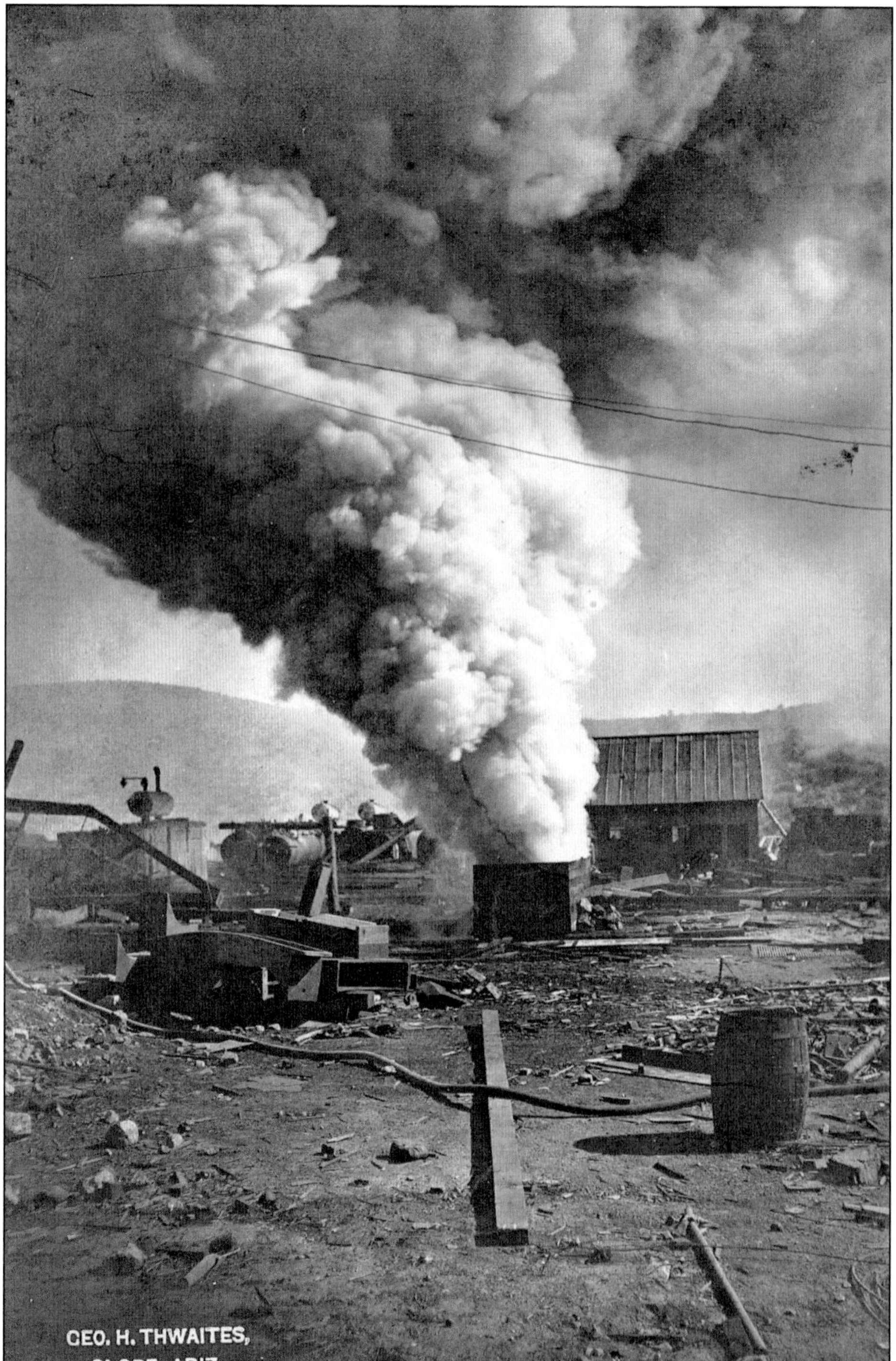

On February 20, 1906, a fire broke out in Old Dominion's Interloper shaft, a ventilation shaft accessible only by a long ladder. Three men were asphyxiated when they entered the shaft and tried to extinguish the blaze.

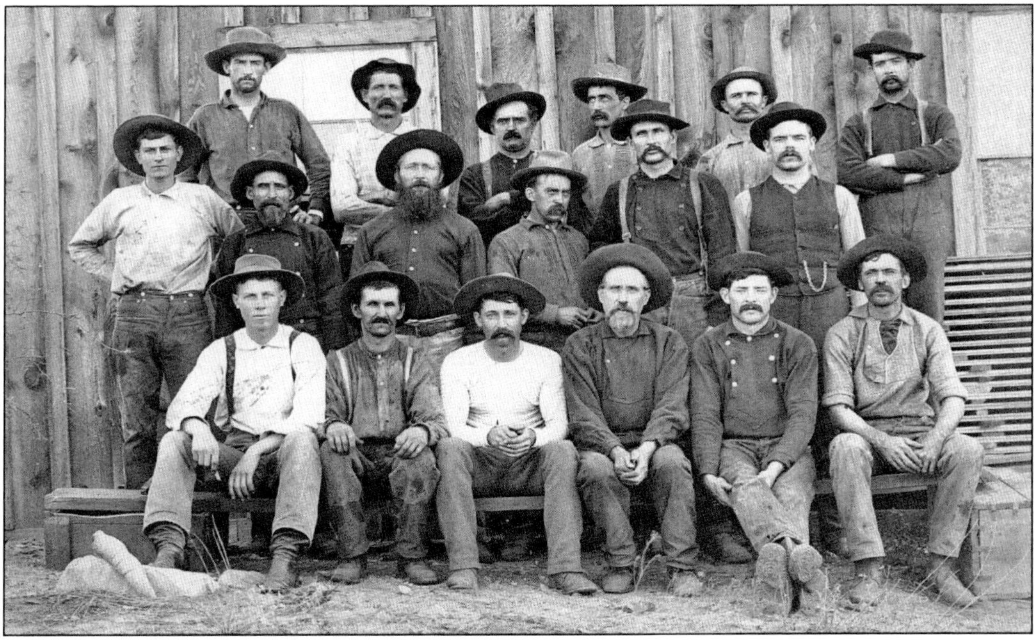

Above, men wearing hats, work shirts, and dungarees are ready for a long, hot shift in the smelter. The man wearing a vest and sporting a watch fob must have been the shift foreman. The office staff on the porch below presents a much fancier picture.

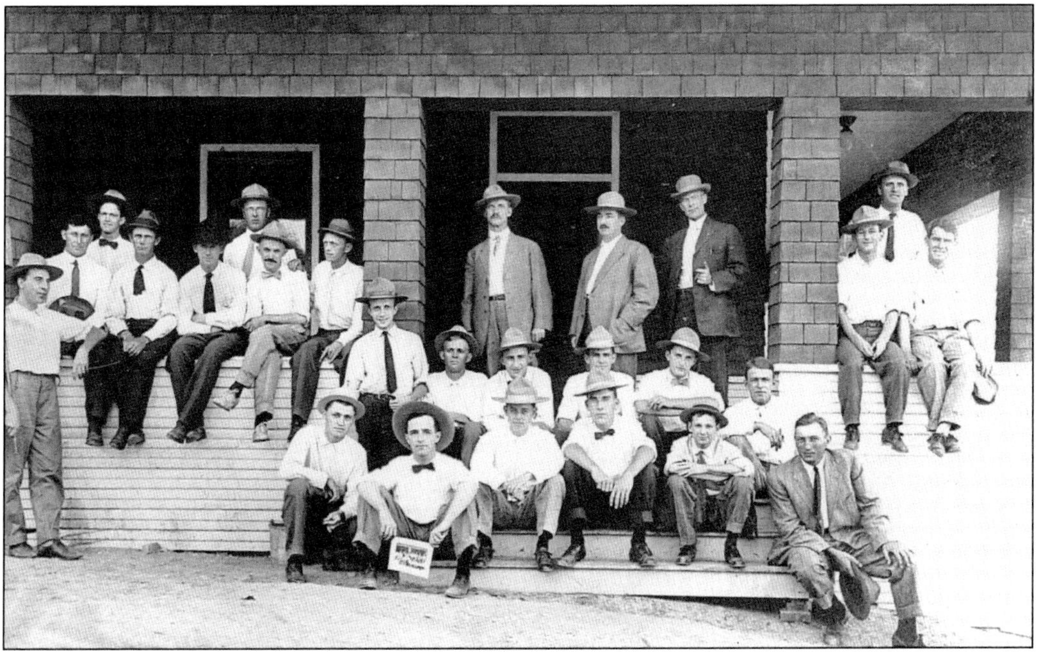

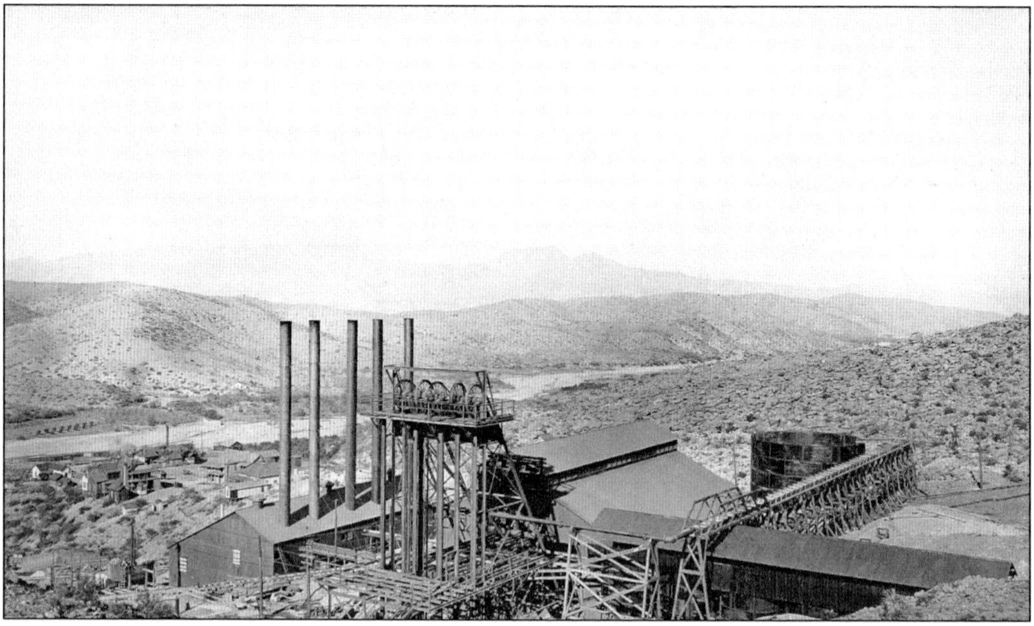

The "A" shaft's headframe and its large hoist house are flanked by a boiler building and ore bins.

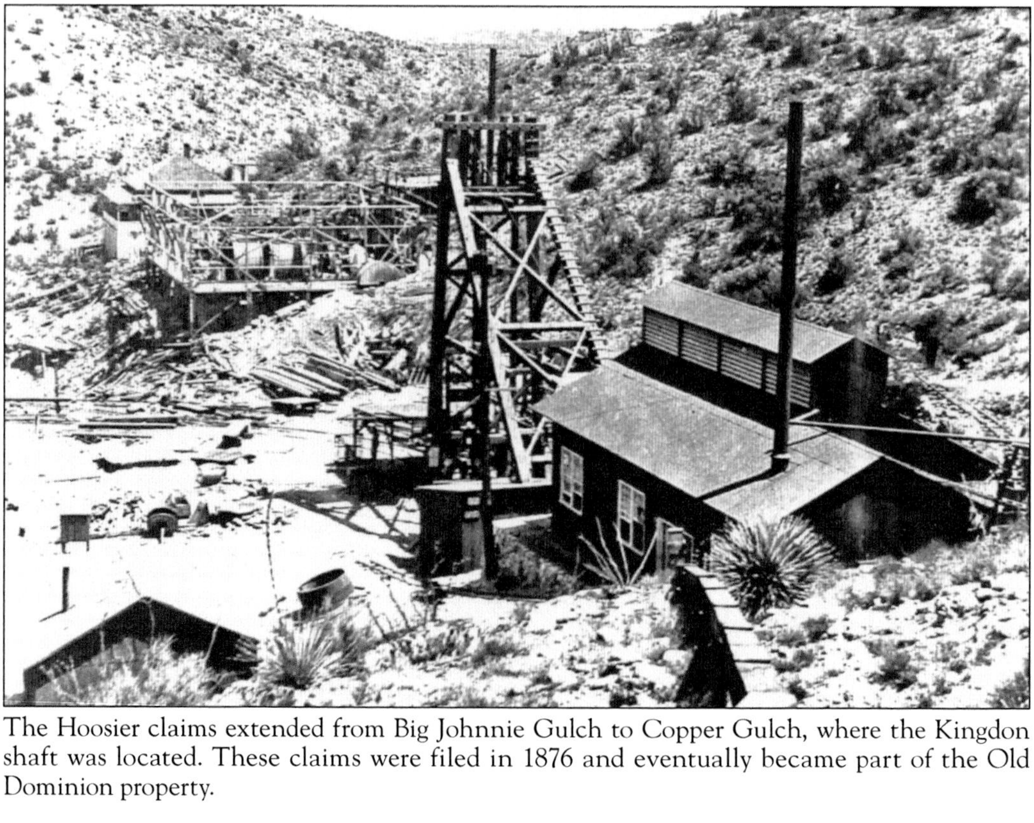

The Hoosier claims extended from Big Johnnie Gulch to Copper Gulch, where the Kingdon shaft was located. These claims were filed in 1876 and eventually became part of the Old Dominion property.

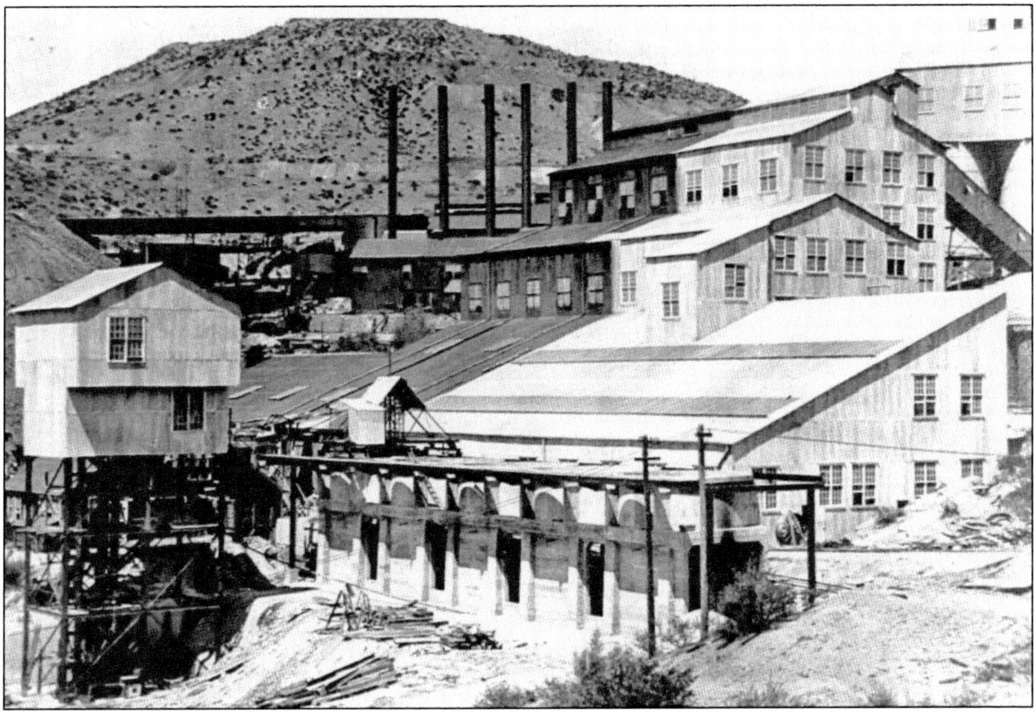

This 1914 photograph shows the old and the new expanded parts of the Old Dominion ore concentrator. Beyond the concentrator, a sixth stack has been added to the boiler building.

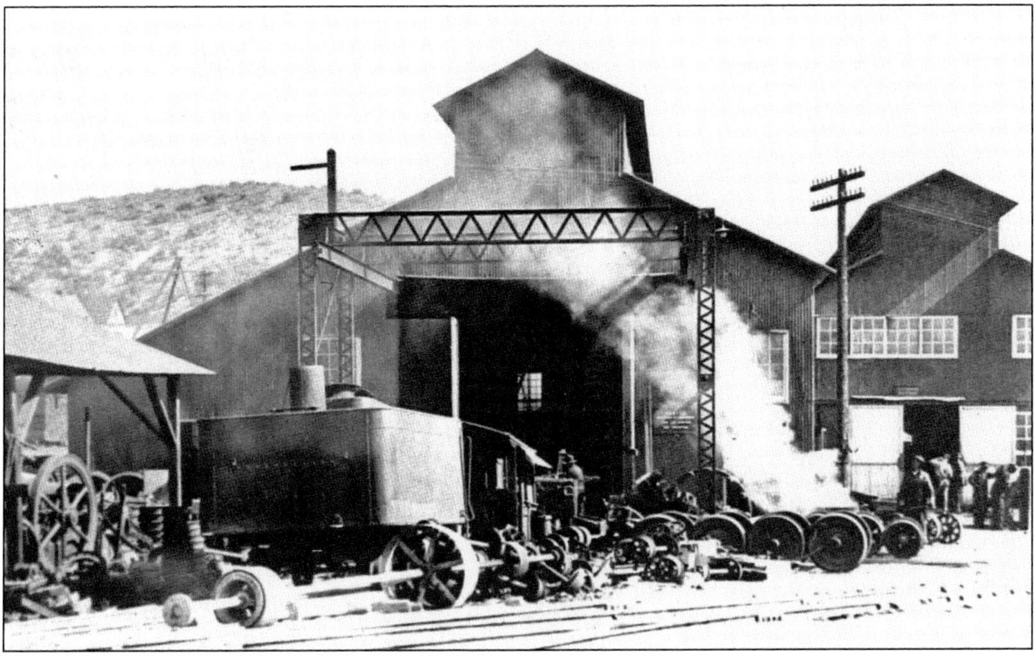

Most of the Old Dominion miners worked underground. On the surface, there were shops for the machinists, carpenters, blacksmiths, and timbermen.

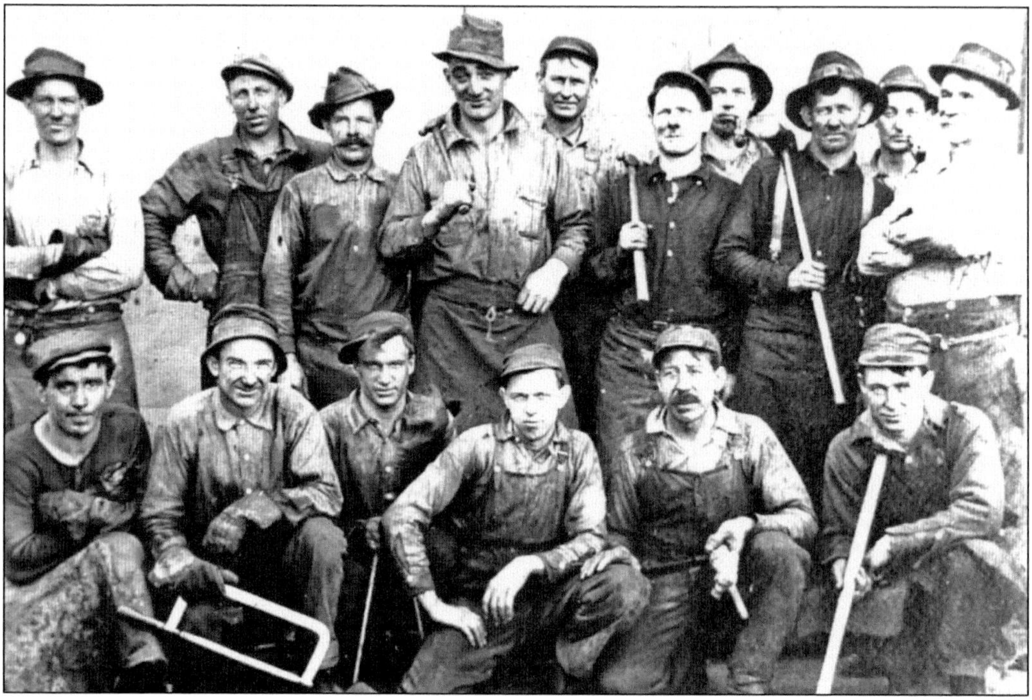

The blacksmiths (above) took time out from their work to pose for this photograph. They are holding some of the tools of their trade. The blacksmiths' shop (below) was equipped with the finest equipment available, including a forge (back left) and a metal turning lathe in the foreground.

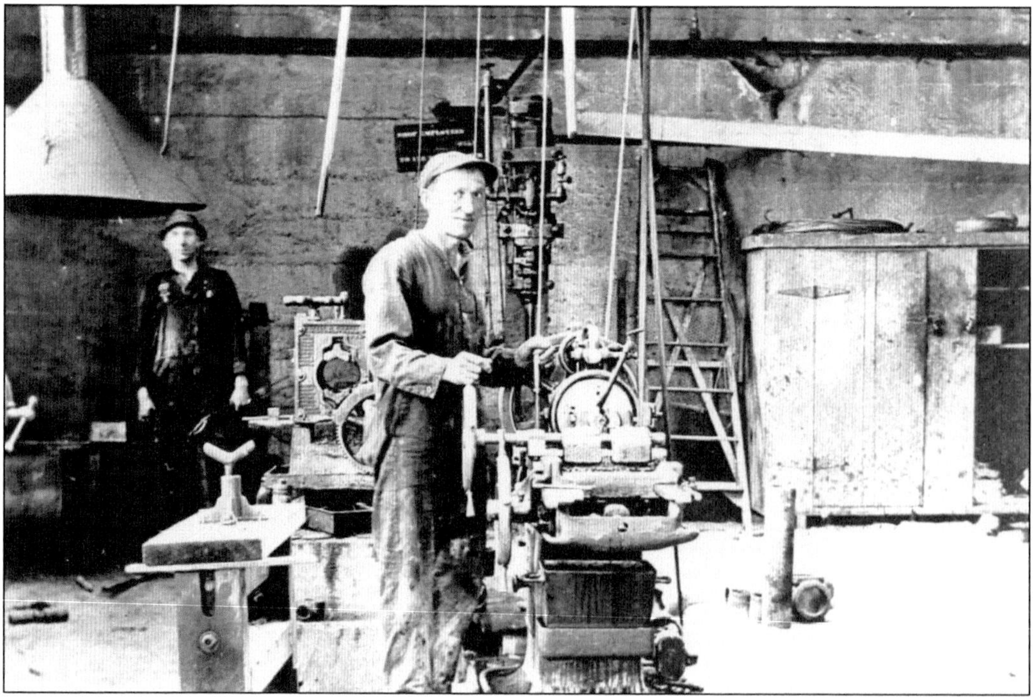

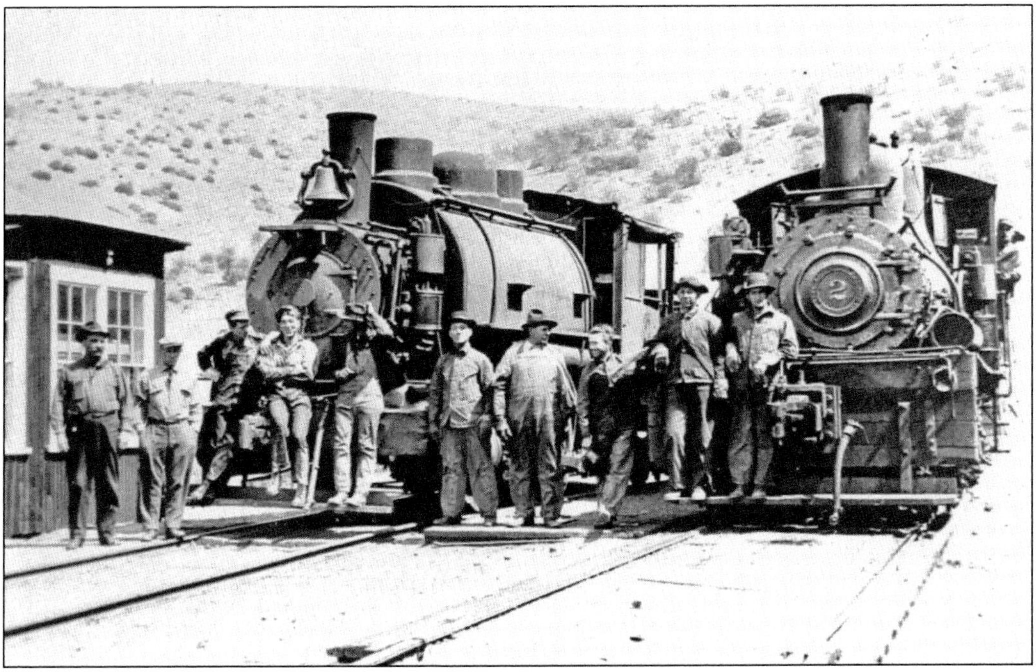

The industrial railroad consisted of main tracks, sidings, spurs, and switchbacks that totaled 6 miles in length. The railroad crew poses with two yard locomotives.

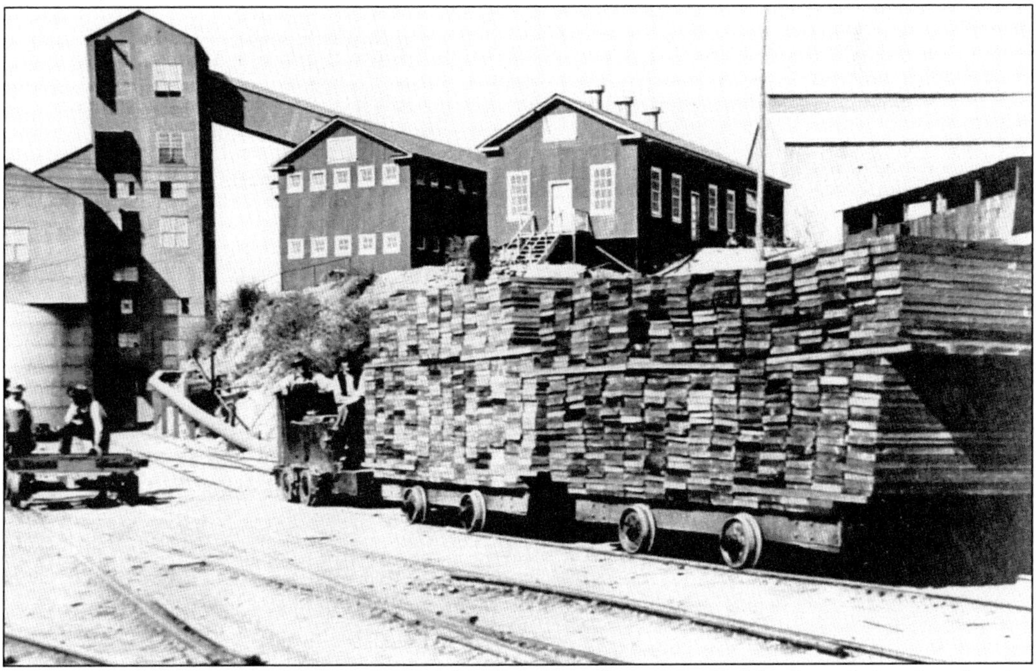

A small gasoline-powered locomotive is hauling two flat cars piled high with lumber for the mines' carpenters and timbermen.

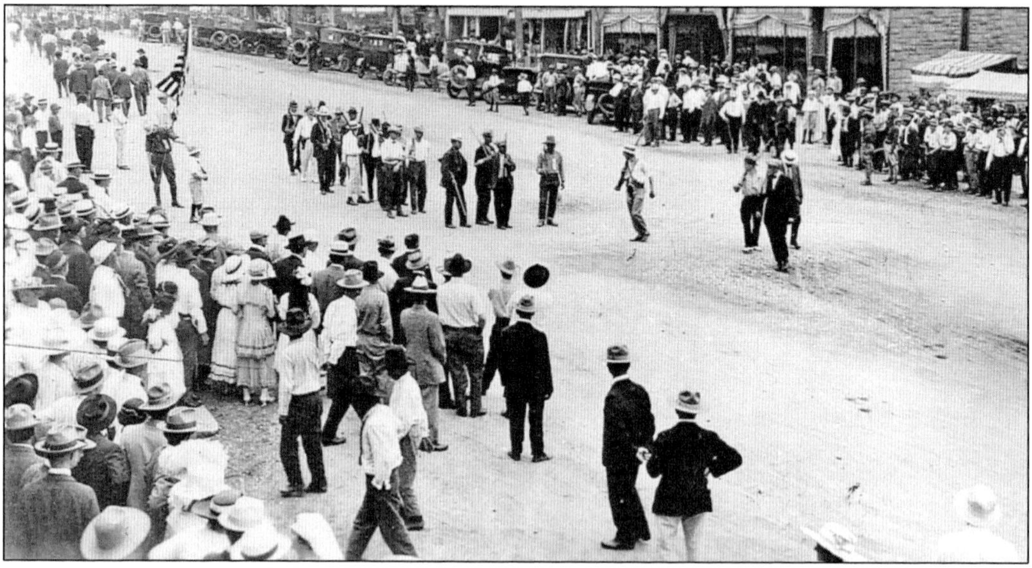

In July 1917, strikers at the Old Dominion Mine were threatening to make trouble, so Sheriff Tom Armer organized the Home Guard, deputizing any adult male with a rifle. Some of them are shown above performing drills before a crowd of onlookers on Broad Street. A few days later, the 17th U.S. Cavalry came to help control the situation. Pictured below are the tents of the soldiers on the mine's slag pile.

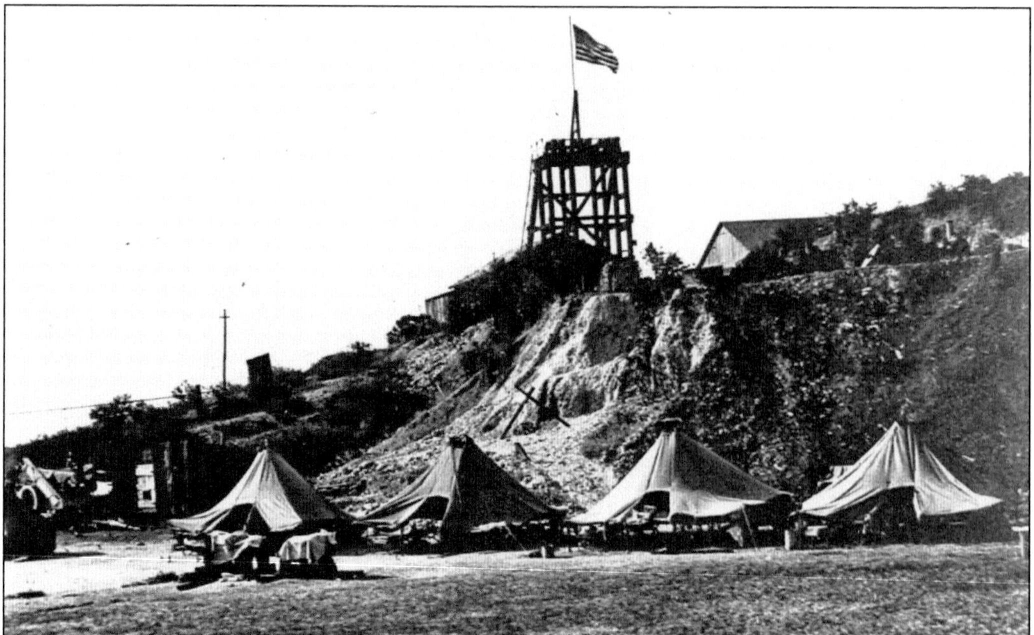

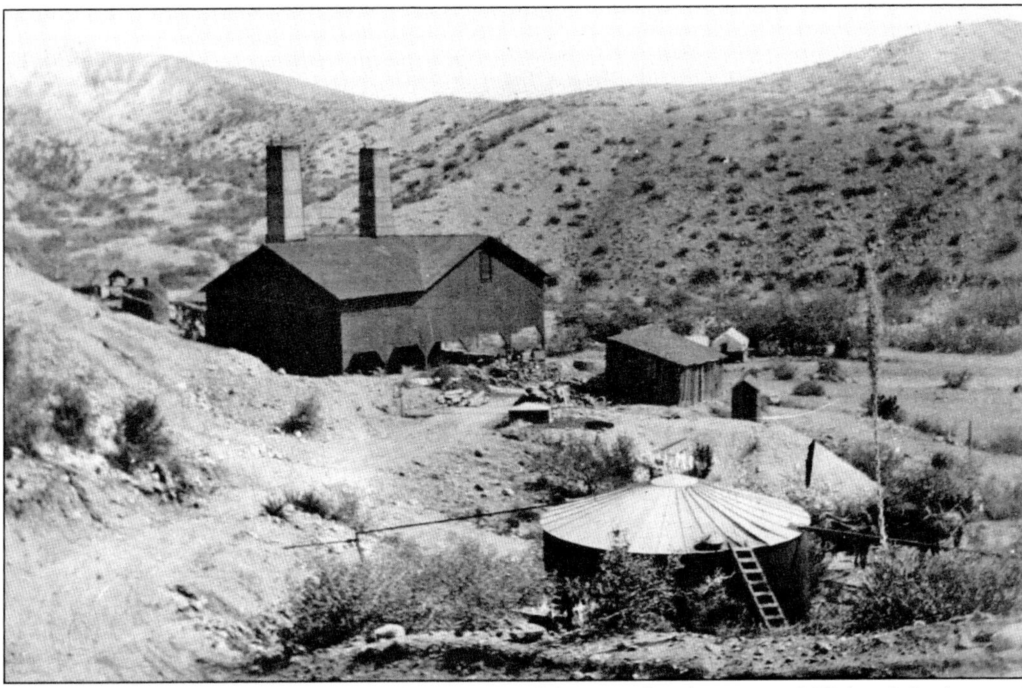

The Black Warrior Mine was located in Lost Gulch several miles west of Globe. It had several surface structures, including the smelter, shops, and a short 18-inch-gauge railroad to haul the ore. The Black Warrior was a profitable copper mine until its sudden decline in 1912.

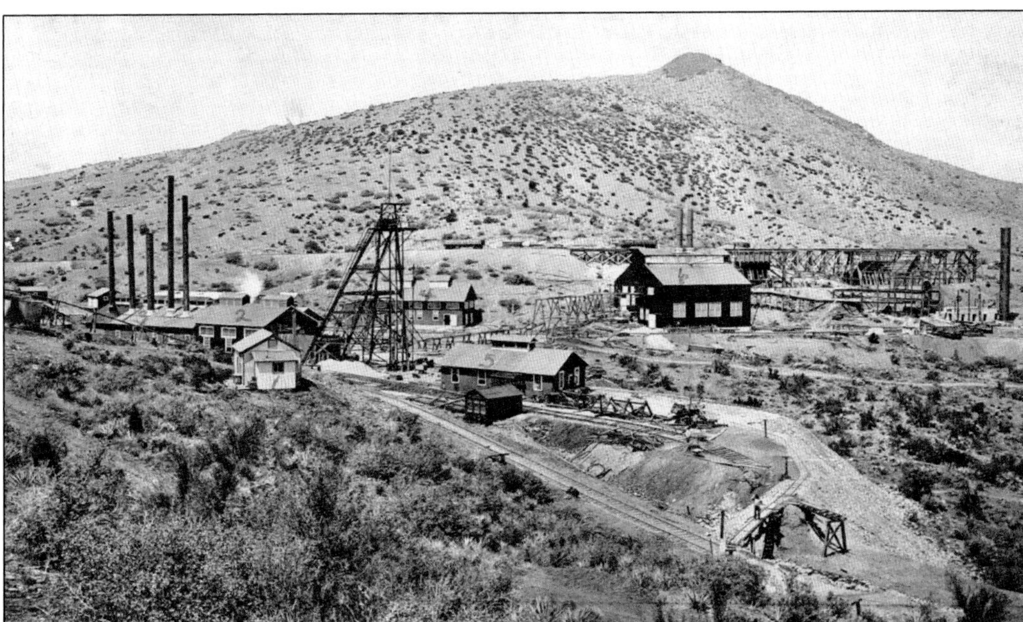

For nearly 30 years, Copper Hill was a busy, thriving mining camp three miles north of Globe. The Arizona Commercial Copper Company is pictured here. Other mines at Copper Hill were Superior and Boston, National, and Iron Cap mines.

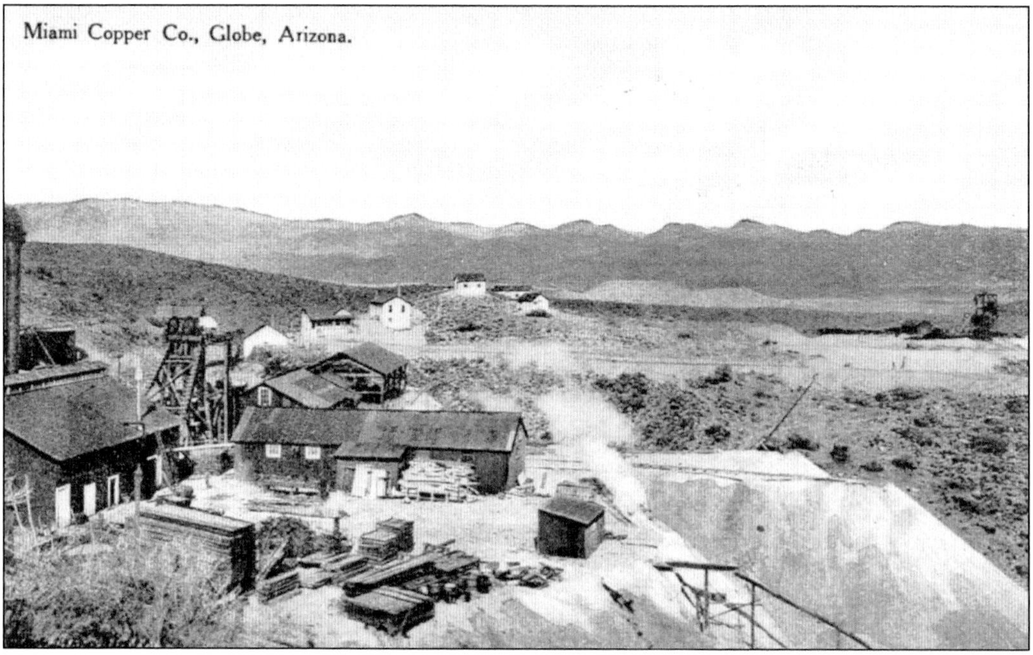

The mine of the Miami Copper Company, under several different names and ownerships, has been operating in Miami for nearly 100 years. It was only a few buildings in 1910 (above). The 1920 photograph below shows the mine's tremendous growth in just 10 years. The large building is Miami Copper's concentrating mill.

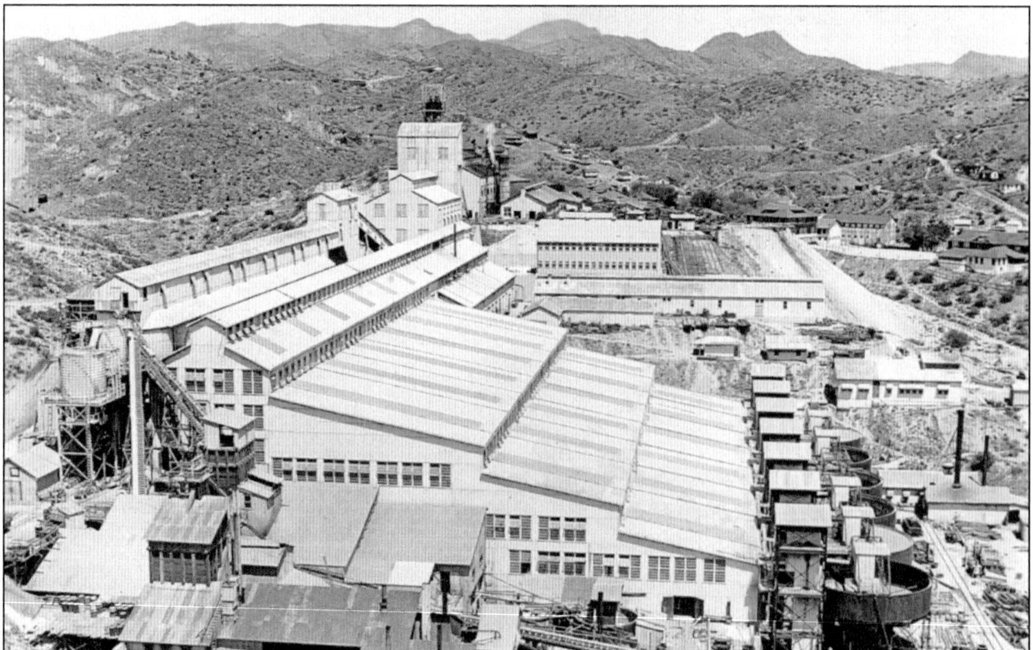

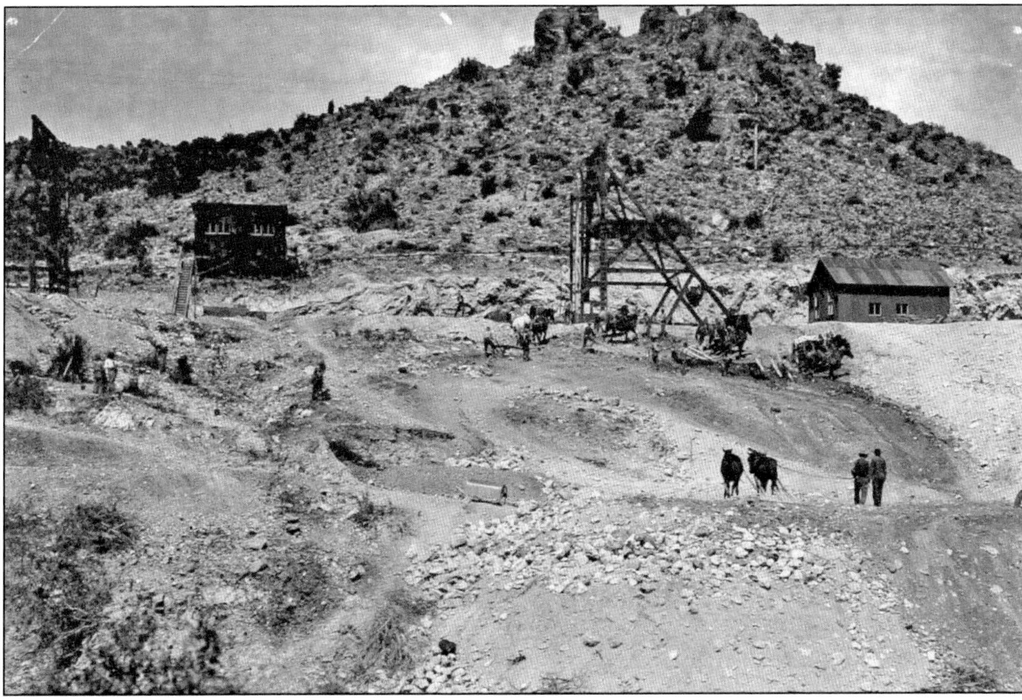

Inspiration Copper Company also began its development over 100 years ago. This is very early construction work at the headframe of the main shaft.

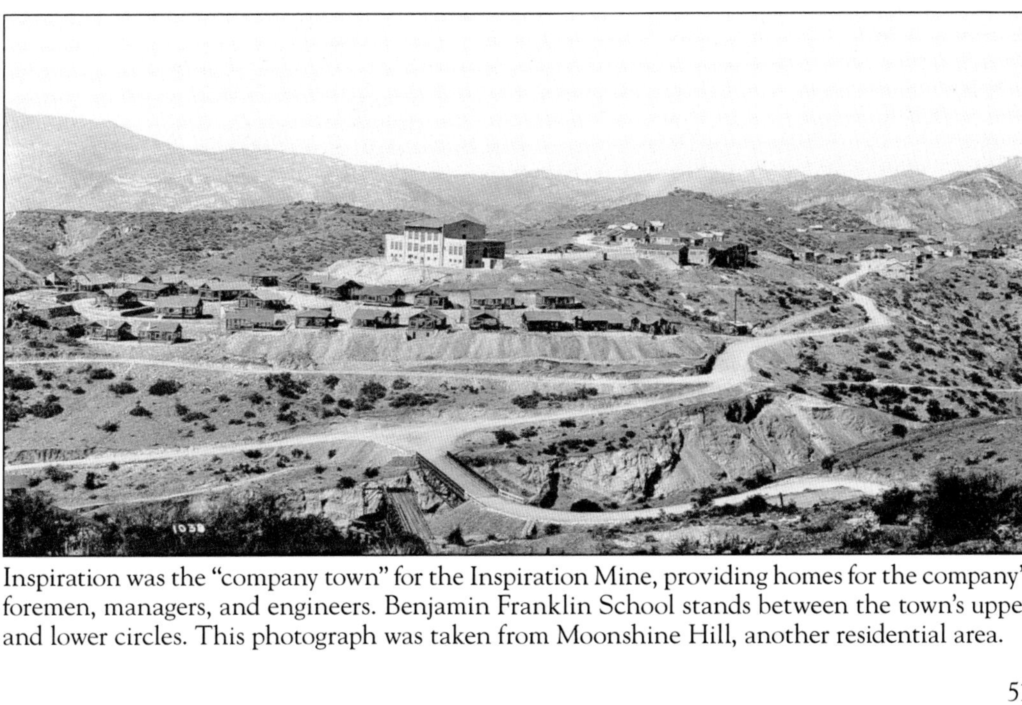

Inspiration was the "company town" for the Inspiration Mine, providing homes for the company's foremen, managers, and engineers. Benjamin Franklin School stands between the town's upper and lower circles. This photograph was taken from Moonshine Hill, another residential area.

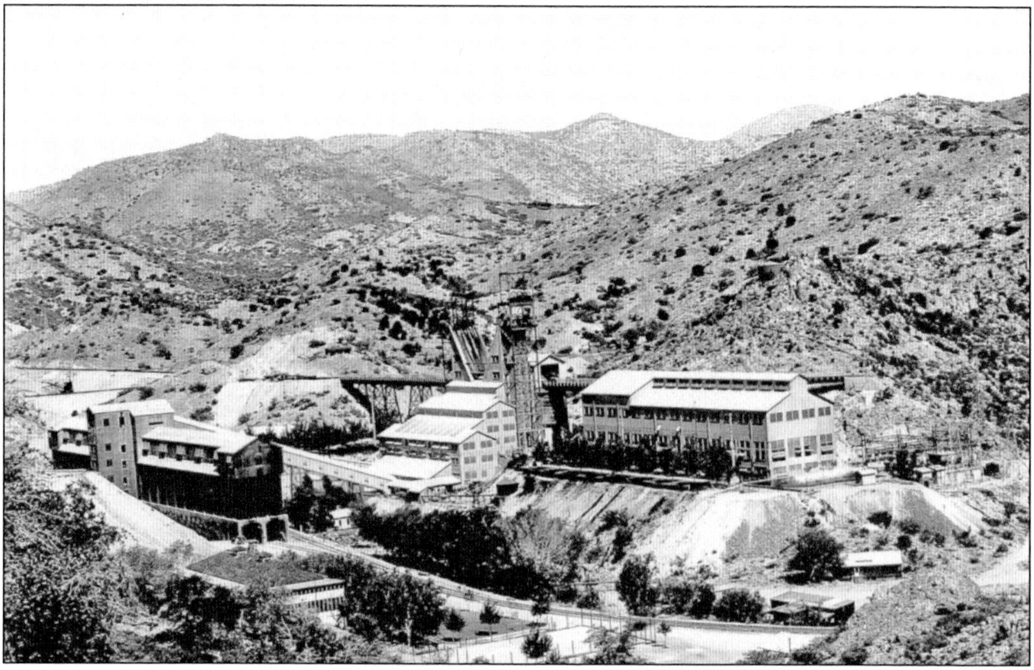

The double headframe of Inspiration Mine's main shaft is surrounded by a mill, storage bins, a boardinghouse, and a tennis court. A portion of the mine's industrial railroad can be seen in the photograph.

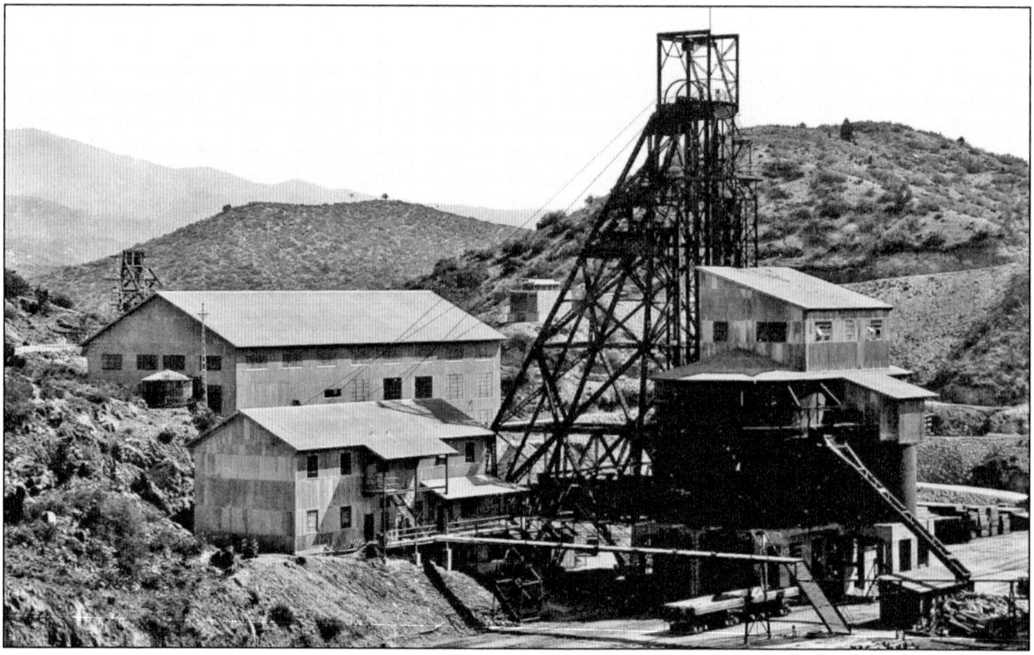

The Live Oak area of the Inspiration Mine was located in a canyon west of Miami. This is the main shaft and its associated surface buildings.

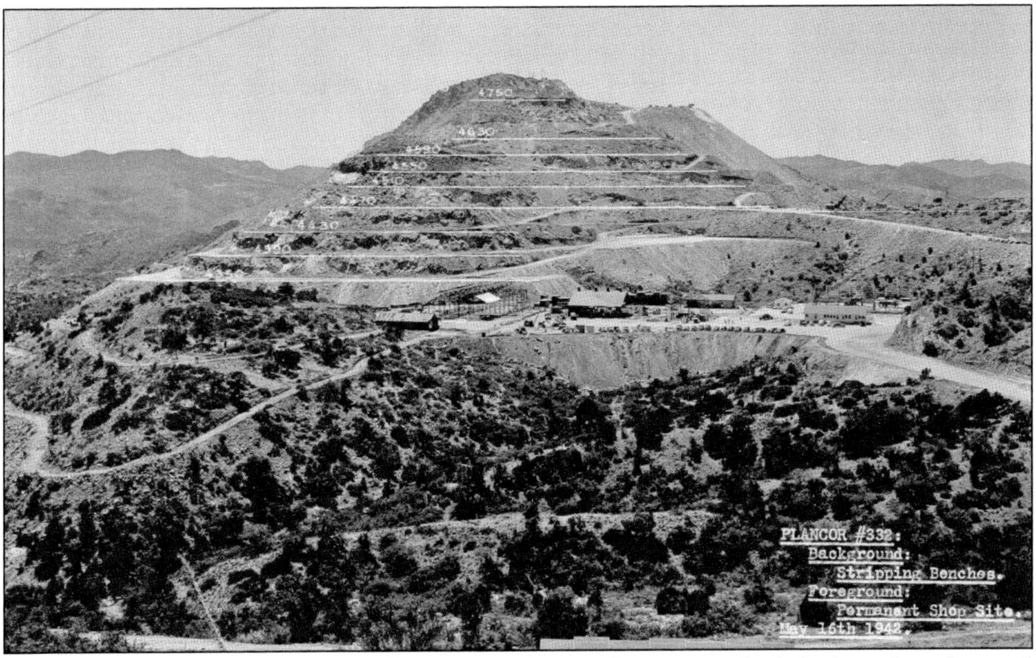

Castle Dome Mine was a division of the Miami Copper Company, which had purchased several small operations in Pinto Valley and combined them around 1940. The tiered "layer cake" site (above) eventually became a deep open pit. The concentrating mill and other structures (below) were later dismantled and moved to a new copper mining site.

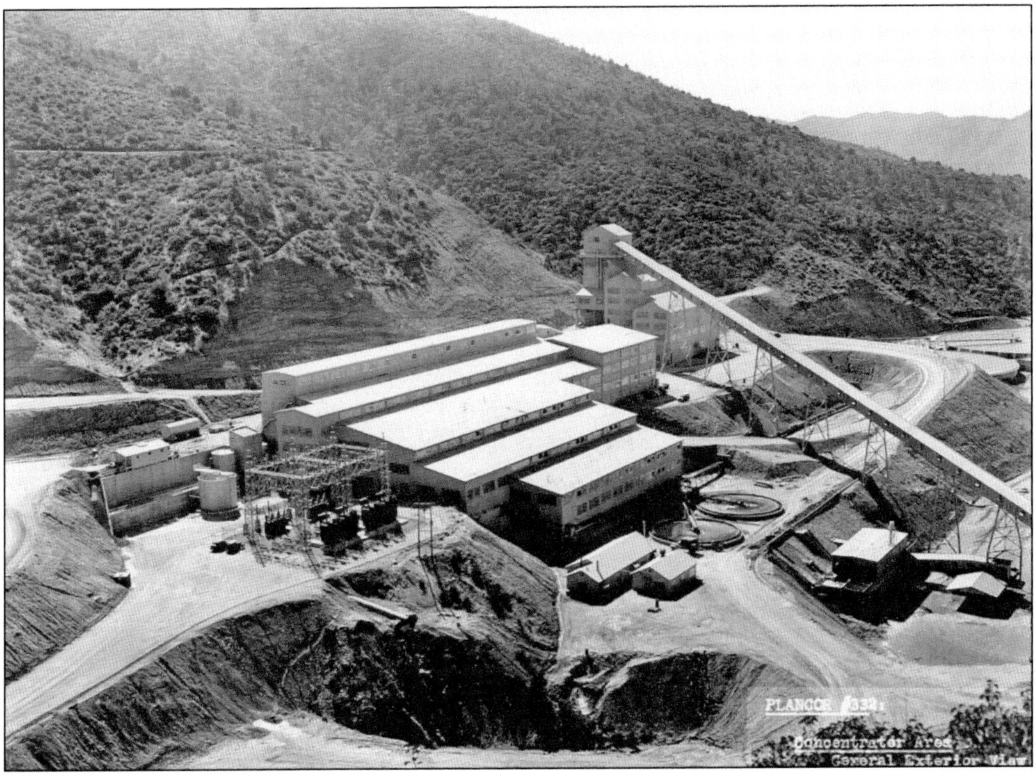

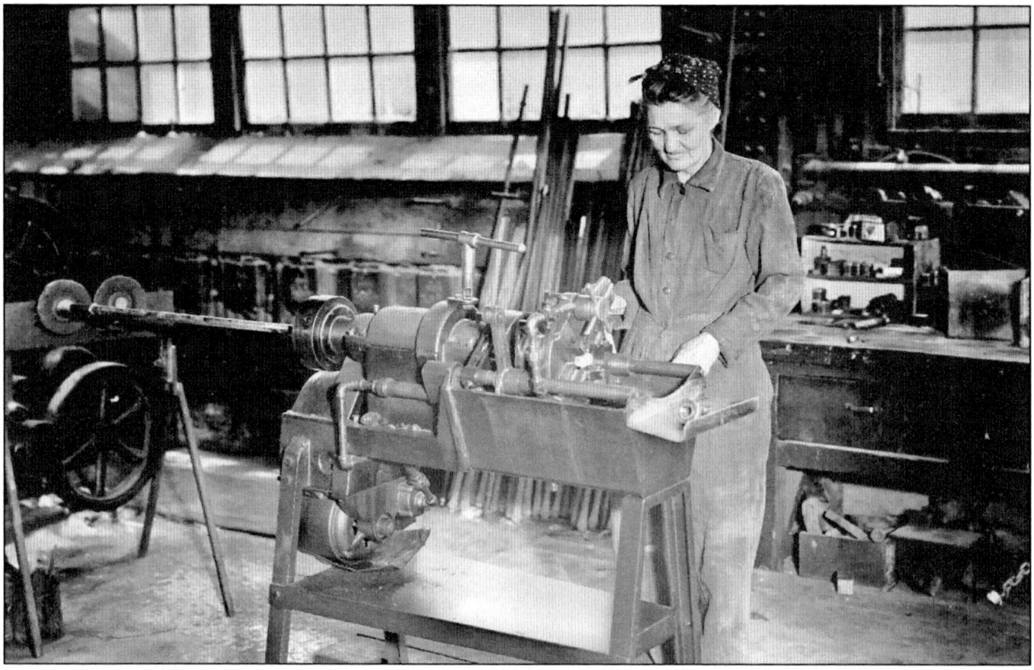

During World War II, Castle Dome was one of the first mines to hire women. This lady is working in the machine shop in 1944.

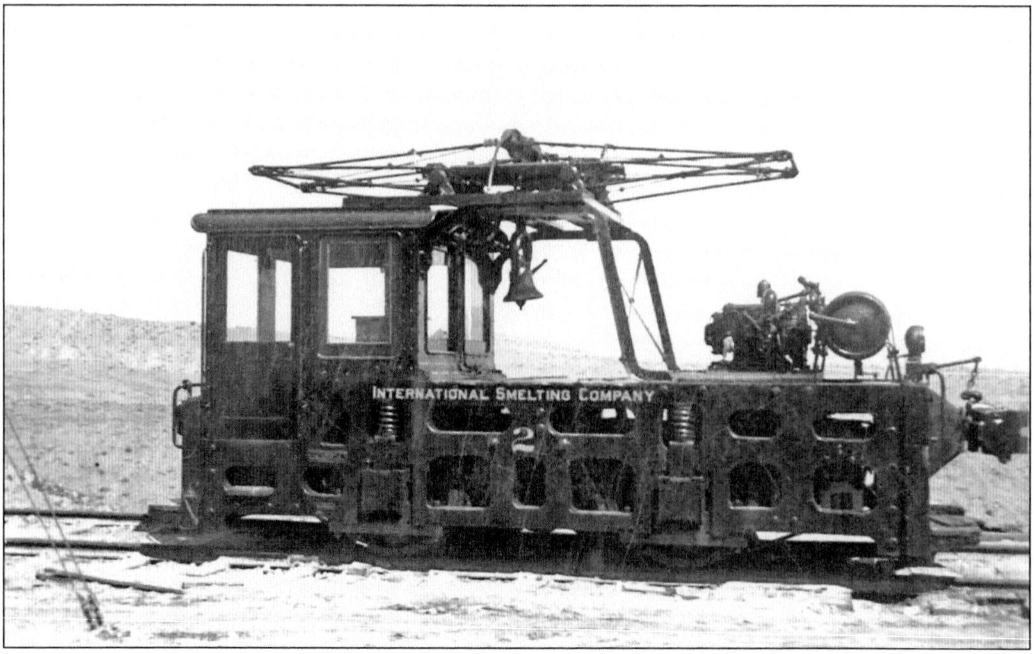

The international smelter was "blown in" on Inspiration property in 1915. The electric locomotive did yard work in and around the smelter.

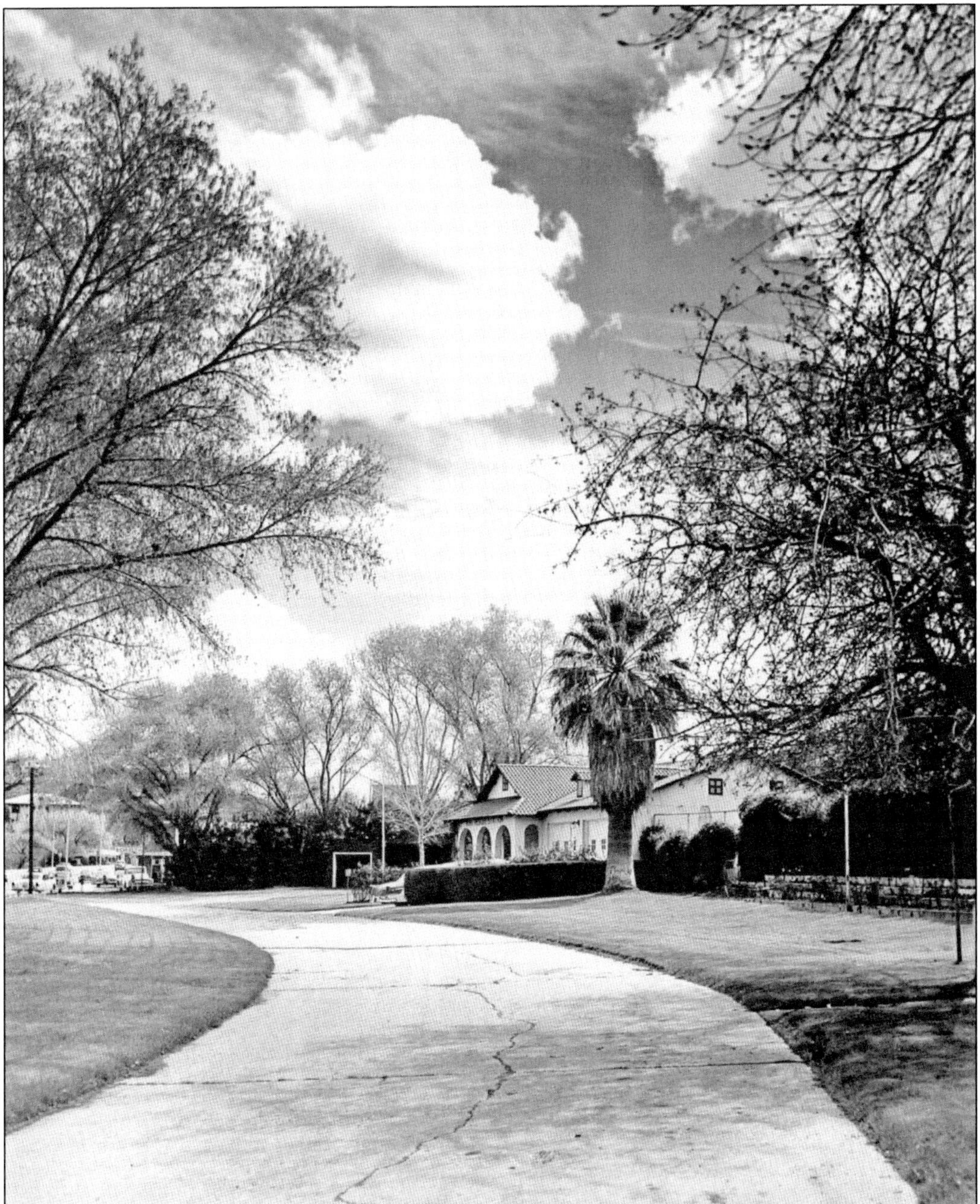

The Globe-Miami Mine Rescue Station, pictured in 1956, opened in 1920 to provide rescue and safety training for local miners. Equipment and supplies were kept in the station, and the station director, Orr Woodburn, and his family lived in the building.

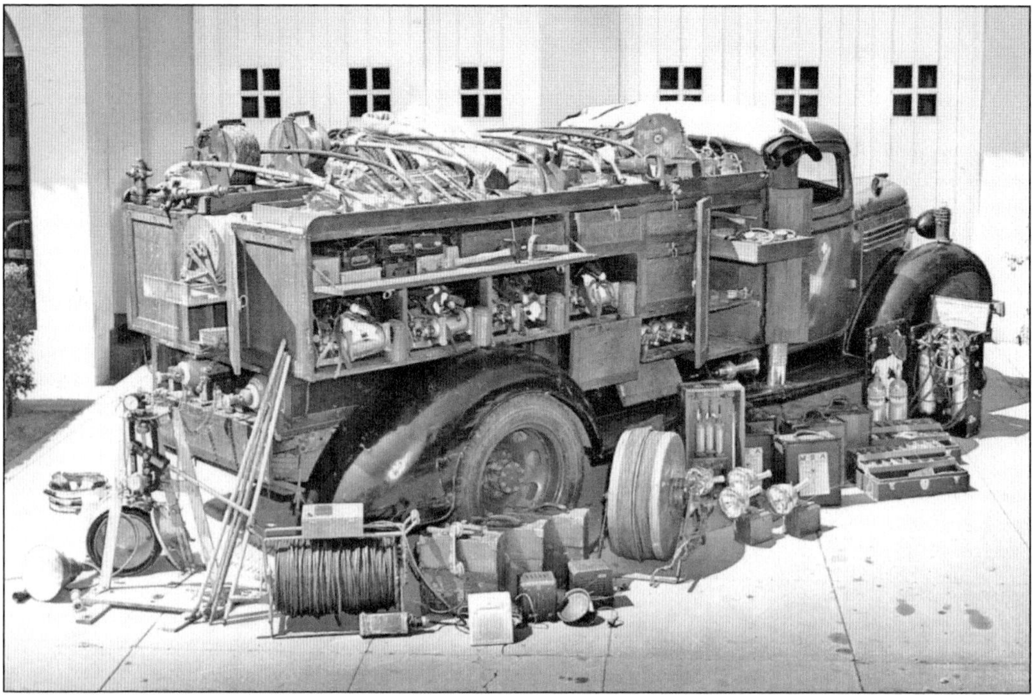

The mine rescue truck was equipped with tools and other gear necessary to respond to accidents, fires, and cave-ins at the mines.

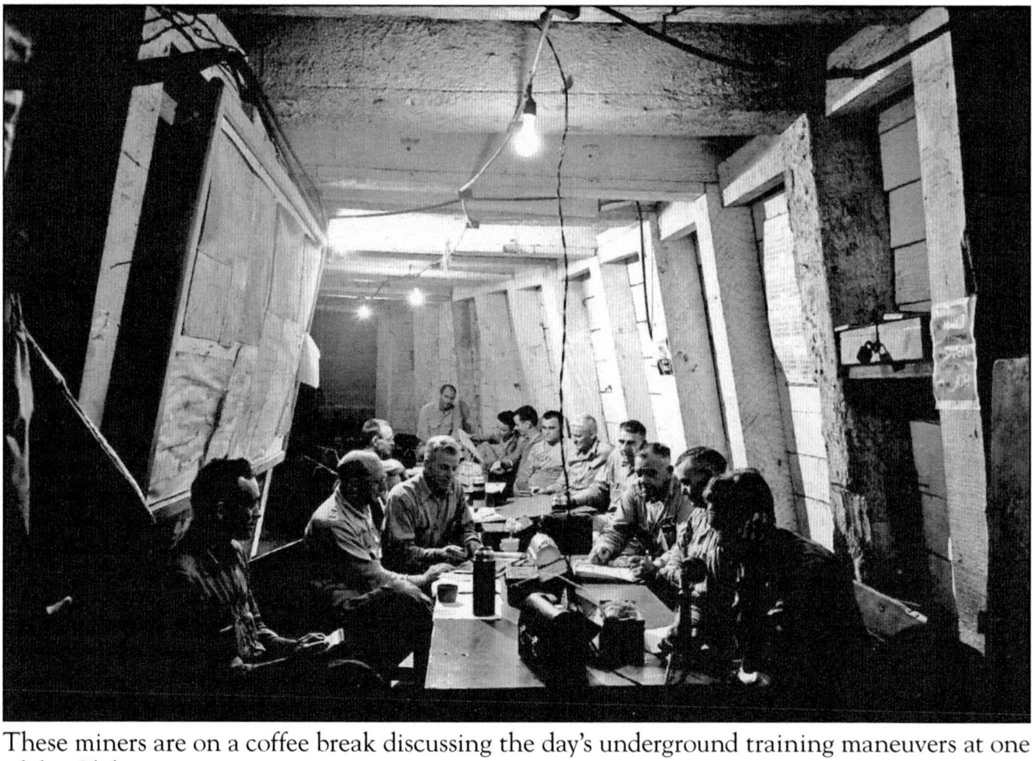

These miners are on a coffee break discussing the day's underground training maneuvers at one of the Globe-area mines.

Four

Buildings and Businesses

"Conditions in the business section of Globe are a revelation to the average stranger who comes to the city expecting to find the usual environs of a mining camp. Far from being a temporary settlement of makeshift buildings, Globe is a city of modern and substantial architecture. Buildings of brick and stone are handsomely finished on the interior," stated the *Arizona Silver Belt* newspaper in 1909. The writer illustrated his point as follows: "The Dominion Hotel is a carefully appointed hostelry, built of stone and brick and the character of its service is excellent."

This description of Globe, of course, was not always true. Globe's first merchant, T. C. Stallo, sold his goods from a tent under a sycamore tree. When he discovered it was illegal to sell liquor because he was operating on federal land, he sold potatoes for $1 each and threw in a small flask of whiskey at no charge.

Globe's commercial buildings were made of adobe blocks until Bremen's sawmill began supplying lumber in 1878. Within a few years, masonry building materials such as locally quarried dacite, tufa stone, and fired brick from Briggs's Brick yard became available

The pioneer businessmen of Globe were a diverse group, some of whom "moved on" from Silver City, New Mexico. Alonzo Bailey came in 1877 and founded the Old Dominion Commercial Company, where George W. P. Hunt later became company president. Harley Hitchcock opened a drugstore in 1879 that became today's Palace Pharmacy. William Ryan arrived in 1881 and started a business that eventually became the statewide Ryan Evans Drug store chain. In 1903, John Joseph Keegan purchased a saloon that had gambling tables on the main floor and a bordello upstairs. Brothers William and Louis Sultan opened a business that later became a Woolworth's.

In 1907, a vendor on Broad Street sold tamales from a steaming bucket. During the nationwide bank panic that year, the Globe Clearing House issued certificates that could be used in lieu of cash. Local merchants were reluctant to accept them, but the tamale vendor cried, "Bring 'em on. I'll take 'em all." Soon others followed his example. The tamale man "stopped the panic of 1907, as far as Globe was concerned," according to *Financing the Frontier* by Ernest J. Hopkins.

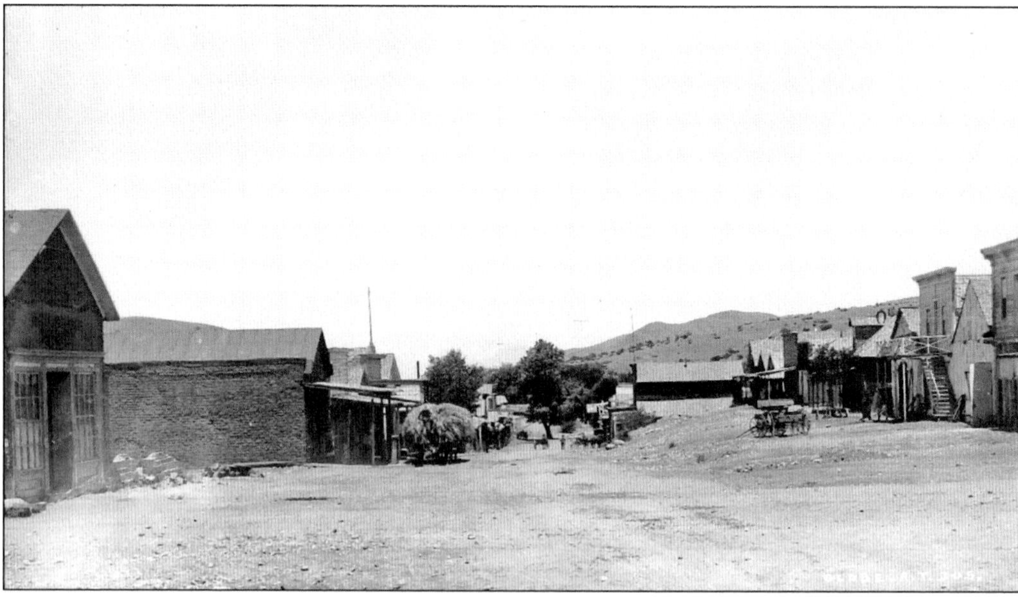

Globe's first businesses were located on North Broad Street near the Pinal Creek Crossing. This view looks north toward the "hanging tree" in the middle of the dirt street. The hay was probably headed for the livery stable.

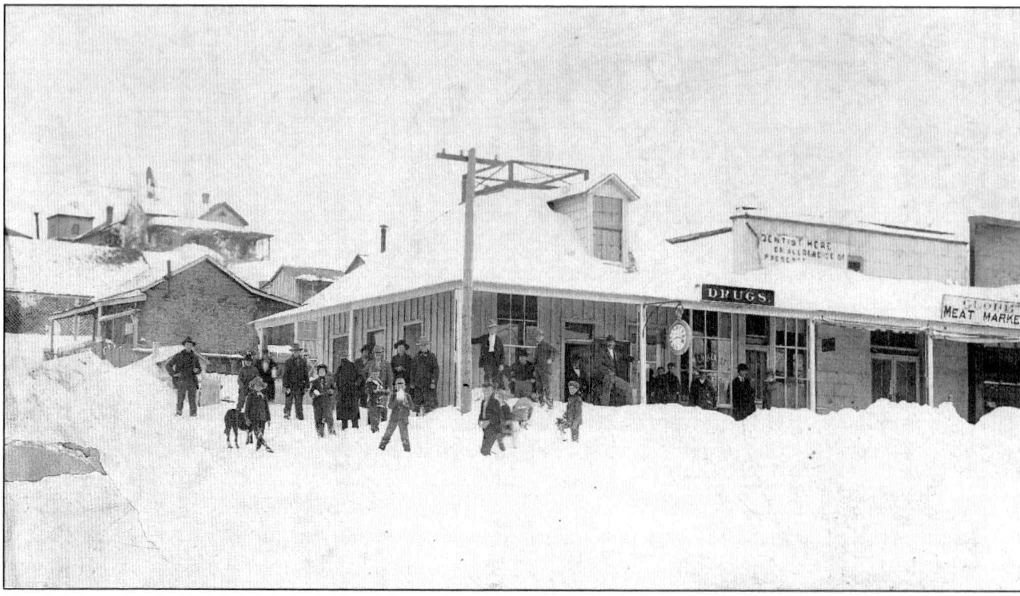

An unusually heavy snow fell on Globe in December 1898. The snowstorm caused the outbound passenger train to stall in a snowbank east of Globe, delaying the train's departure for three days.

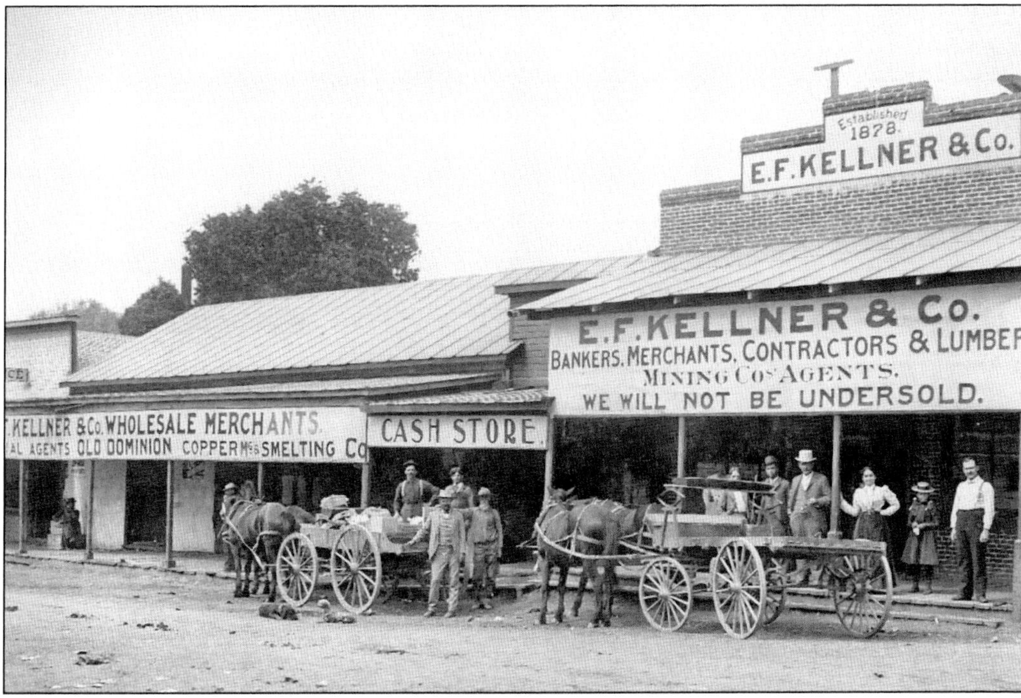

Ernest Kellner, pictured above in the white hat, founded Kellner Mercantile in 1878. The prominent signs tell it all! He later acquired farming and ranching properties, a stockyard, and a second store in Phoenix. He stands beside the teller's cage in his "cash store" in the photograph below.

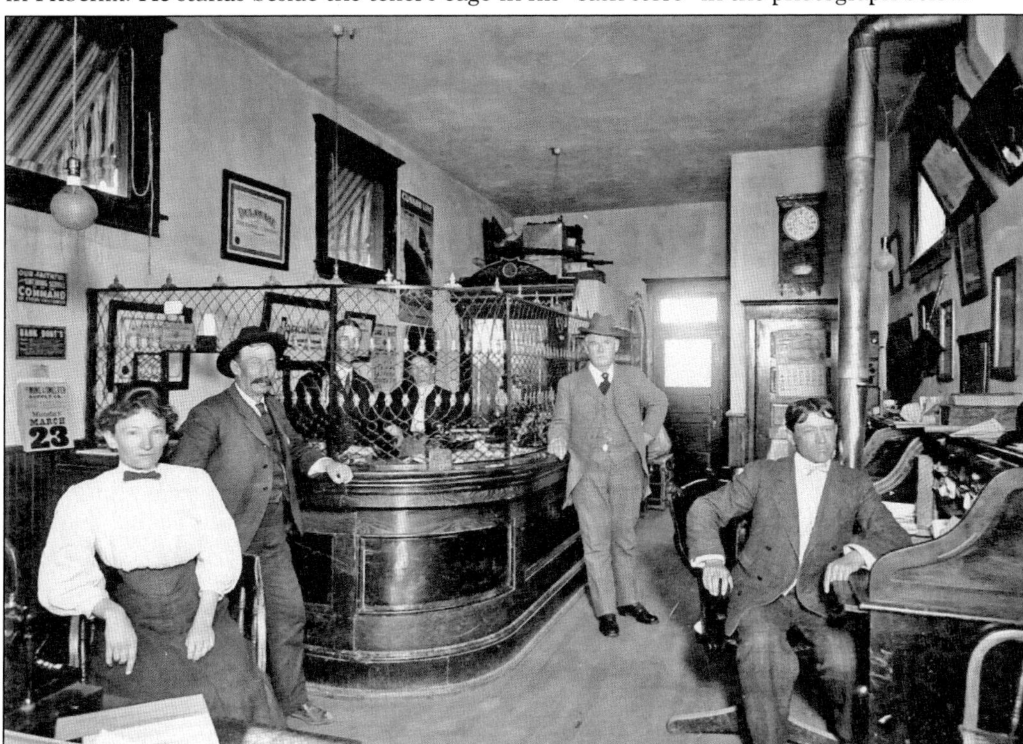

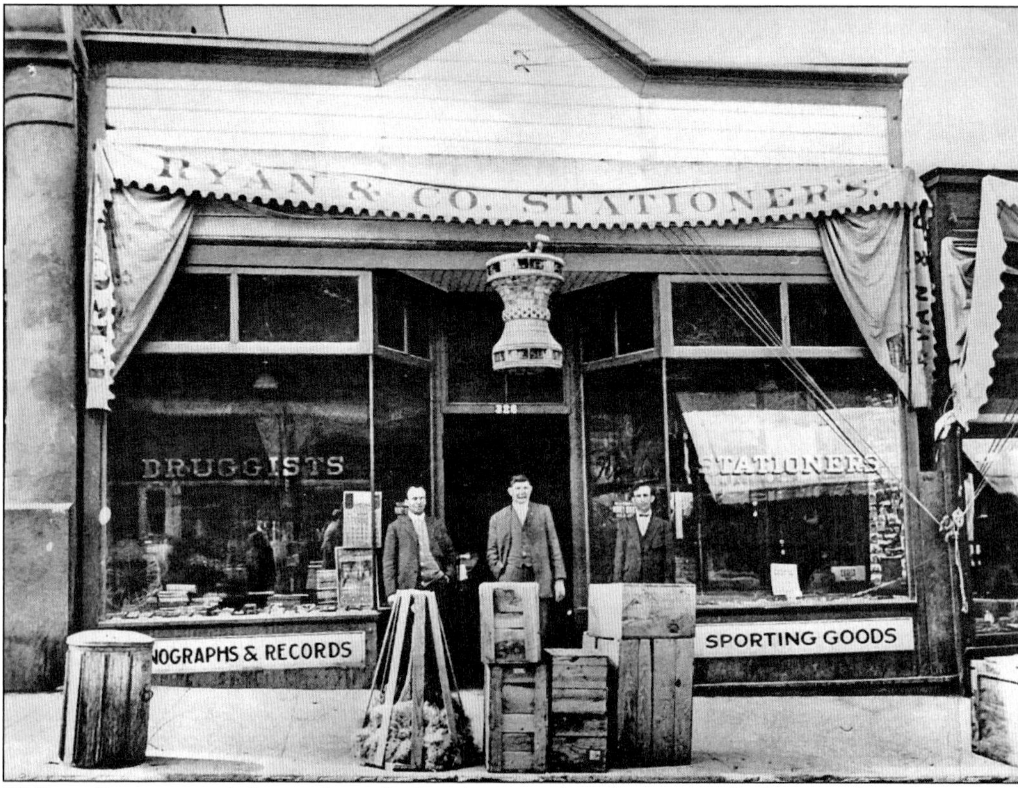

William Ryan carried the mail, worked and invested in the mines, dealt in cattle, and operated a dairy before he established Ryan and Company Stationers in 1904. The business expanded to offer other merchandise, and in 1908, he hired a pharmacist. Ryan later formed a partnership with Larry Evans, and they developed the Ryan Evans Drugstore chain statewide.

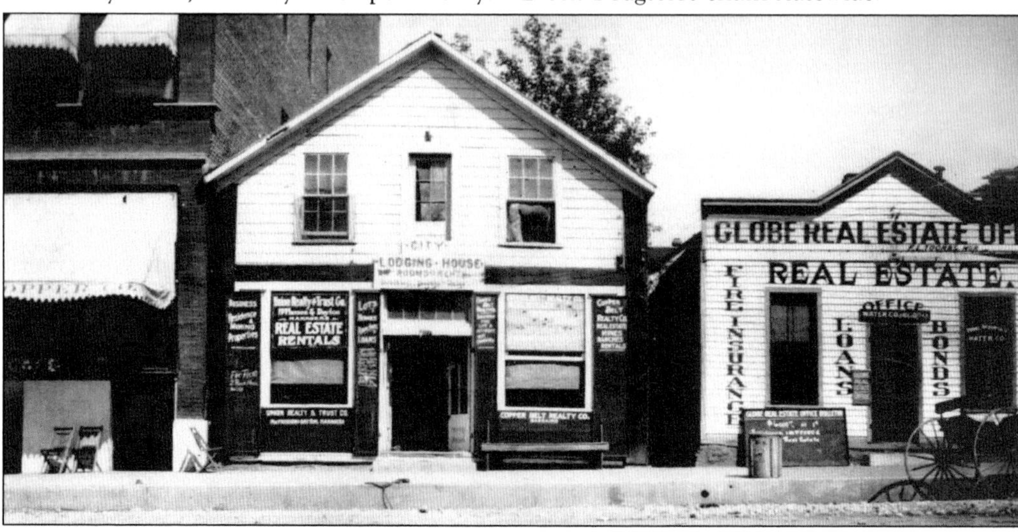

This two-story building, photographed *c.* 1916, was home to the Globe Realty and Trust Company and the Copper Belt Realty Company. The City Lodging House offered rooms upstairs. The adjacent building also housed a real estate business as well as a place to buy insurance or bonds, arrange a loan, or pay your water bill.

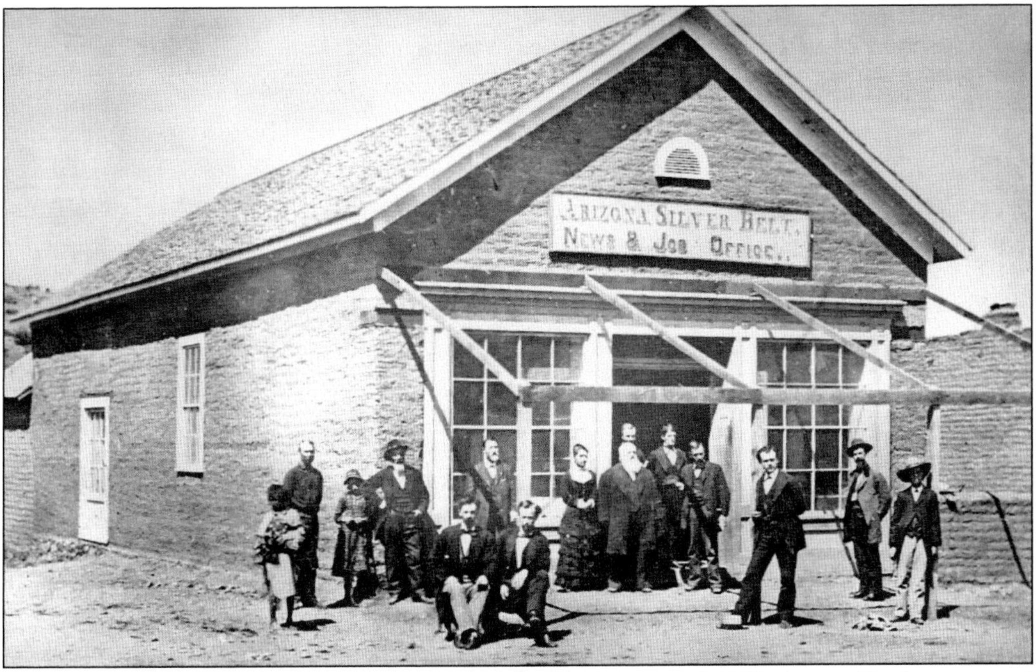

The Arizona Silver Belt office was built of adobe blocks around 1878. Aaron Hackney moved his printing equipment into the building and began publishing the *Arizona Silver Belt* newspaper. Hackney is the bearded man at the door; his nephew and partner, Joseph Hamill, is in the right foreground. Hackney lived in an apartment at the back of the building.

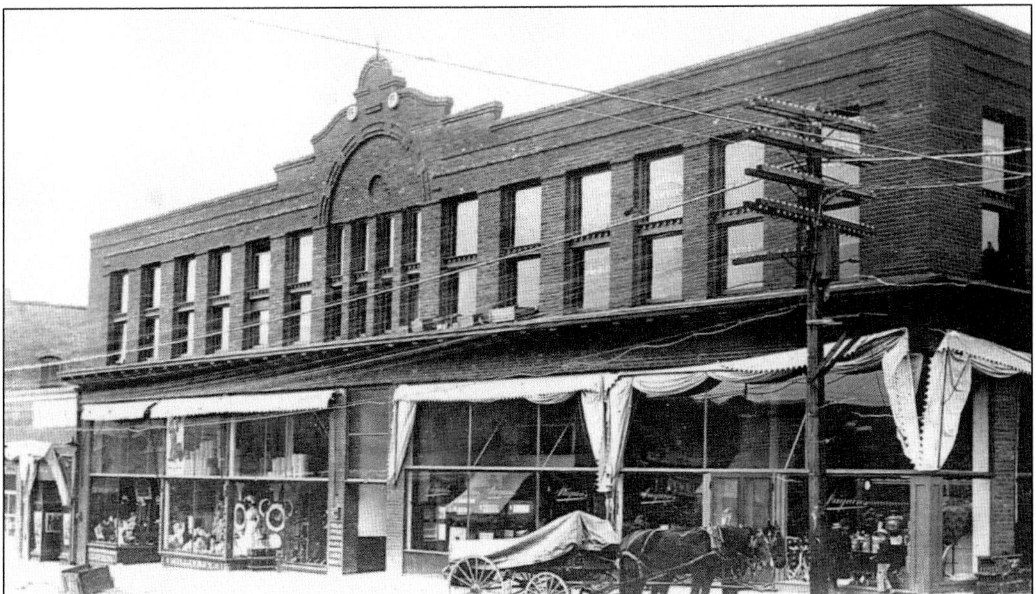

Because of its architectural style, Black Jack Newman's Globe office building became known as the Colonial Building. Initial tenants were Brown's Millinery and Naquin's Furniture Store. During the 1940s, a bowling alley was located in the building. The Colonial Building was razed in the 1950s to make room for a wider Broad Street, then U.S. 60 through Globe.

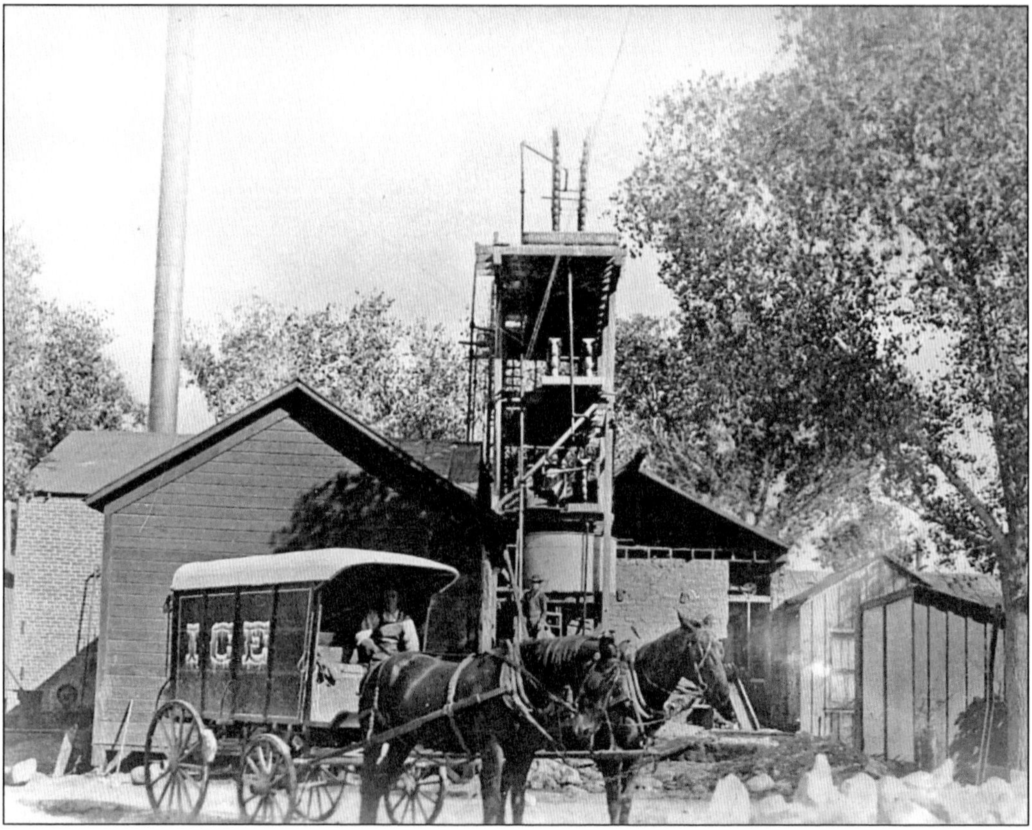

At first, Globe's ice supply was blocks of ice cut from frozen ponds in the Pinal Mountains and hauled into town. In the early 1900s, ice was provided by the Globe Ice Company near downtown Globe. Globe Ice was delivered to saloons and meat markets in a horse-drawn ice wagon.

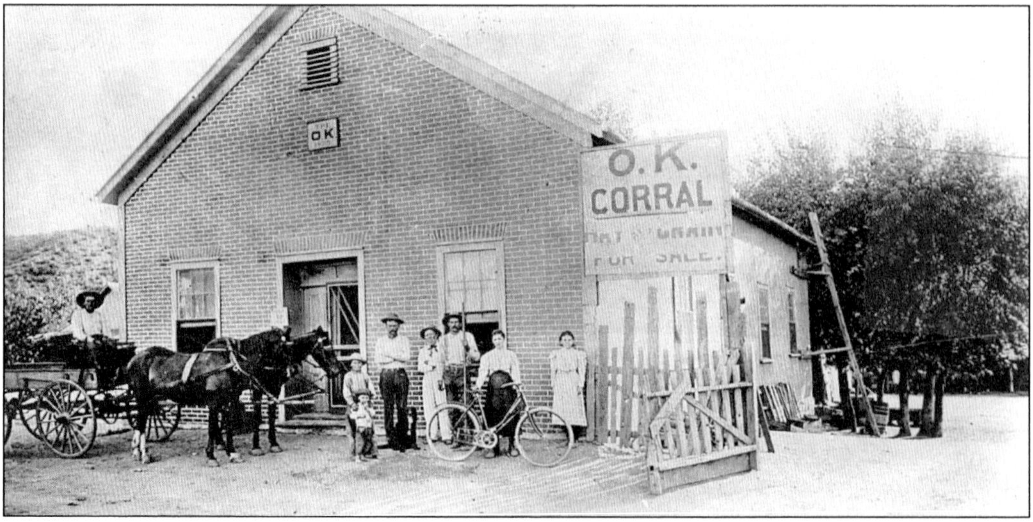

W. P. Kelsey's O.K. Corral sold hay and grain, provided horse-drawn tallyho wagon parties, and rented wagons and horses for hauling and traveling. Kelsey later became one of the first automobile dealers in Globe.

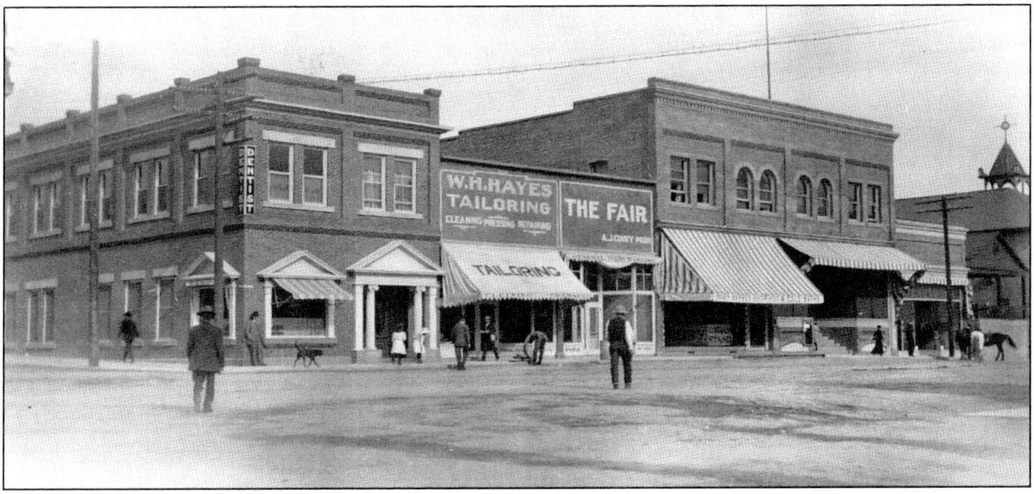

Jones Mortuary and the Federal Building anchor this section of Broad Street. Tailor W. H. Hayes advertised, "We will combine fashionable fabrics, distinct style and new ideas with brains in an endeavor to make you the best suit you ever wore." The Fair offered ladies' and men's clothing "to the well dresser."

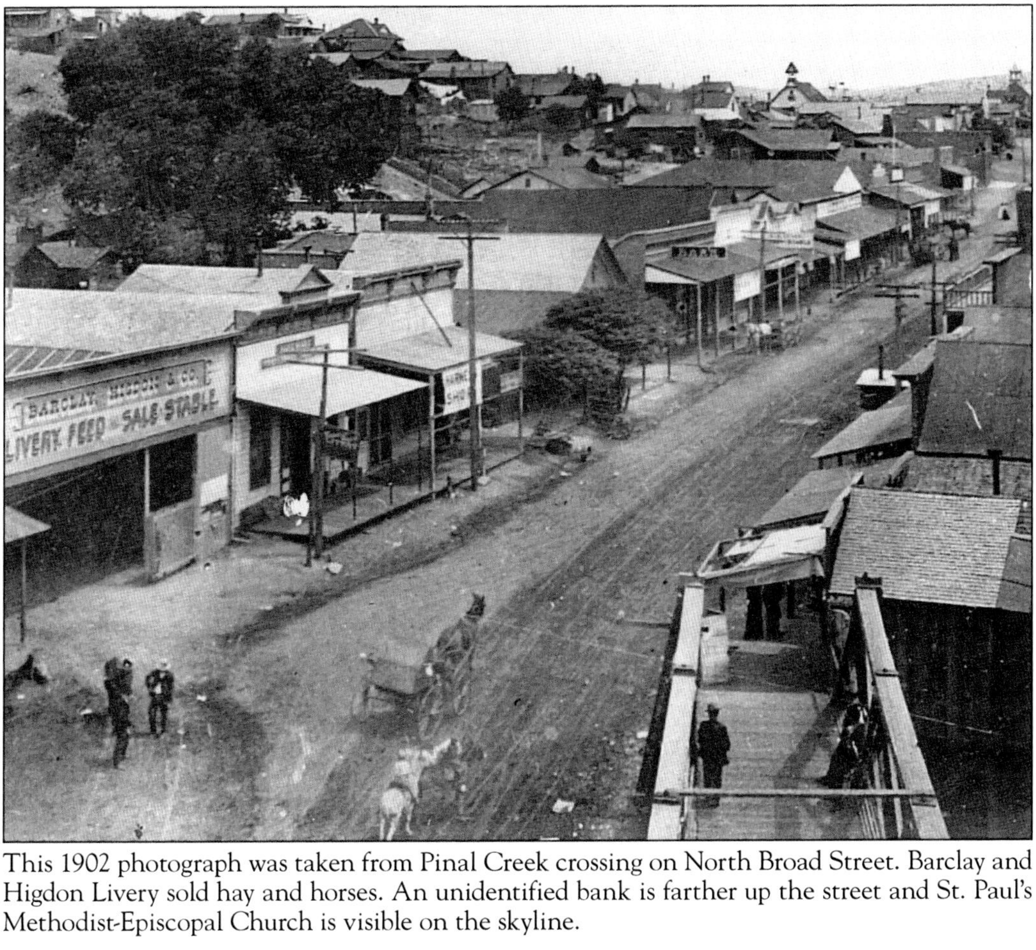

This 1902 photograph was taken from Pinal Creek crossing on North Broad Street. Barclay and Higdon Livery sold hay and horses. An unidentified bank is farther up the street and St. Paul's Methodist-Episcopal Church is visible on the skyline.

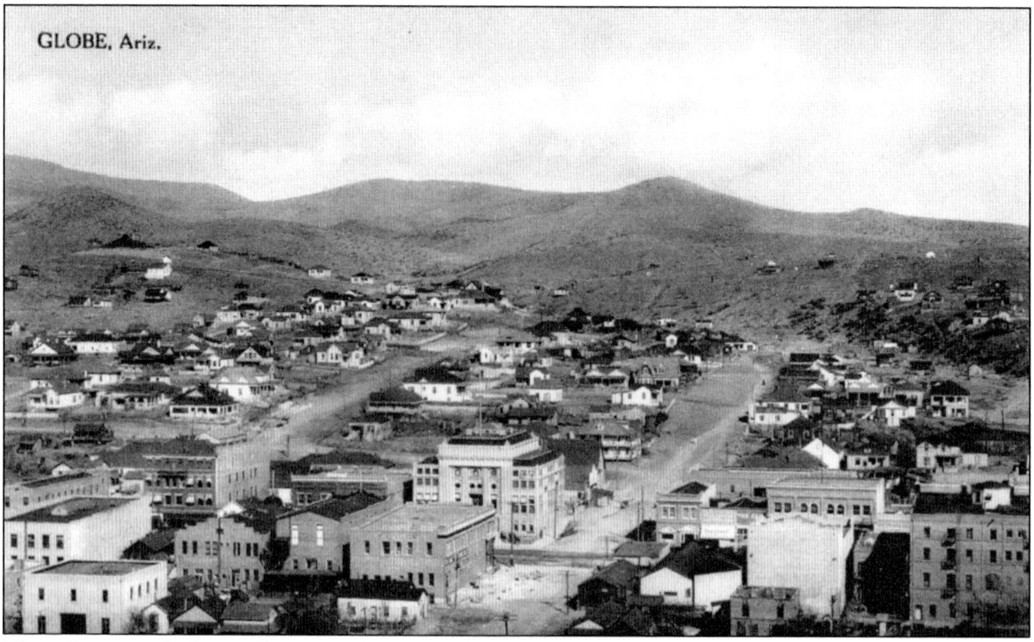

This photograph shows the central part of Globe's business district *c.* 1910. Thirty years earlier, the city's commercial district was developing four blocks to the north (left). The prominent structure in the center of the picture is the three-year-old Gila County Courthouse.

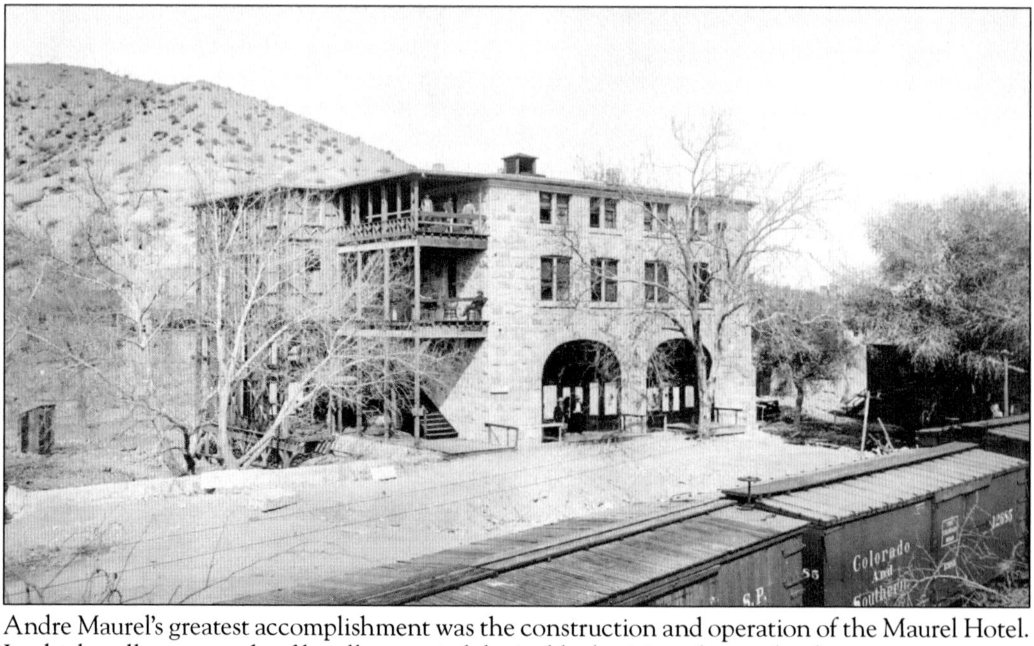

Andre Maurel's greatest accomplishment was the construction and operation of the Maurel Hotel. Its thick walls were made of locally quarried dacite blocks. Maurel served as his own stonecutter, a skill he had learned in France. Large stone arches, cozy porches, and a spring-fed swimming pool lured out-of-town guests to the Maurel Hotel.

The Globe Elks Building was erected on Mesquite Street in 1910. Robert Ripley's *Believe It or Not* featured it as the world's tallest three-story building. Local legend is that the number of bricks needed was overestimated, but the contractor just kept adding them until they were gone.

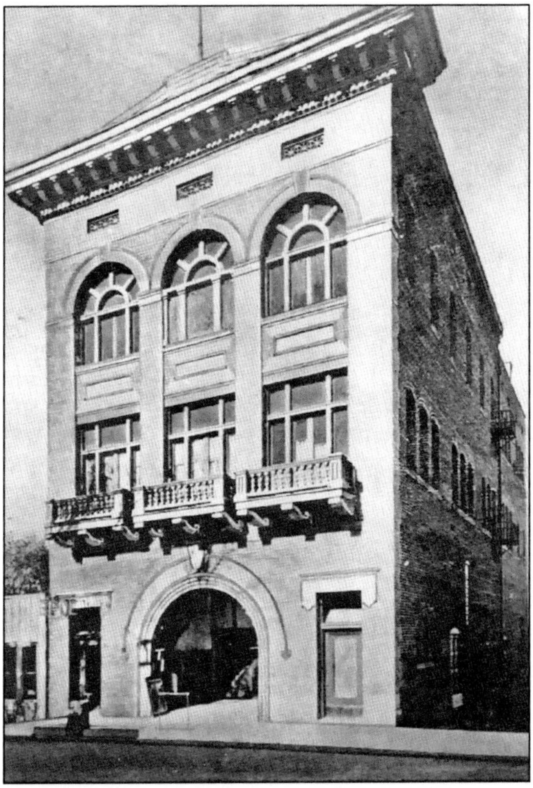

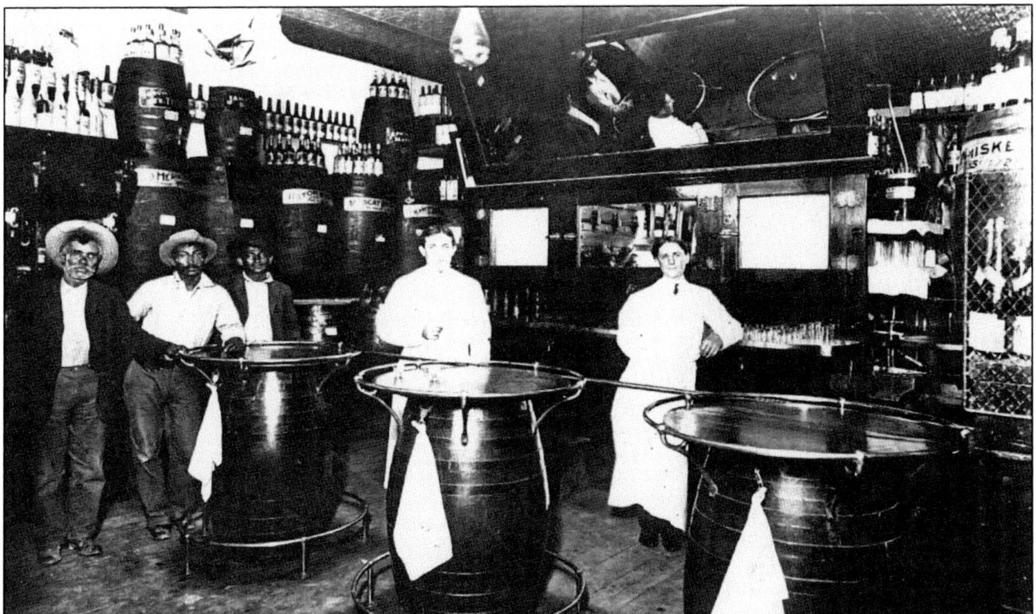

The saloons in Globe advertised that they sold fine wines, whiskey, and other liquors. Did anyone drink beer in those days? You bet! The Parlor offered Tony Faust Beer, "recommended by physicians throughout the world," and Keegan's Saloon suggested ordering the biggest "schooner" of beer in town.

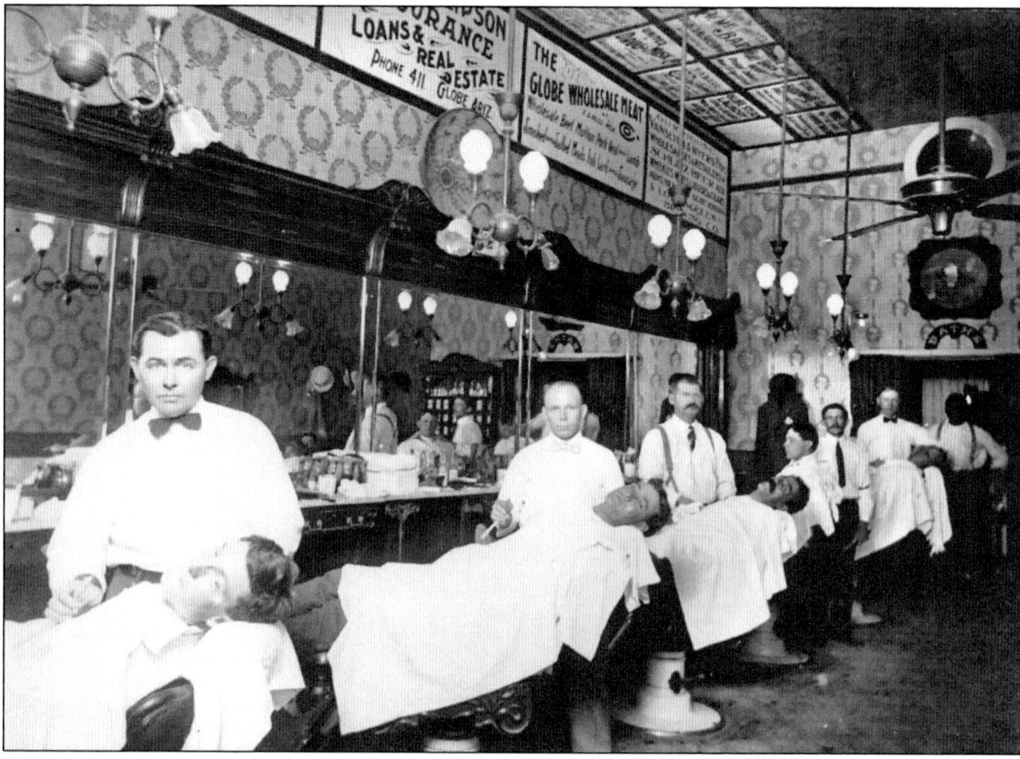

In 1908, the Newport Barber Shop was a popular place to get a trim and shave, the latest news, some advice, and the same old joke as last week.

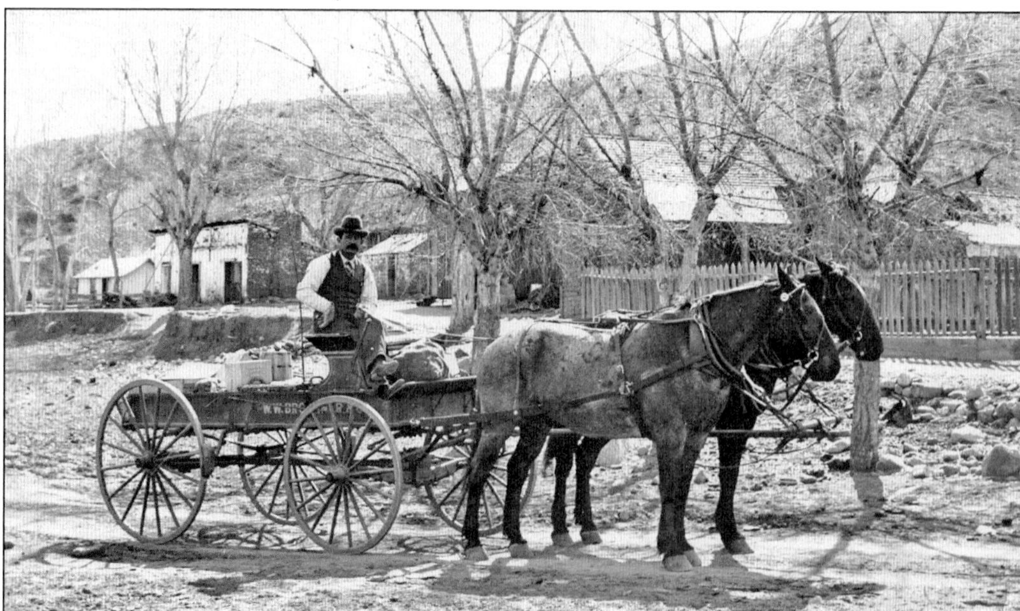

The driver of this wagon is delivering goods ordered at the W. W. Brookner Store. William Webb Brookner advertised his business as "The Big Store." He was also a partner in a trading post at old San Carlos and served five terms as the treasurer of Gila County.

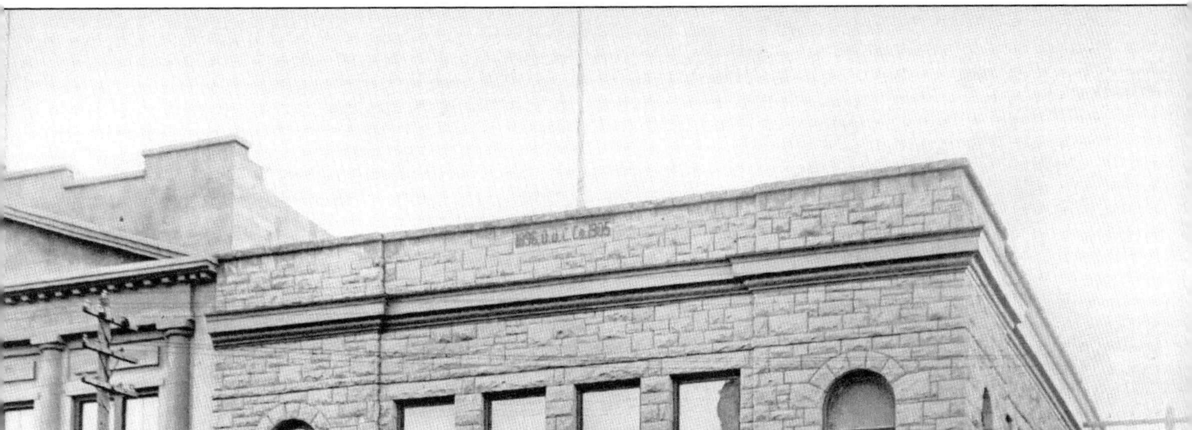

The Old Dominion Commercial Company operated in this building for 25 years. The business, founded by Alonzo Bailey, was first located at Broad and Mesquite Streets. When it outgrew the building in 1904, the business moved to its new structure just one block away at Cedar Street. The new store was made of locally quarried stone and completed within one year at a cost of $30,000. Bailey retired a year later. By this time, George W. P. Hunt had been president of the corporation for five years. Under his direction, it became the largest business on Broad Street. In 1928, the Old Dominion Commercial Company went out of business. The J. C. Penney Company moved into the building that year. The company displayed and sold J. C. Penney merchandise on the main floor, the mezzanine, and the bargain basement. This store in Globe was one of many small-town stores that were closed by the parent company in the 1990s.

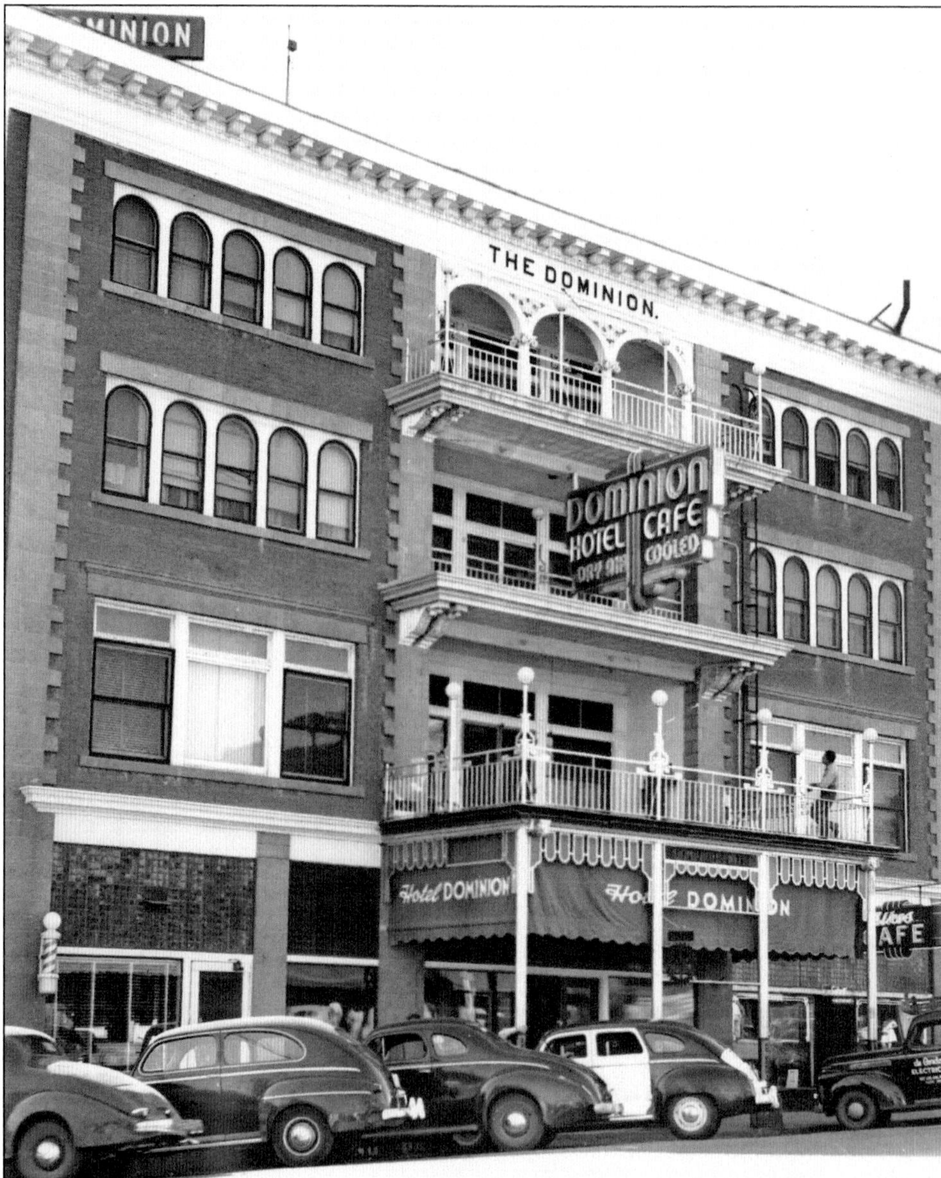

The 1906 Dominion Hotel brought prestige, comfortable lodging, and fine dining to the city of Globe. Construction of the Classic Revival building was financed by John B. "Blackjack" Newman and Samuel L. Gibson. Hotelier Alfred Hansen assisted with the plans and James Creighton from Phoenix was the architect. The hotel opened to the public on September 6, 1906. The hotel had 80 rooms, 30 of which had private baths. The first floor had a grand lobby, a billiard room, and fine restaurant. The furnishings were the best: lush carpets, chandeliers, marble counters, and copper handrails. Modern conveniences included electric lights, hot and cold running water, steam heat, and a well-stocked wine cellar. Local people enjoyed cocktails in the Cactus Room or socializing in the lobby. Guests came from far and wide. Theodore Roosevelt was a guest in 1911, as were Calvin Coolidge and Will Rogers in 1931. On December 23, 1981, a fire severely damaged the upper two floors. Within a few months, the grand old hotel was taken down to make room for a parking lot.

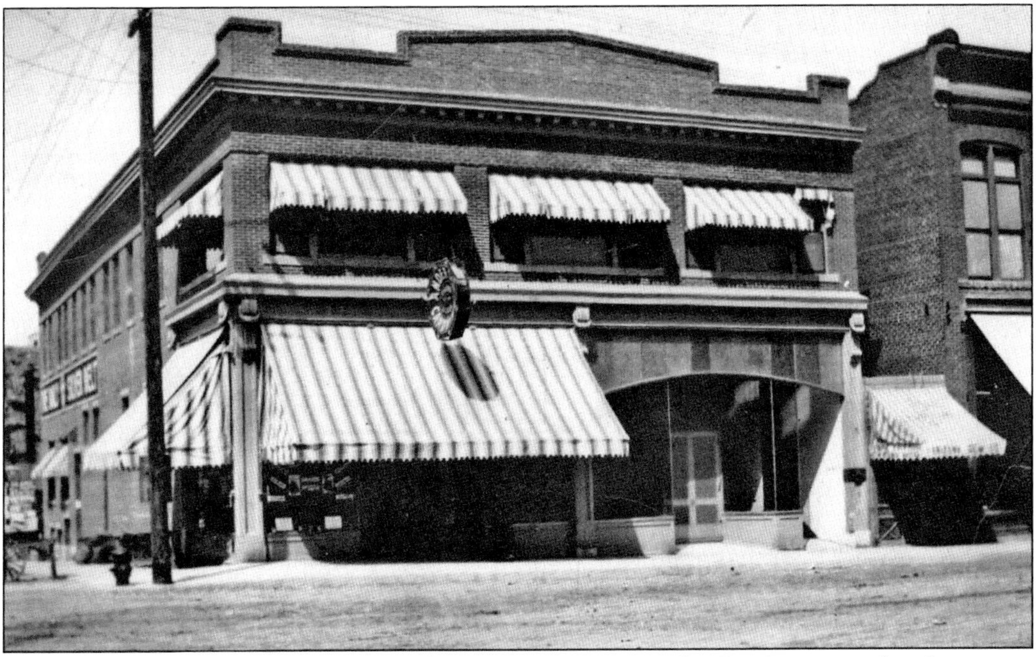

Rumanian immigrant Nathan Amster chose mining as a career, but he also invested in downtown Globe properties. The Amster Building became an attractive addition to Broad Street in 1909. Several different businesses have operated in the building and almost all have included a drugstore.

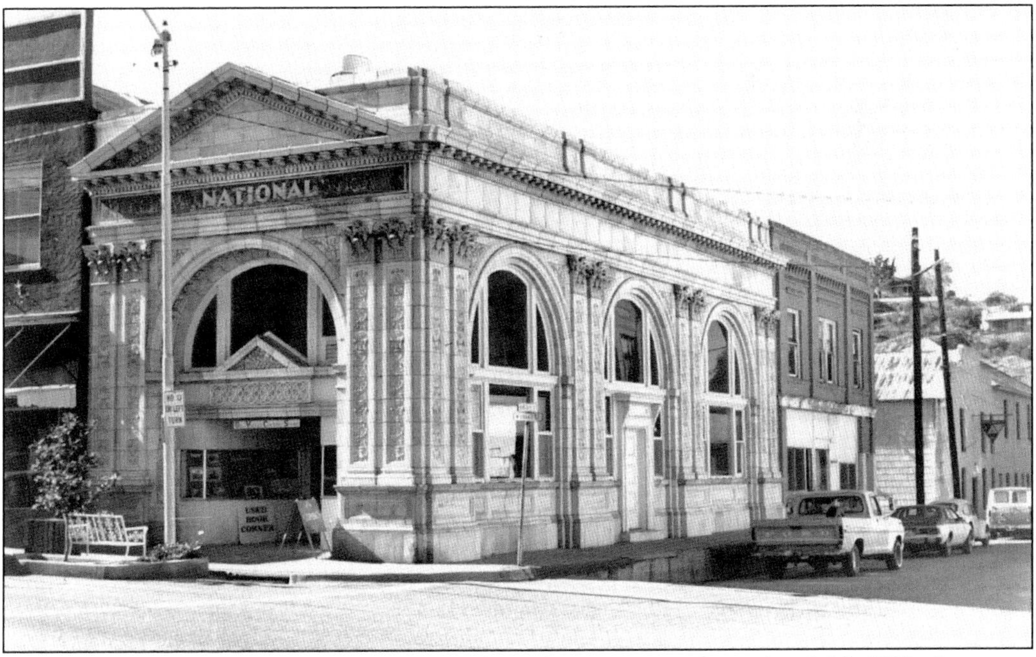

When the employees of the Valley National Bank came to work on April 25, 1933, they were greeted by two men who were intent on robbing the bank. The thugs locked two men in a vault and pushed two tellers into a closet. Bank manager Paul M. "Tuck" White nervously unlocked the main vault, and the robbers sped off with $34,000. Only one of the culprits was apprehended, and his half of the loot was recovered.

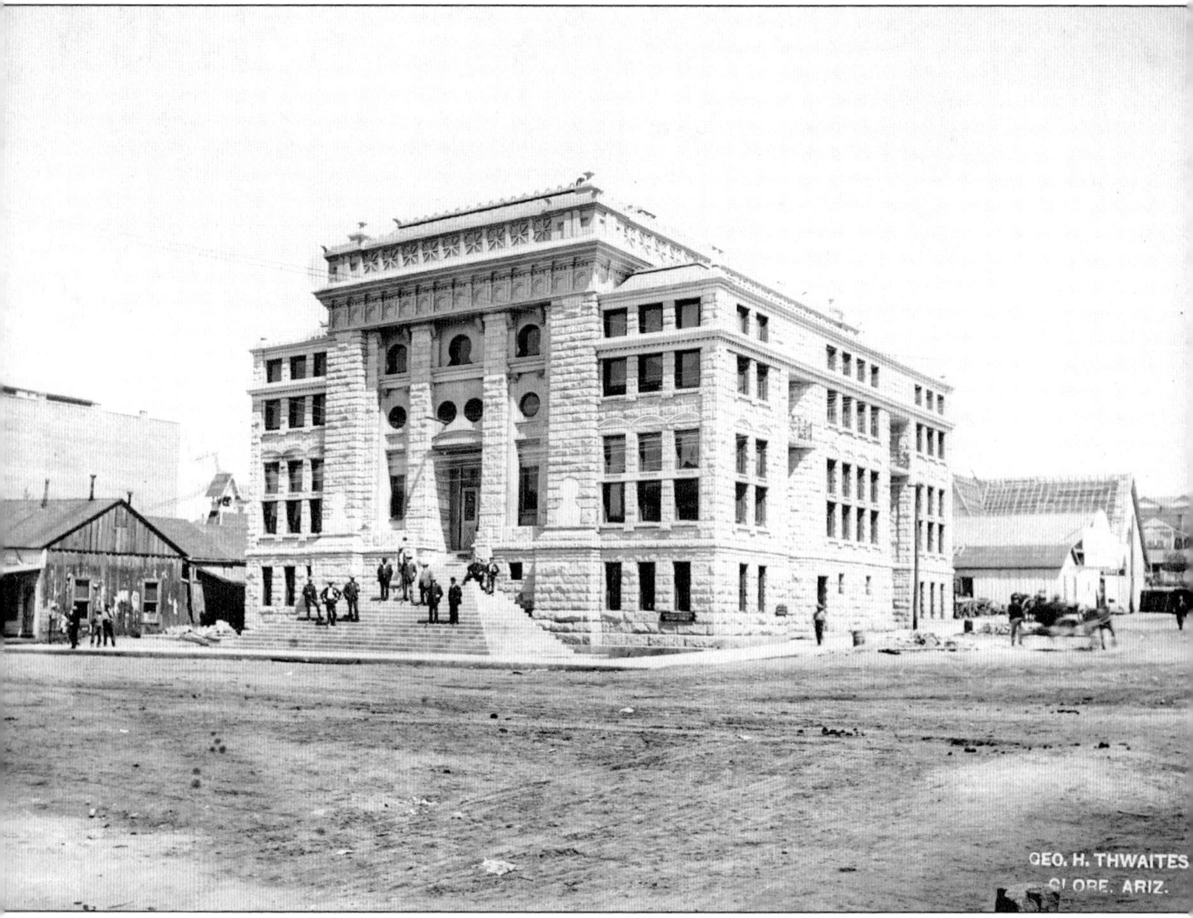

The men on the steps can be mighty proud of the impressive new Gila County Courthouse. The original courthouse that sat on this site was razed in 1906. The stone blocks from the old building, plus more from a nearby quarry, were used on the new structure. The sheriff's office and 16 jail cells occupied the ground floor. On the next story, the county conducted its official business. The third level housed a courtroom, judge and jury chambers, and the law library. The sheriff and his prisoners moved to an adjacent building in 1909. The courthouse served the people of Gila County for 70 years. In 1984, the building became the Cobre Valley Center for the Arts. The center displays and sells fine arts and crafts and offers theater, youth theater, and music and dance instruction to the community.

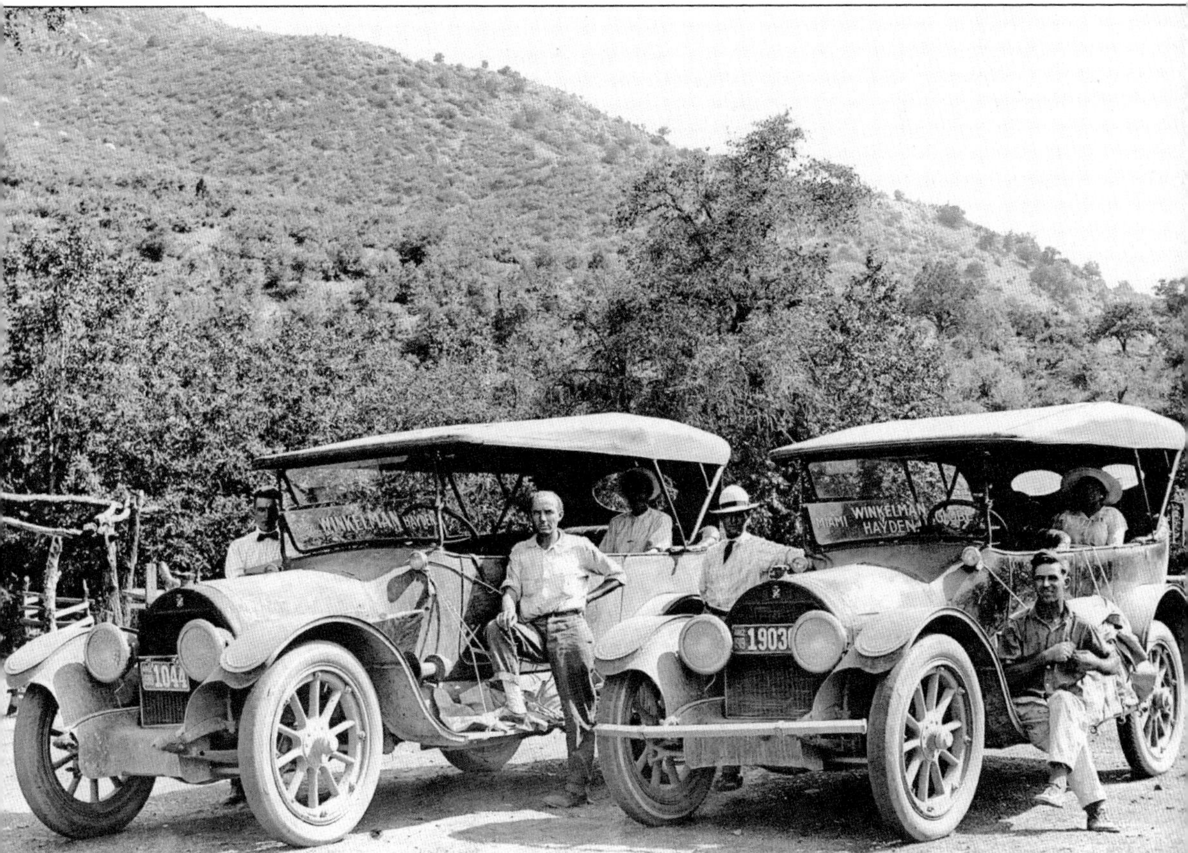

The Short Line Stages ran two Cadillacs between Globe-Miami and Hayden-Winkleman in 1919. This photograph was taken at the Martin Wood ranch at El Capitan, midway between the communities. Pictured are, from left to right, an unidentified man, Jack Pate, Cal Simpson, and Charles Allen; the women sitting in the Cadillacs are unidentified. Auto stages offered faster and more comfortable transportation than that provided by horseback, buggy, stagecoach, or train. W. P. Kelsey's O.K. Corral added automobiles to its merchandise in 1911 and started an auto stage line over Pioneer Pass in the Pinal Mountains to Kelvin and Mesa. He also opened a stage line over the Apache Trail, where he was in competition with the Gila Valley Transportation Company. They operated with a 1909 Pierce Arrow and a 1912 Overland. Starting in 1915, passengers on the Southern Pacific Railroad had the option of leaving the main line at Bowie and boarding a coach of the Arizona Eastern Railroad to Globe. After a night at the Dominion Hotel, they rode a Velie or Cole auto stage over the scenic Apache Trail to Phoenix.

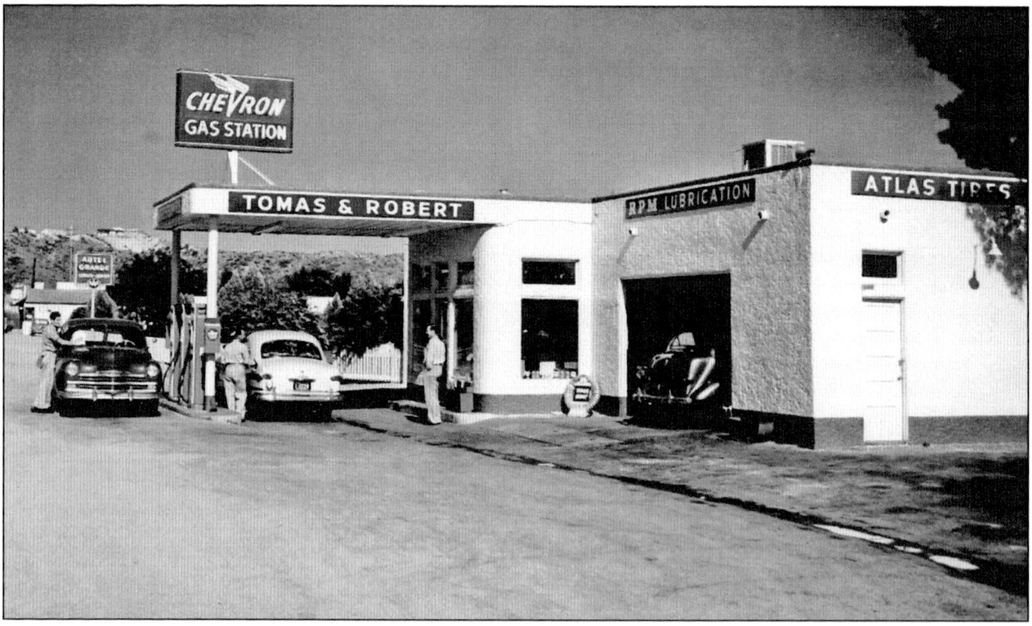

The Tomas and Robert Chevron station, pictured around 1950, was a full-service business. The attendants are seen filling the gas tank and washing the windshield.

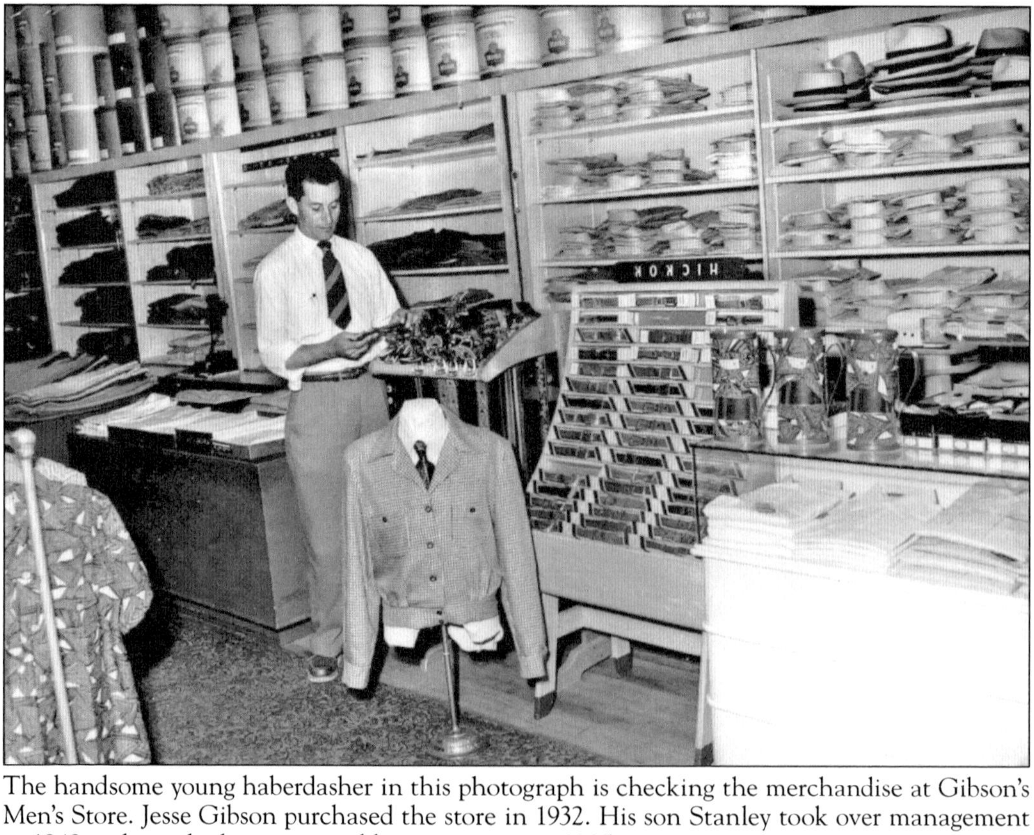

The handsome young haberdasher in this photograph is checking the merchandise at Gibson's Men's Store. Jesse Gibson purchased the store in 1932. His son Stanley took over management in 1949 and ran the business until his retirement in 1995.

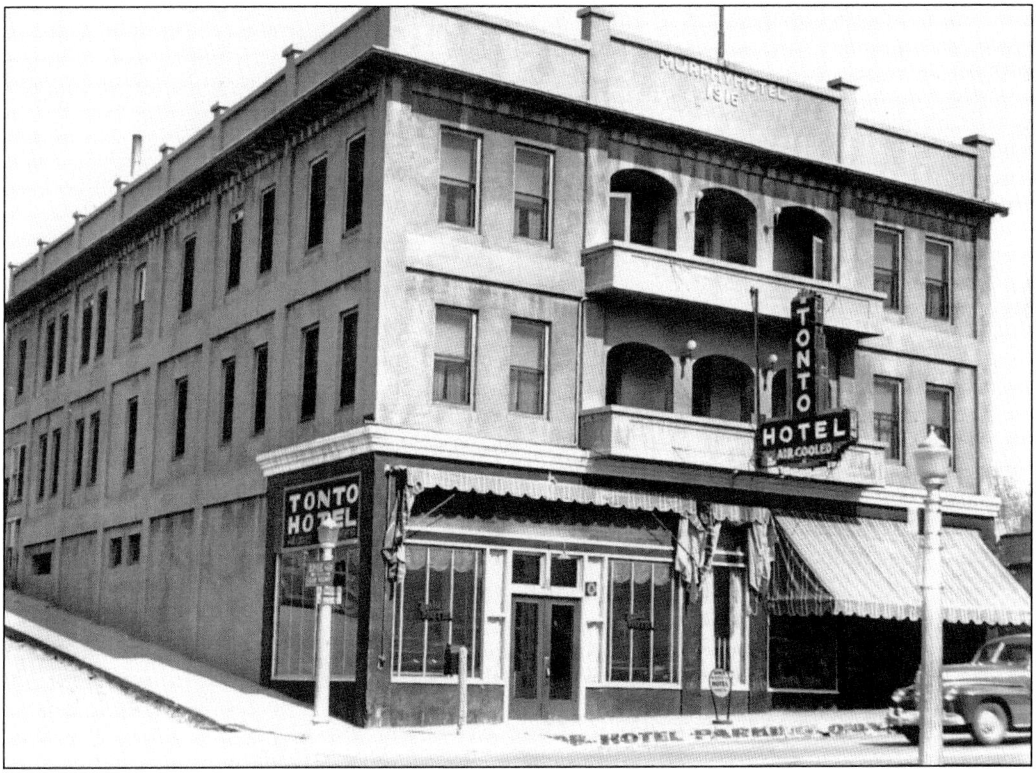

The Murphy Hotel was built in 1916 by Denis Murphy. The hotel later became the Tonto Hotel, owned and operated by Albert C. and Josephine Hachtel. A daughter, Marie Hachtel, spent her long career at Globe High School teaching business subjects and coaching the girls athletic teams.

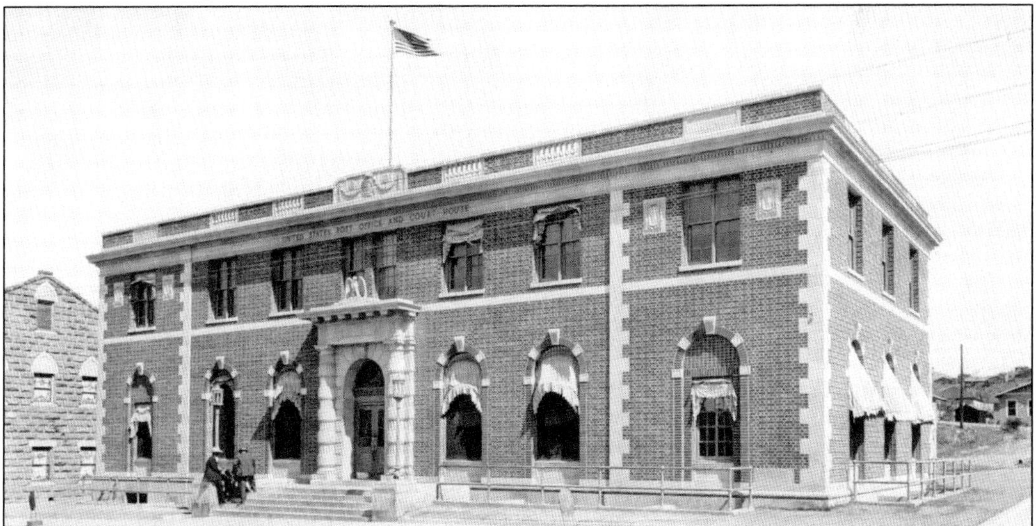

The Globe Post Office was established in 1876. It was located in several Broad Street locations until 1910, when a new Federal Building was erected on Broad Street. In 1927, a new, larger Federal Building was built a block away. Both buildings had the post office on the ground floor and federal courtrooms upstairs.

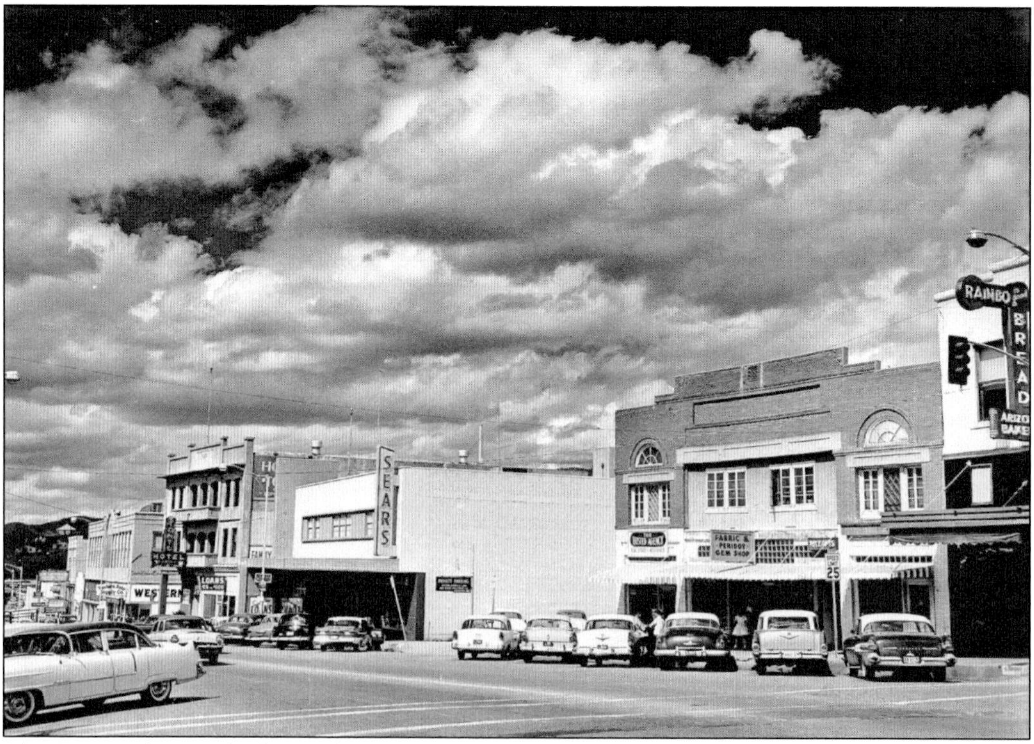

The Dime Theater (right in the above photograph) presented live shows and movies for 20 years. In about 1929, it was converted into office space, stores, and apartments. The main tenant around 1950 was the Fabric and Peridot Gem Shop. The buildings below are, from left to right, the Amster Building, the Odd Fellows Hall, the Hamill-Gibson Building, the Masonic Temple, and the Old Dominion Commercial Building. These structures continue to give Broad Street its historic ambiance.

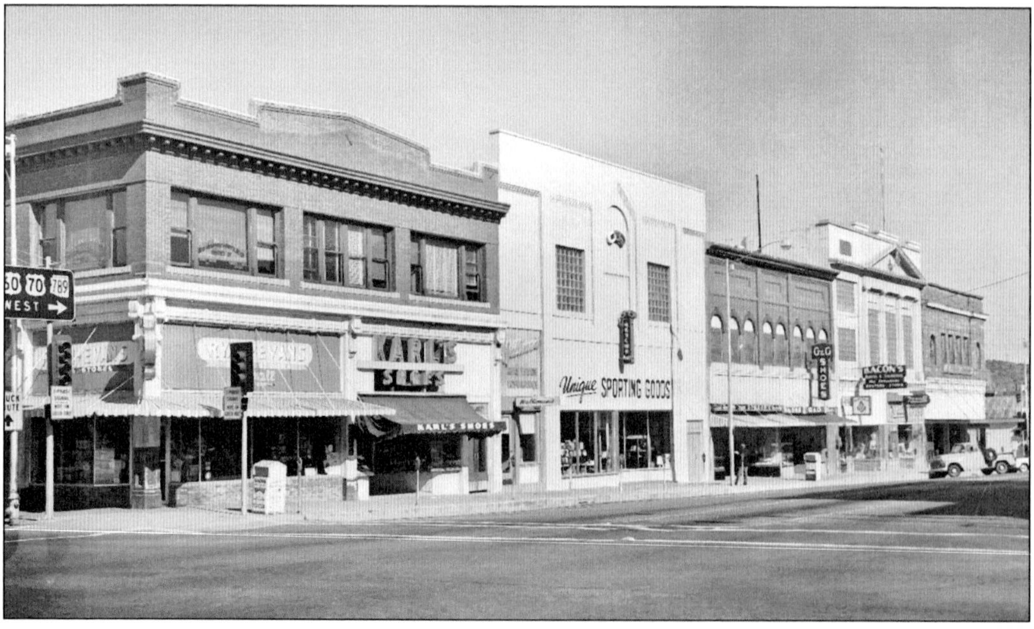

Five

Schools and Churches
the Four "Rs"

The first R is for religion. The other three stand for readin', 'ritin', and 'rithmetic. It took only a few years for churches and schools to become part of life in Globe.

The Reverend John Wingar traveled over rough mountains and through canyons from the town of Pinal to Globe to start religious services. For many weeks, he hiked 60 miles round-trip to be with his parishioners. On November 7, 1880, the St. Paul's Methodist-Episcopal Church dedicated its new place of worship. The brass bell in the tower of the church became known as "God's Alarm Clock." It called people to church services, weddings, and funerals, and rang out in times of danger. It tolled somberly during the night when two men were lynched on nearby Broad Street.

Other congregations—Baptist, Catholic, Episcopal, Presbyterian, Lutheran, and Latter-day Saints—were formed over the next three decades, each serving the spiritual needs of its members. Most of their historic church buildings are still in use today.

A former rooming house on Broad Street served as Globe's first school. Classes began in this small adobe structure in 1882. Four teachers guided the education of all the grades. It was Globe's only school until Central School opened in 1897.

As early as 1883, several small schools appeared in the rural areas around the town. The Little Blue School in Six Shooter Canyon and schools at Wheatfields, El Capitan, and Copper Hill taught the three "Rs" to children from the area mines and ranches. The schools also served as social centers where community meetings, programs, potlucks, and dances were held. The dances were often attended by people from many miles away.

In Globe, the Ball Ground School was built on South Hill Street. In 1918, the large new Hill Street School was erected on that site. Two nearly identical schools were built in opposite ends of town in 1908, and both were given identical four-room additions nine years later. For just a few years, Globe's black students attended the Dunbar School on Euclid Street.

Classes for Globe's high school students were first held at Central School. When that became overcrowded, the students and teachers moved to the second story of the Globe Bakery downtown. An attractive new high school was built in 1914.

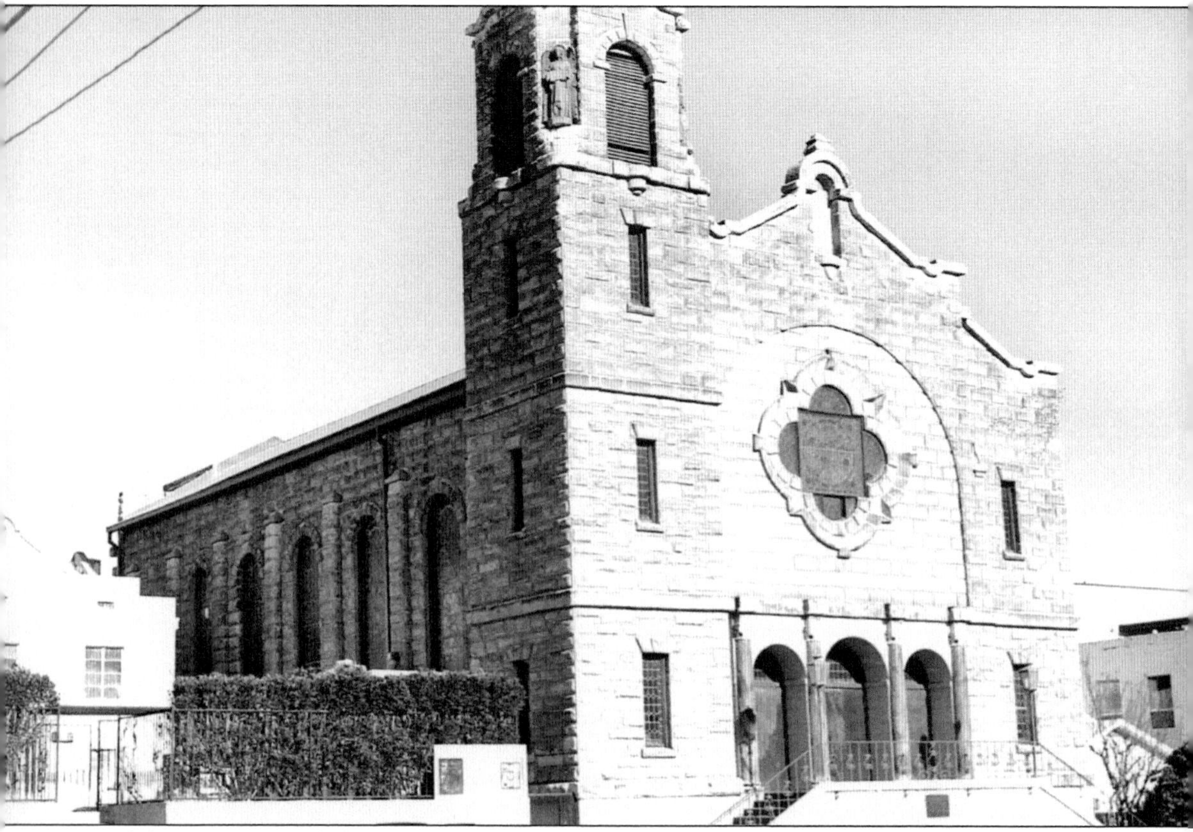

Globe's Roman Catholics purchased a church from the Baptists in 1890. They had been meeting with circuit priests in members' homes for over a decade. In just 10 years, the building was replaced by a sturdy adobe structure. This too became inadequate for the growing congregation. Fr. Virgil Guenevrier came to Globe in 1915 and immediately began to make plans for a large new edifice. Guenevrier served as the general contractor. He solicited funds, ordered materials and furnishings, hired workers, and supervised the job himself. The beautiful building, made of native tufa stone, was dedicated in September 1918. It featured a prominent bell tower, Emil Frei stained-glass windows, copper-clad entry doors, and an Italian marble altar. In the 1980s, extensive restoration and renovation were done to both the interior and exterior of Holy Angels Catholic Church.

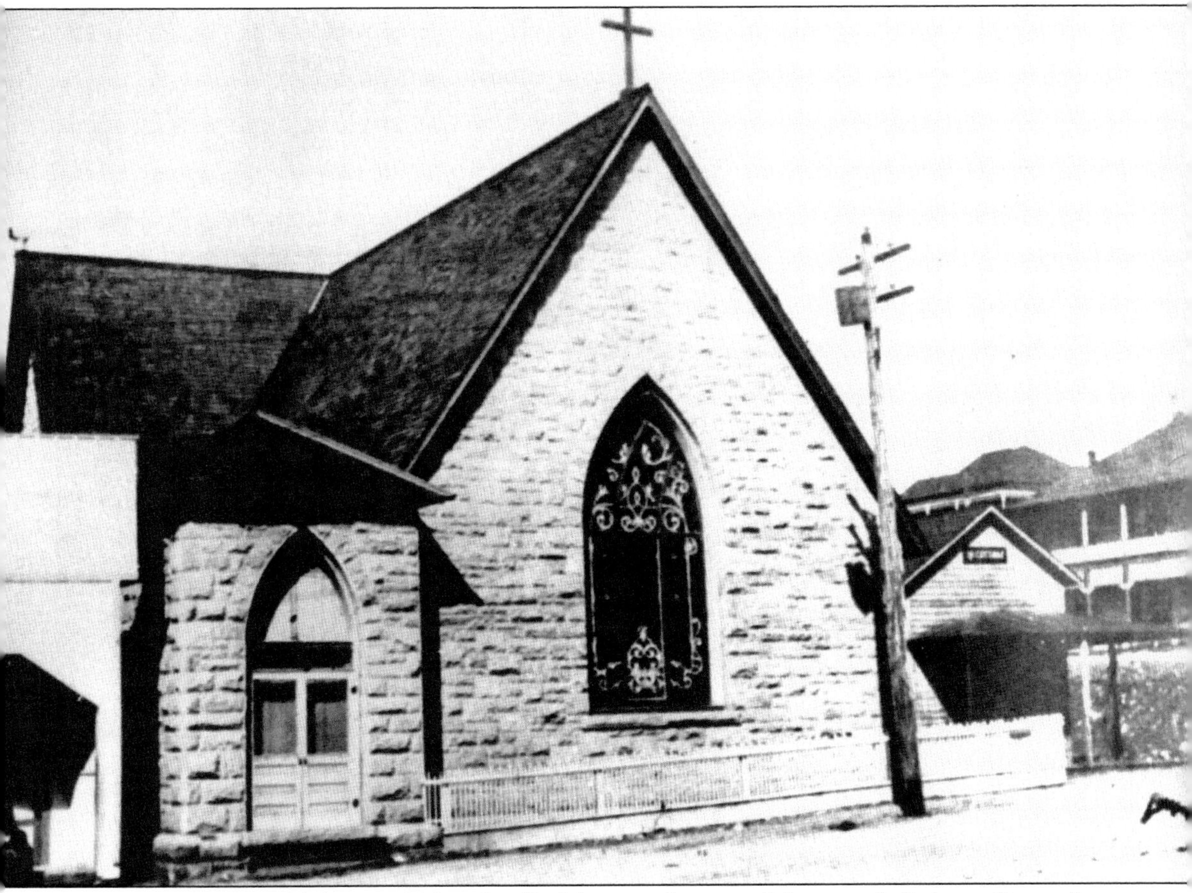

A stranger came to Globe in 1899 and called for a gathering of the town's Episcopalians. A worship service was held and an offering taken. Later the unknown man was seen wagering his money at a local saloon. Organizational meetings were held later in October 1899. By the end of the month, the group had established St. John's Episcopal Mission and engaged a resident clergyman. After purchasing a lot for $500, the parishioners voted, in 1909, to start construction on a place of worship. The next year the cornerstone was laid, and work proceeded a little at a time, as money for wages and materials became available. The front stained-glass window was purchased with money earned by the women of the St. John's Guild. Other windows were added through donations and memorials. Finally, the roof was completed in 1908, and the building was ready for use.

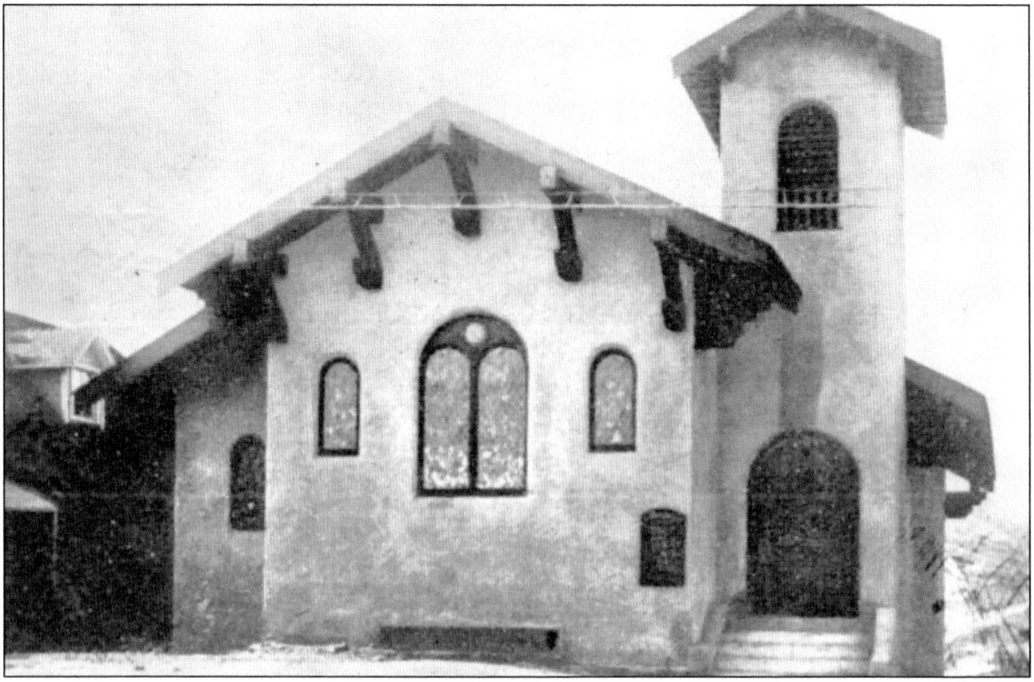

"I had no idea that my tenure here would be so long." Rev. Edmund Loew wrote this in 1983, about halfway through his 35-year ministry at the First Presbyterian Church of Globe. The church was founded in 1908. Eleven pastors preceded Reverend Ed.

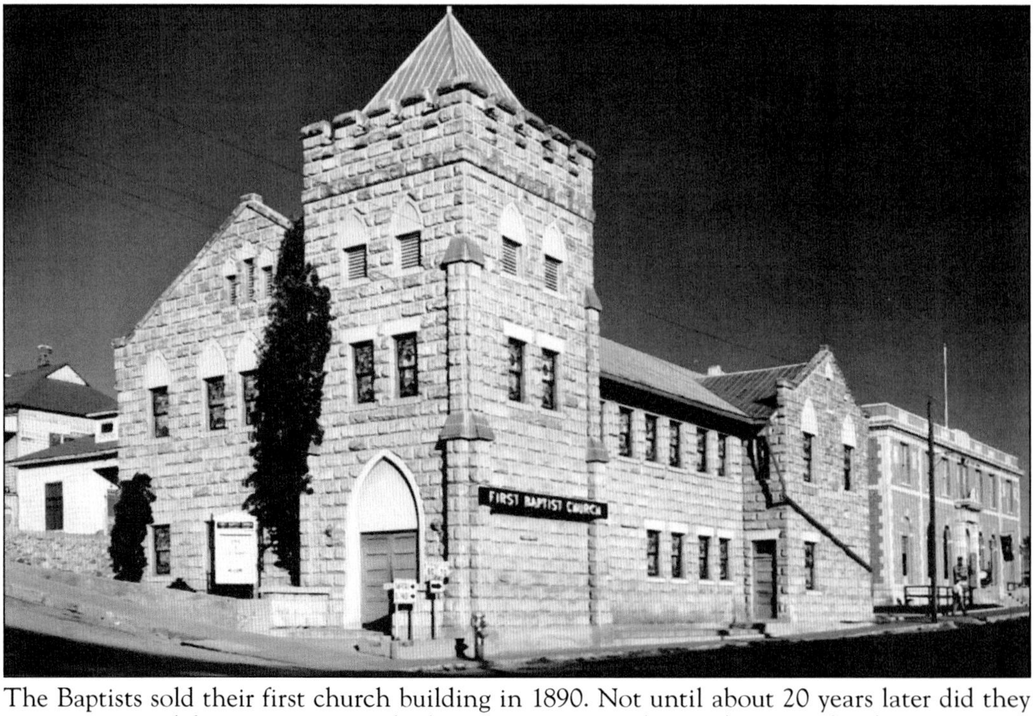

The Baptists sold their first church building in 1890. Not until about 20 years later did they put up a second frame structure, which in turn was razed to make room for this impressive stone building.

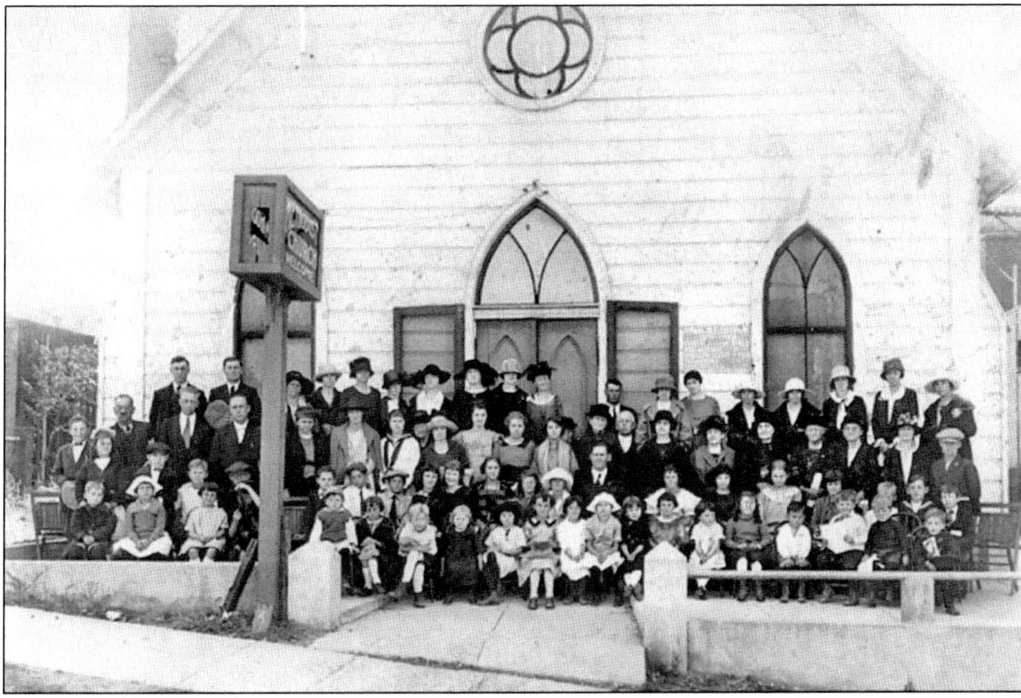

Most of the Methodist congregation poses in front of their 40-year-old church *c.* 1920. The Sunday school class (seen below) was taught by Mrs. Hammond, who shared a love for fancy hats with the young girl on the left.

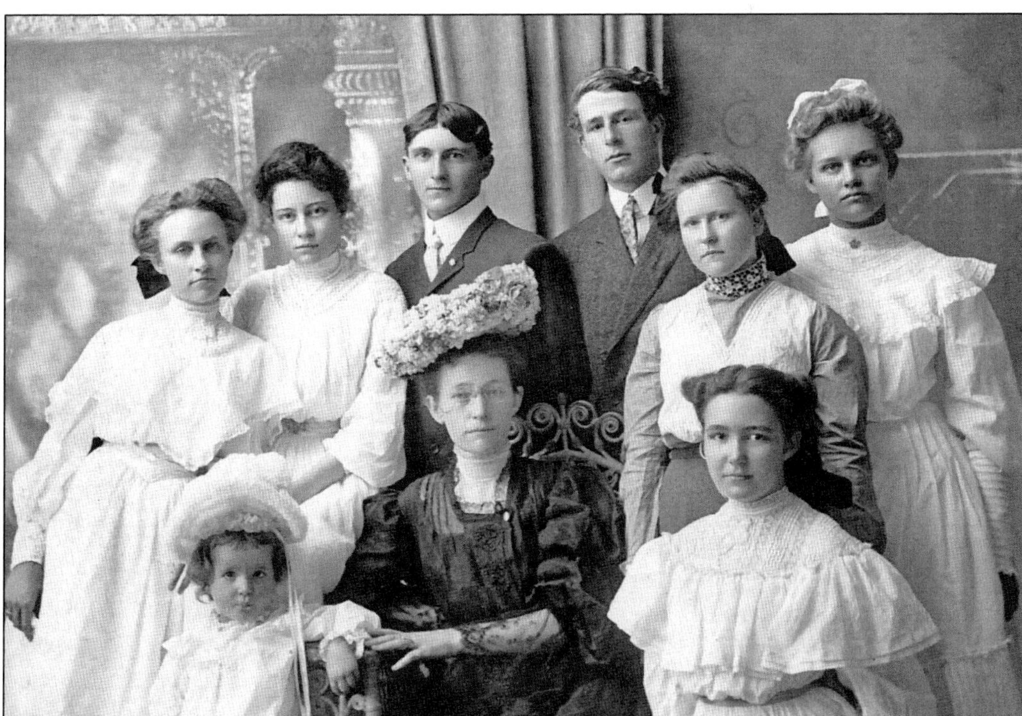

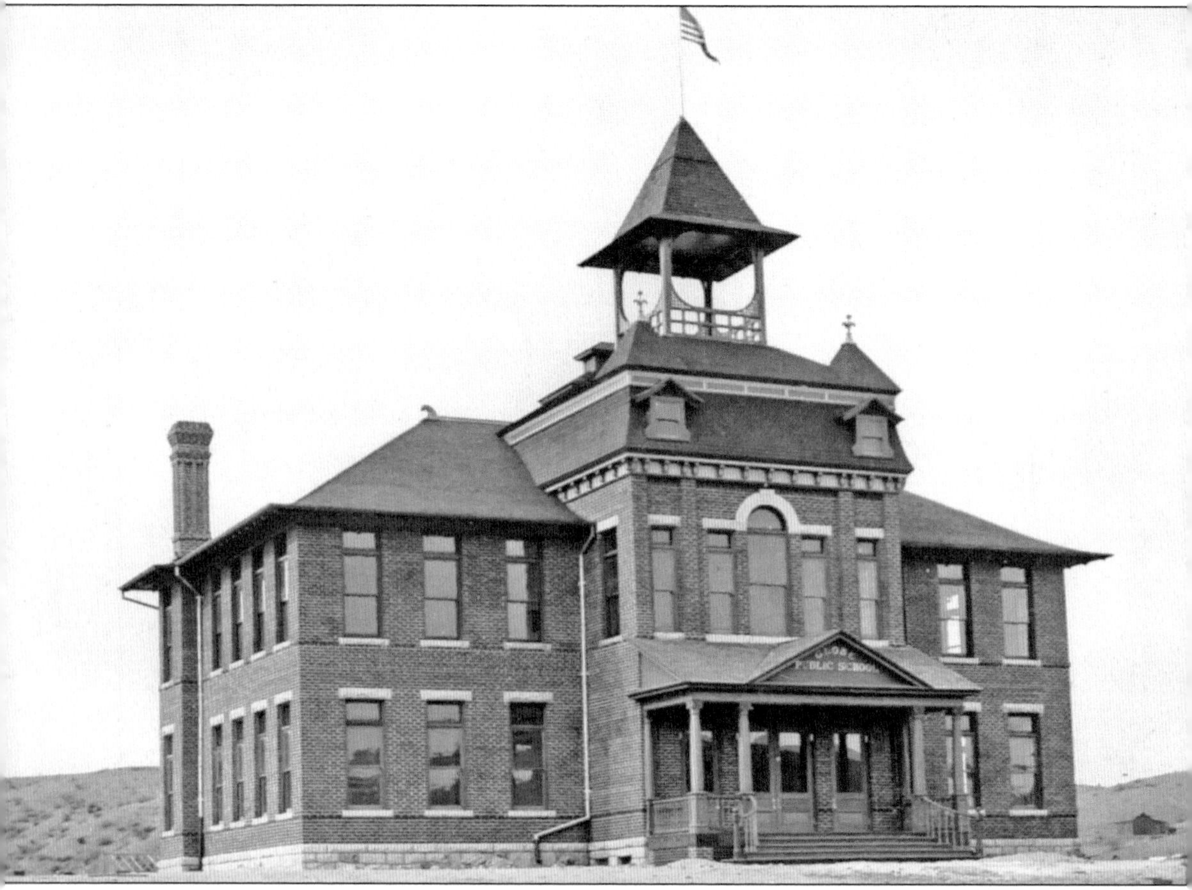

On June 18, 1896, an election was held to approve the construction of a new school in Globe. The measure passed by a two-to-one margin. The Central School was completed in 1897 at a cost of $7,000. It was a much needed addition to the school system and a striking presence on the hill overlooking the city. For 84 years, hundreds of teachers taught thousands of students at Central School. In 1941, the building also housed an aircraft school with classes in template layout, welding, riveting, and mechanics. Some classes were held at Cutter Airport. The program was funded by the Civil Aeronautics Administration.

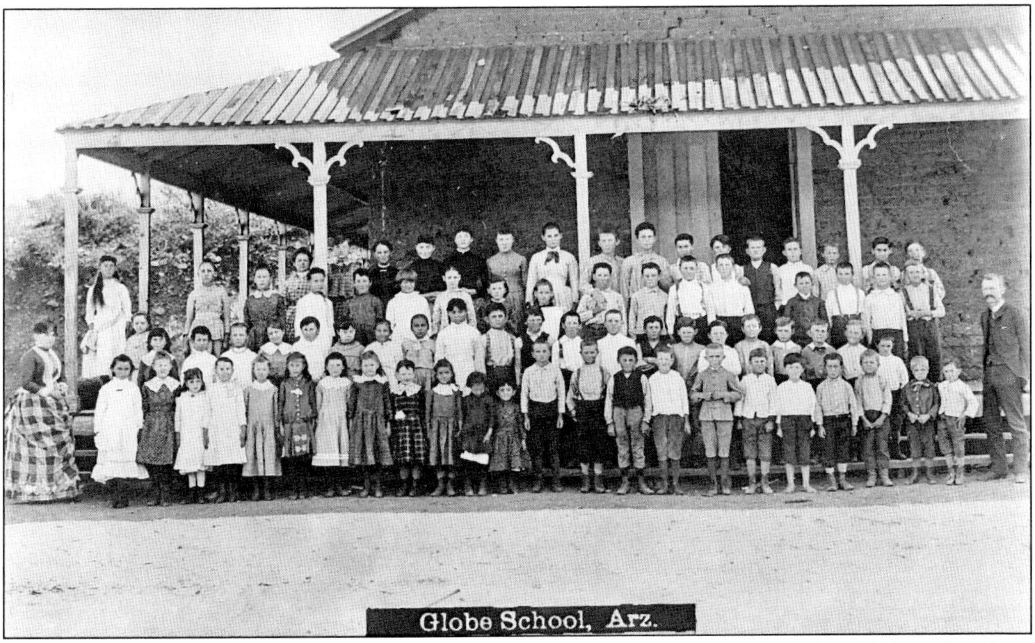

The entire student body poses on the wooden front porch of the old adobe Globe school on Broad Street *c.* 1895.

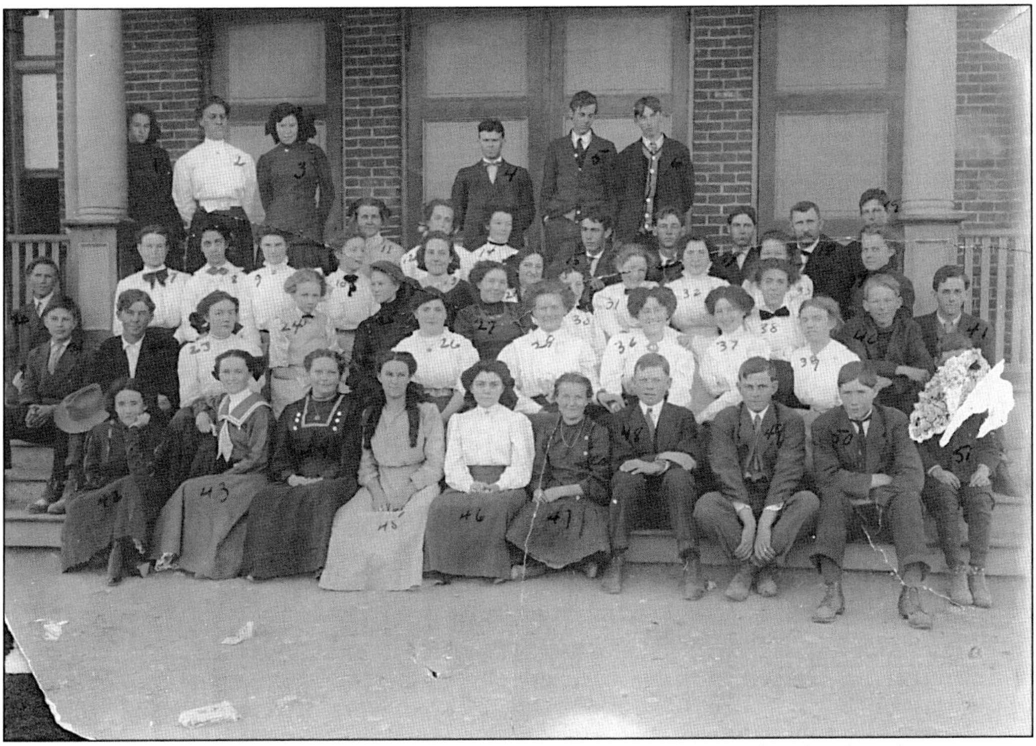

Judging by the suits and ties and pretty dresses, this group of Globe High School students appears ready for graduation *c.* 1910.

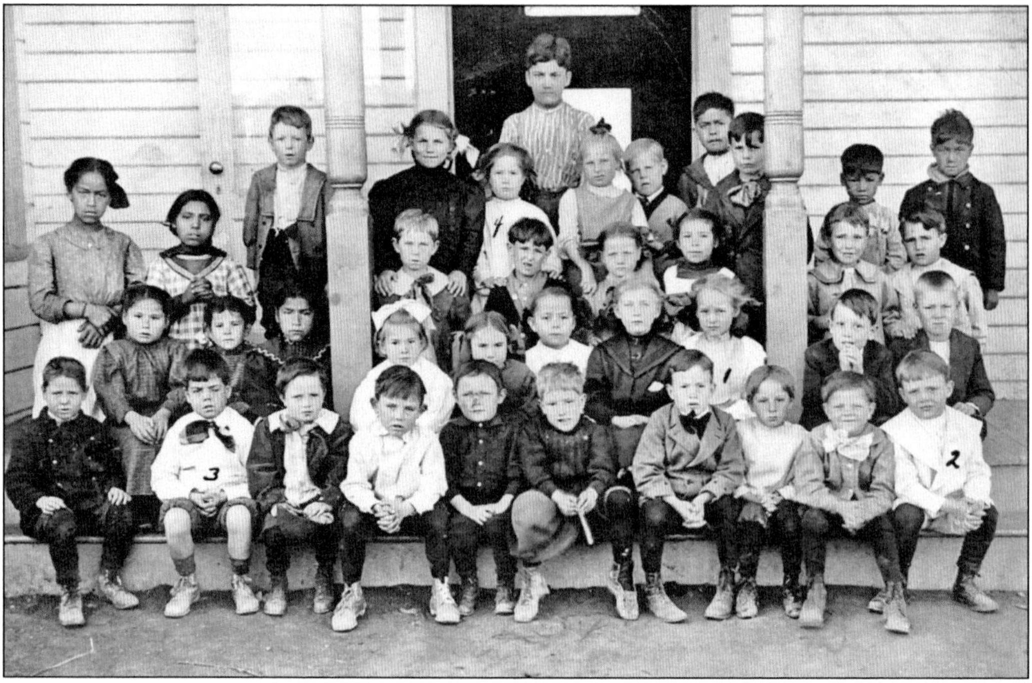

The only teacher at the Ball Ground School looks over her charges on the pillared porch in 1910. Students identified are Harriet Heiner (1), Fred Nave (2), Orme Lewis (3), and Grace Wrightman (4).

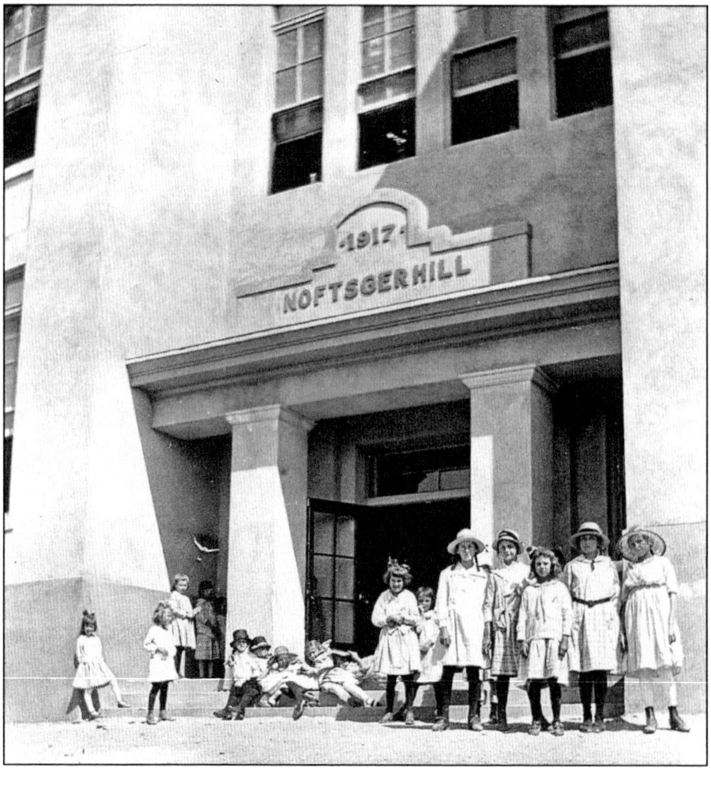

The first-grade class at Noftsger Hill School stands at attention in their 1920 class photograph.

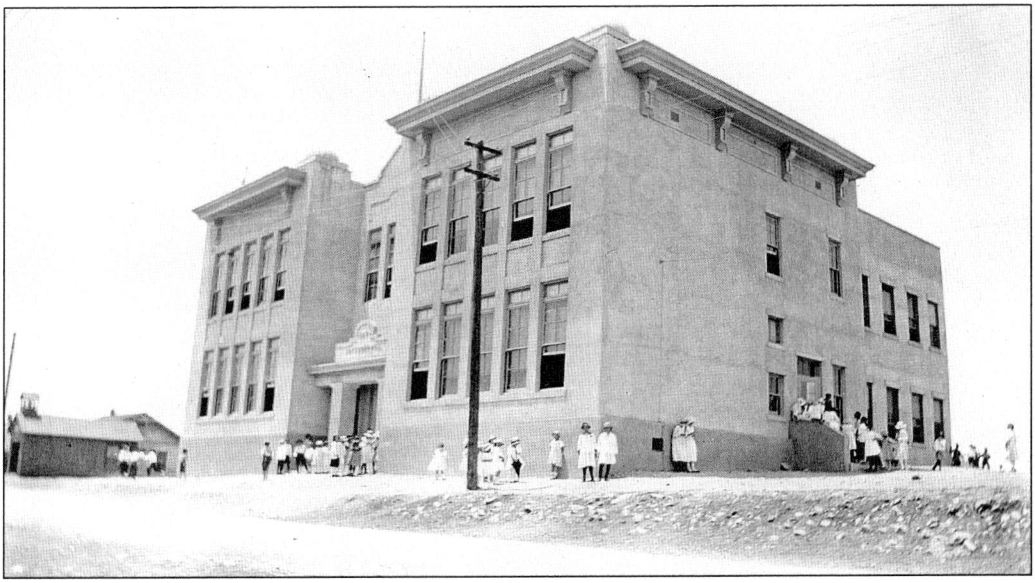

Some students are posing while others are ignoring the photographer in front of Noftsger Hill School about 1920. This building is still in good repair on Noftsger Hill and serves as a bed and breakfast inn.

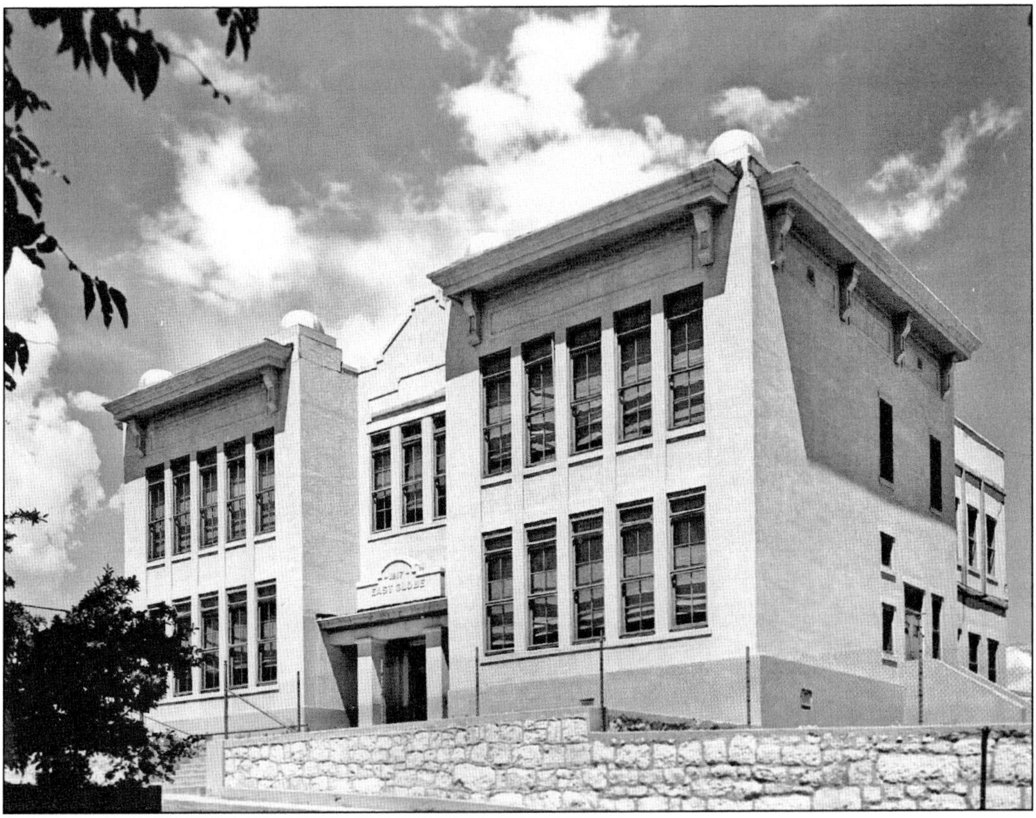

The East Globe School was enlarged by the addition of four spacious classrooms in 1917. The Noftsger Hill School had an identical appearance.

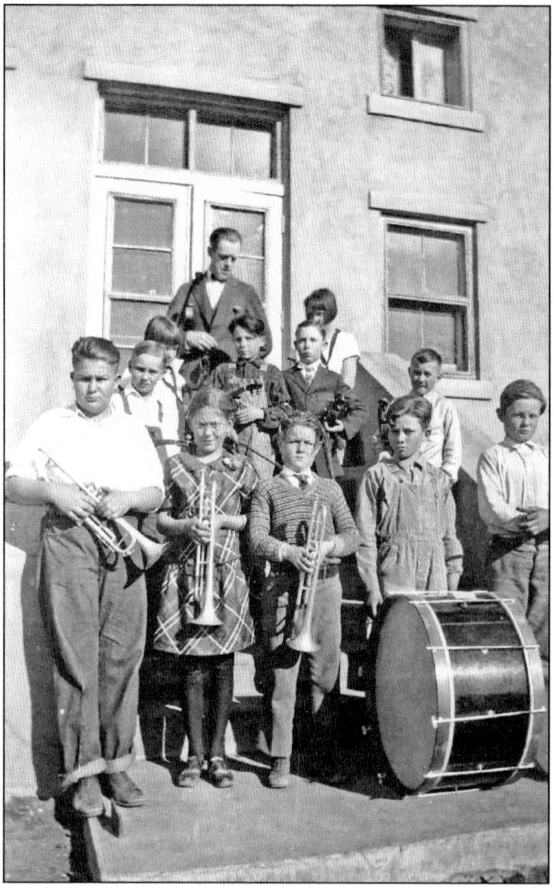

This small school band (left) is standing on the side steps of East Globe School. Later these students would join others from Globe and additional rural schools to form the Globe High School Band. The sharply dressed high school band members pose in front of the school below.

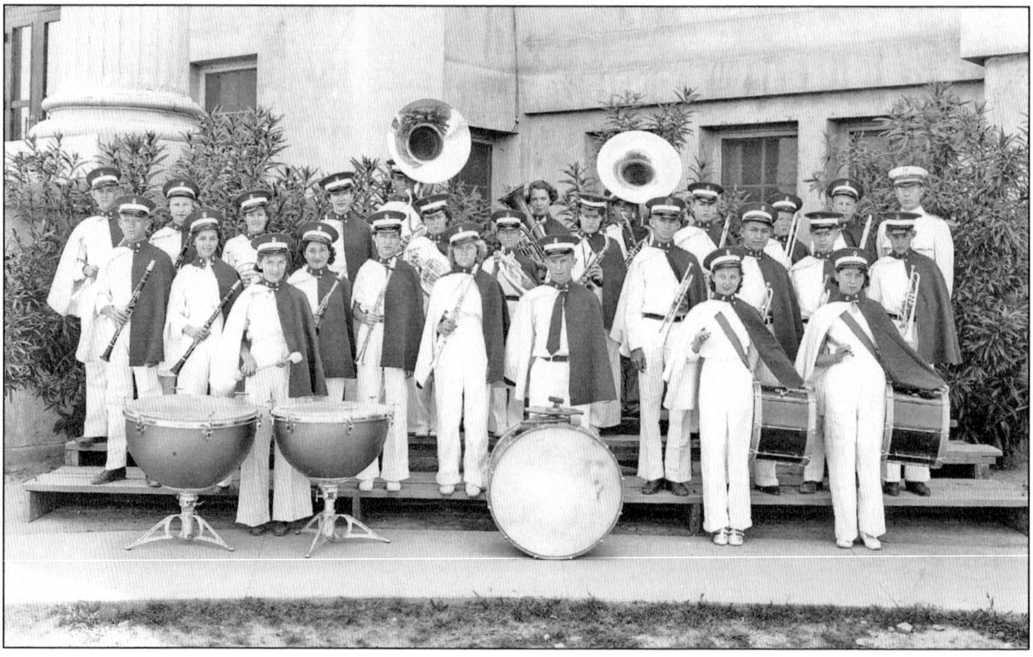

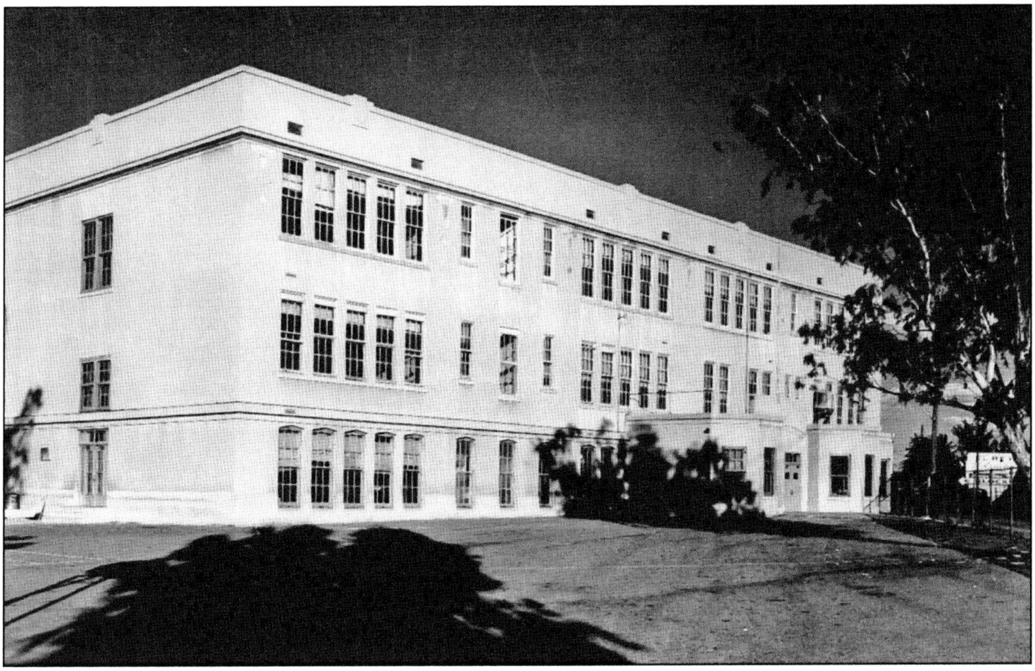

The Hill Street School replaced the one-room Ball Ground School in 1918. The addition of this building, the almost new high school, and other existing schools satisfied the educational needs of Globe for four decades.

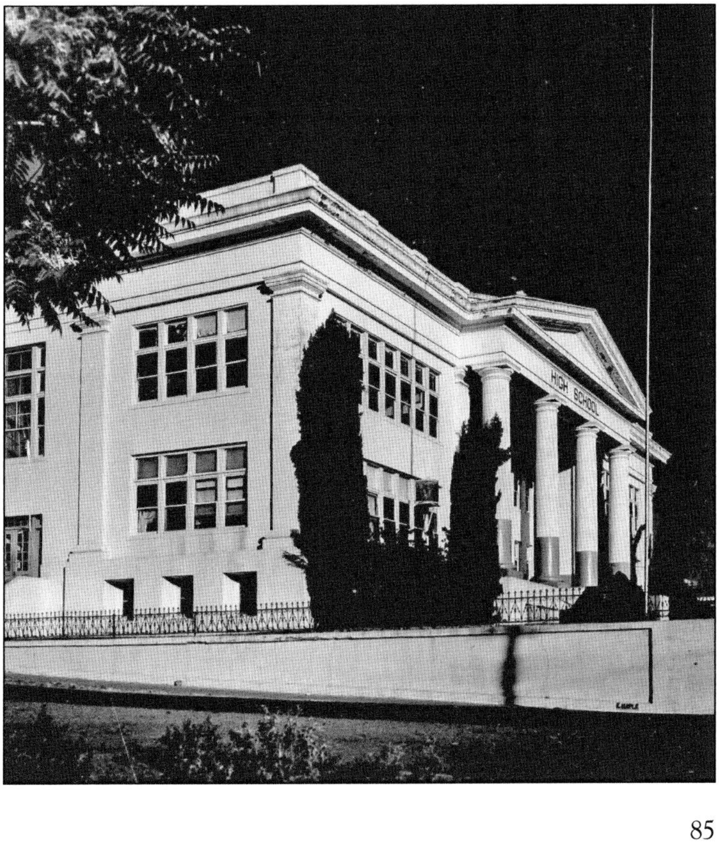

The people of Globe were proud of their attractive new high school when it was dedicated in 1914. Old-timers are pleased that it still serves its purpose today, while educators and students say it is time to move on.

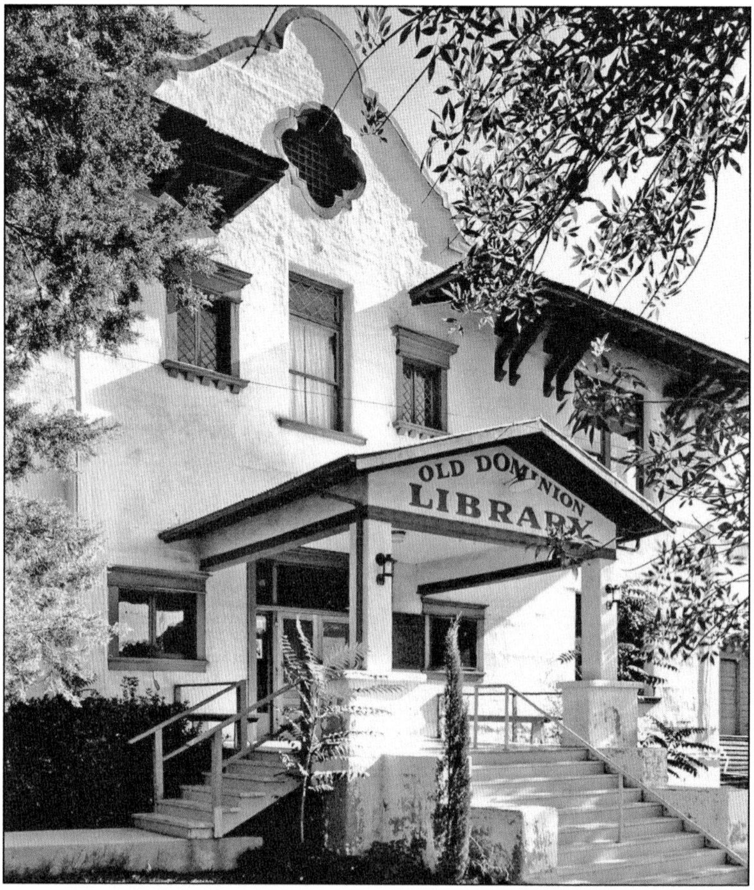

The Old Dominion Library was built in 1908 in memory of three men who died in a mine shaft fire. The building was first used as the North Globe Town Hall. In 1915, it was turned over to the Women's Club of Globe for use as a library. The interior was well-appointed and comfortable. The table in the foreground has a *Time* magazine with a photograph of Pres. Harry Truman on the cover. On March 11, 1981, a tragic fire completely destroyed the Old Dominion Library.

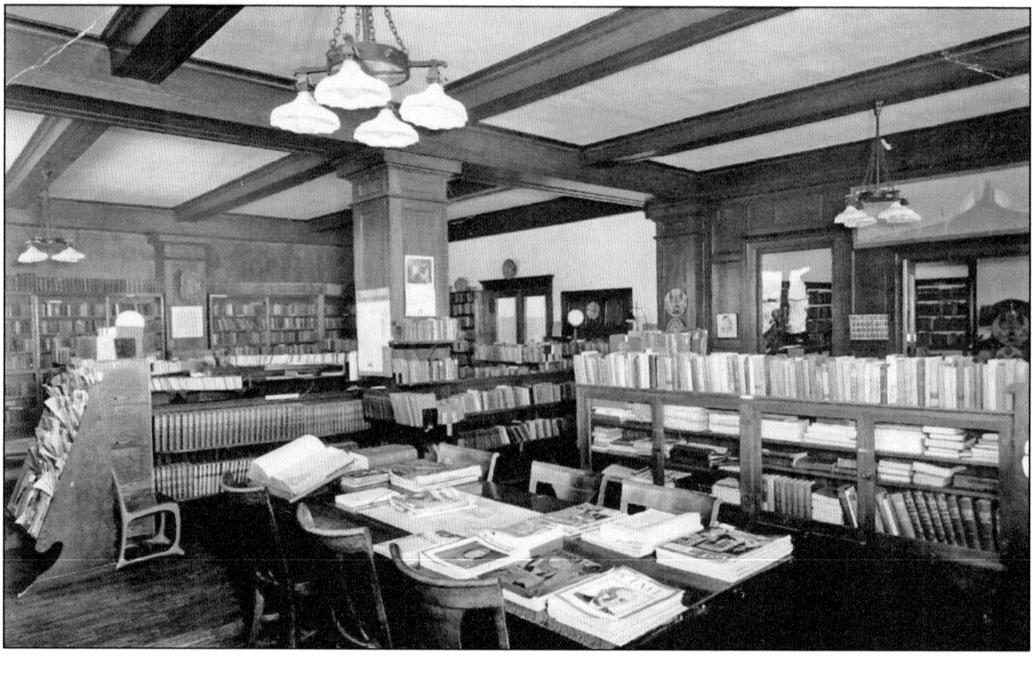

Six

Entertainment, Sports, and Diversions

The first prospectors, miners, and ranchers came to the Globe area in the 1870s. Saloons, gambling, and brothels were not far behind. In just a few years, a variety of more acceptable leisure activities were available to the people of the growing town. In 1910, the *Arizona Silver Belt* published the following description:

> "The social life of Globe is singularly agreeable for those who care to grasp the many advantages which it has to offer. The city is fortunate in having several attractive theaters and a long list of fraternal organizations, which afford recreation and interest to a great many people. Nature has also made Globe's climate and location peculiarly fit for outdoor sports. Baseball thrives and gets hardy support from the people. Riding and driving are pastimes available any time of the year. The great Pinal Mountain range offers grandeur of scenery, broad valleys, seemingly endless distances and many a quiet woodland retreat where every care that assails the busy mortal may be forgotten in the soothing embrace of Nature."

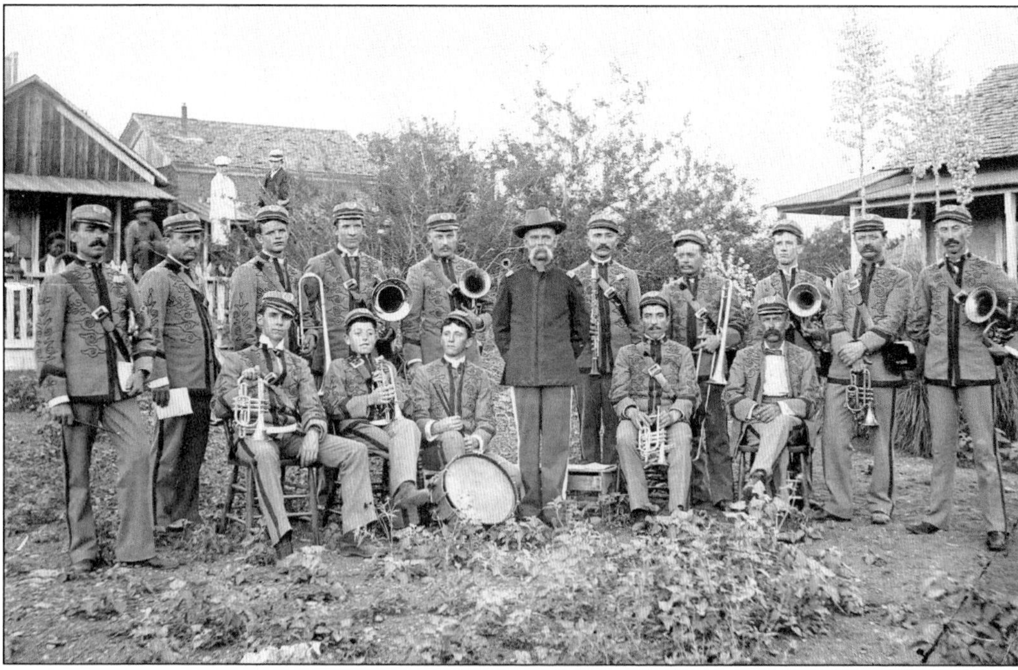

The Globe City Band was organized in the 1890s and played at many community gatherings for more than 100 years. In March 2007, the band regrouped and gave a concert during the Globe Centennial Celebration.

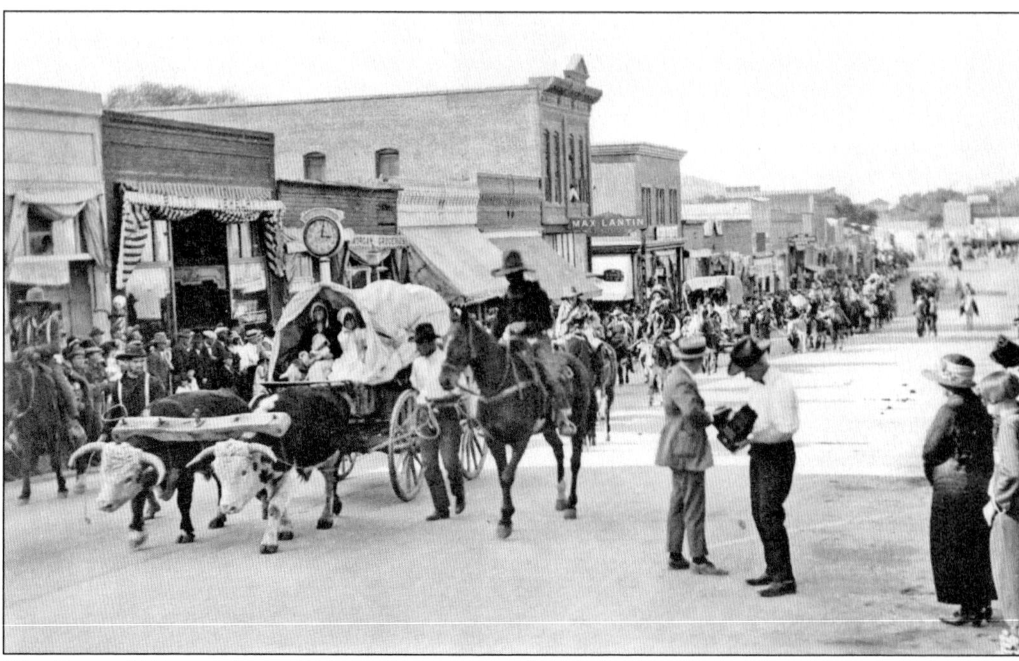

The Days of '49 parade in 1924 passes by the pedestal clock in front of Cubitto's Jewelry Store. The yoked oxen were one of the highlights of the parade.

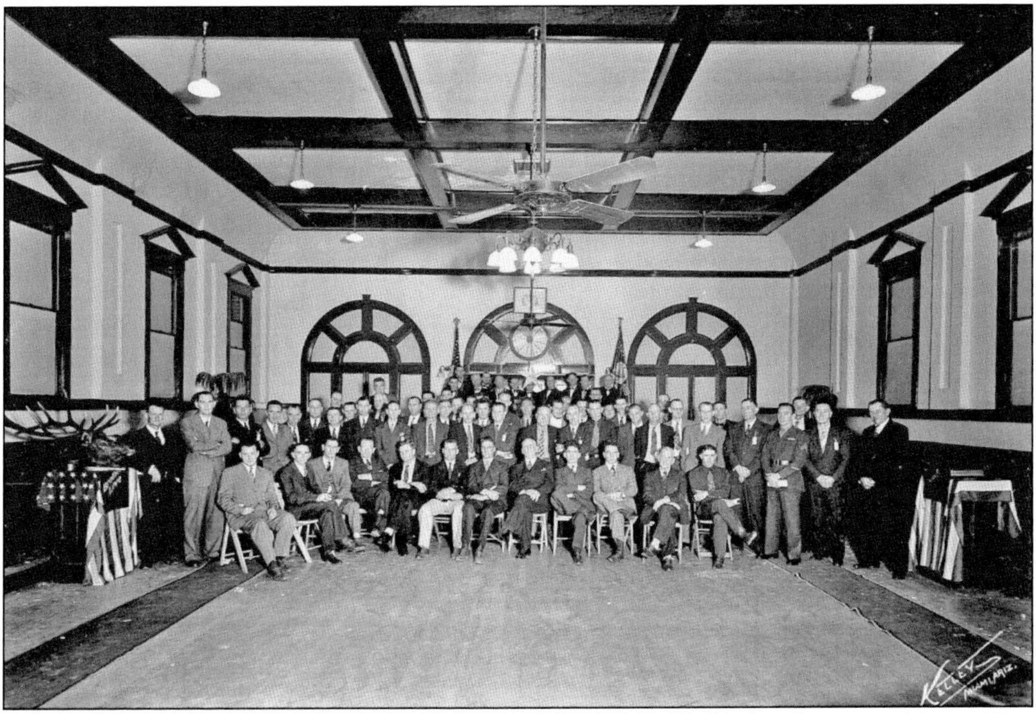

Members of the Globe Elks Lodge 489 are gathered in their third-story clubroom (above). The Elks were active in community and fraternal events, and they sponsored parades, festivals, beauty pageants, and dances. They never missed an opportunity to set up a refreshment stand. The Elks horse-drawn float (below) is waiting for the parade to start. The gentlemen with the top hats are members who will march with the float in the parade.

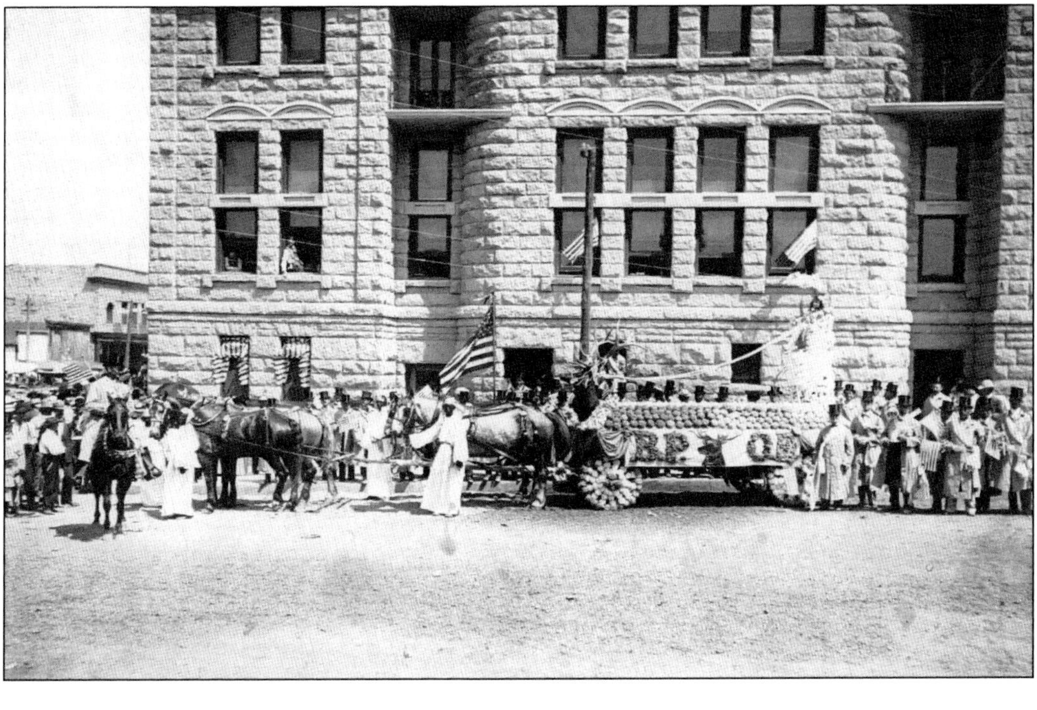

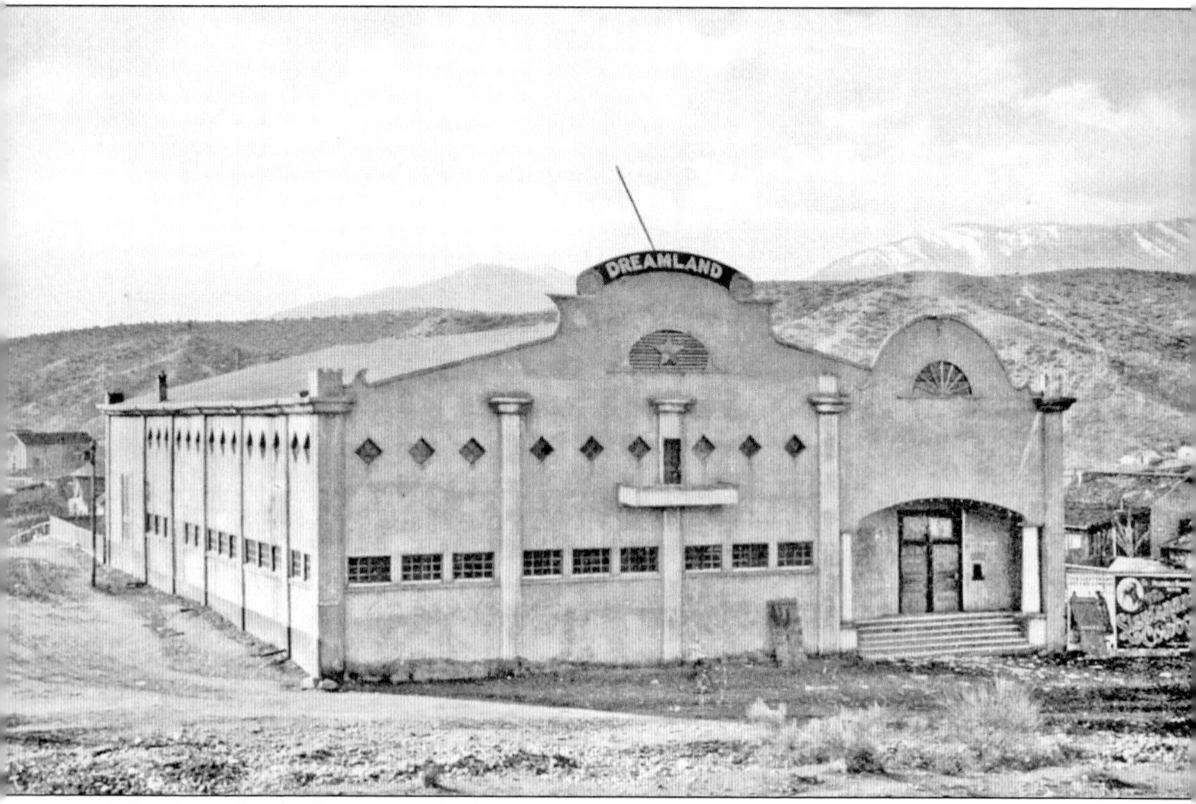

The Dreamland Theater was built in 1905. On May 31, 1907, a traveling theater troupe was scheduled to perform *The New York Idea* at the Dreamland, but their train from El Paso, Texas, had many delays on its way to Globe. At 8:00 p.m., the waiting audience was told to expect a two-hour delay. The theatergoers spent a pleasant time in conversation and camaraderie, and the curtain finally went up at 10:00 p.m. The audience was enthralled with the performance. Minnie Maddern Fisk, the star of the show, later wrote: "It was no ordinary audience and the company gave no ordinary performance. In the canyon theater there was a warmth as well as a brilliance, and it was assured by the most overwhelming response the play had ever produced."

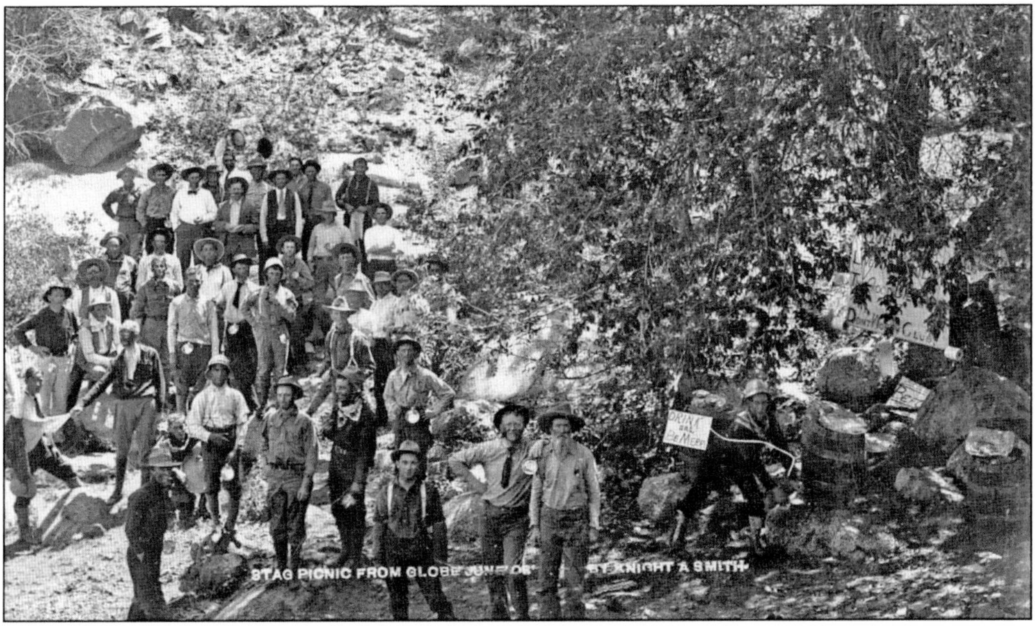

Membership in the "Don't Worry Club" was open to any adult male with some free time and a couple of bucks to pay for food and beer. Their typical meeting was a picnic in the Pinal Mountains. Kegs of iced beer were brought up in a wagon and a good time was guaranteed for all.

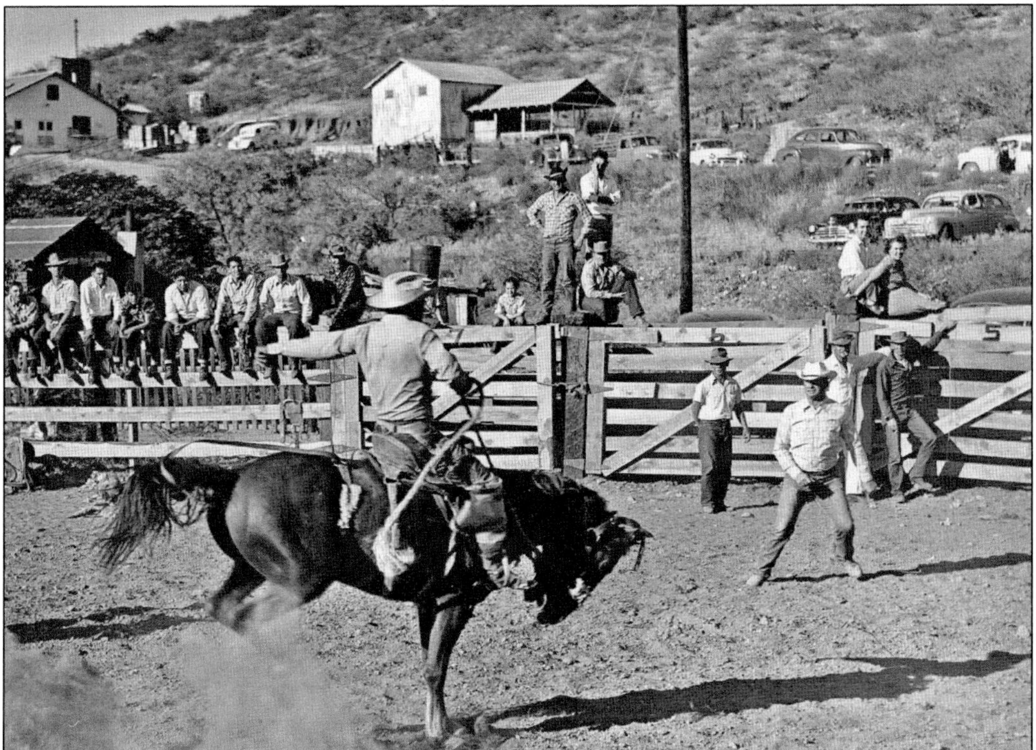

A group of spectators watches approvingly as a Globe cowboy gets the better of a bucking horse c. 1950.

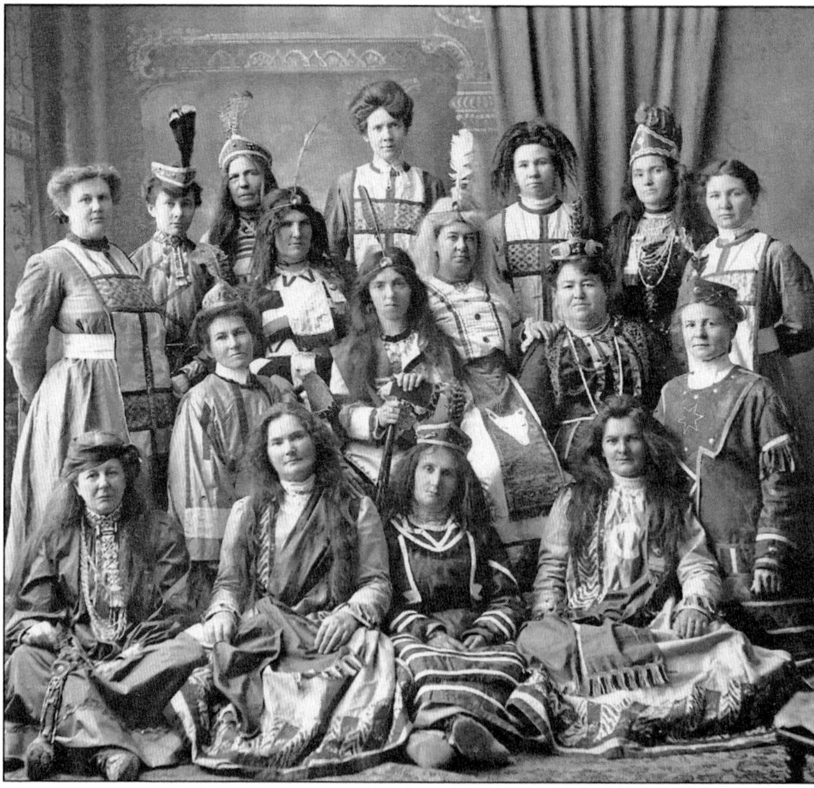

The Daughters of Pocahontas are named for the daughter of Algonquin chief Powhatan, and they emulate her virtues of kindness and courage. Pictured is the chapter from Globe.

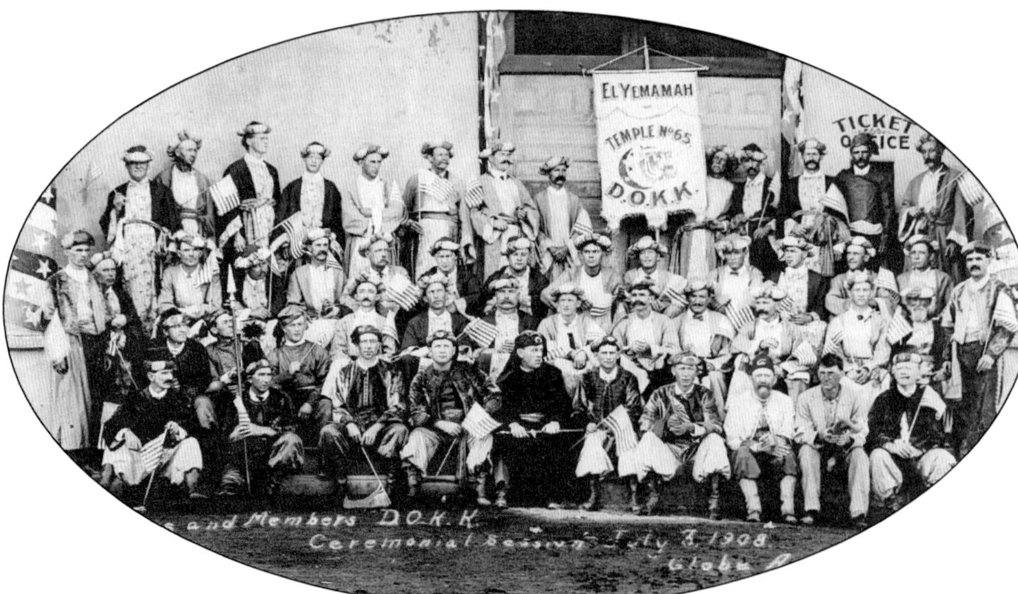

Pictured here on July 3, 1908, is the Globe Temple of the Dramatic Order of the Knights of Khorassan (DOKK). The national governing organization is the Imperial Palace, and their motto is "Lift up the fallen." The DOKK is associated with the Knights of Pythias, and a popular saying is, "It's a privilege to be a Pythian and a pleasure to be a Dokey."

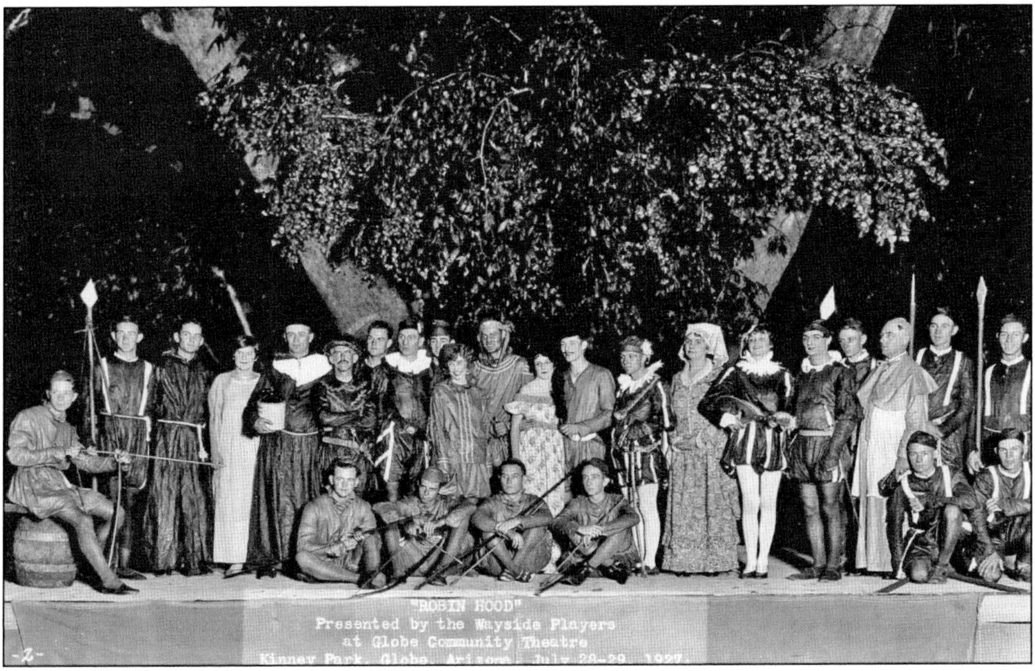

The play *Robin Hood* was performed on the outdoor stage at Globe's Kinney Park on July 28 and 29, 1927. The local cast posed in costume under one of the large sycamore trees in the park.

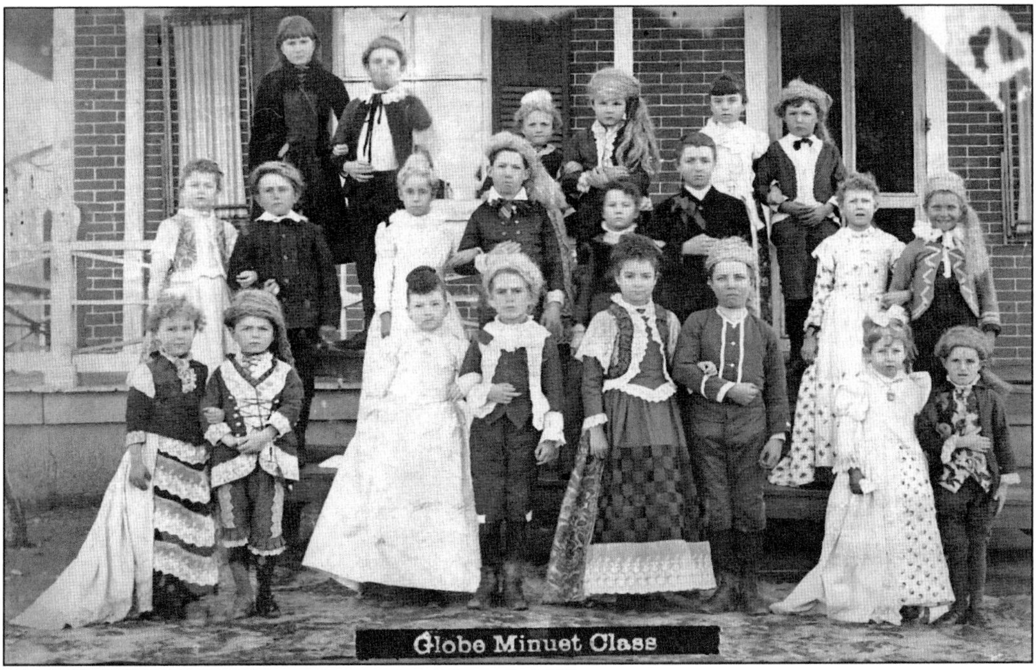

The young members of the Globe Minuet Class, dressed in their finest dancing costumes, are ready to demonstrate their latest steps.

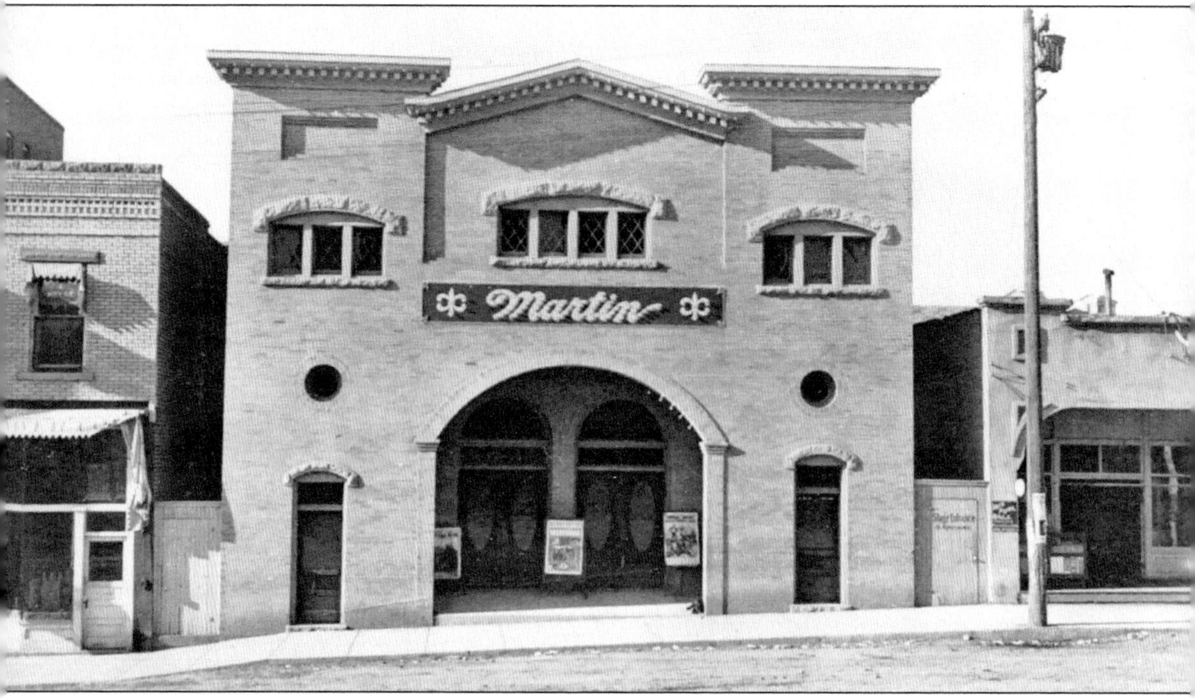

Globe's early theaters offered vaudeville acts, minstrel shows, drama productions, local talent shows, and even boxing and wrestling matches. The first theater in Globe was the Main House. It was replaced by the Dime Theater in 1910. The first movies were shown at St. Elmo's Saloon around 1910. The Martin Theater was built in 1915 by Charles Martin, a local entrepreneur. The Moorish-style structure was one of the finest on Broad Street. It later became known as Alden's Theater. The beautiful building was razed in 1970.

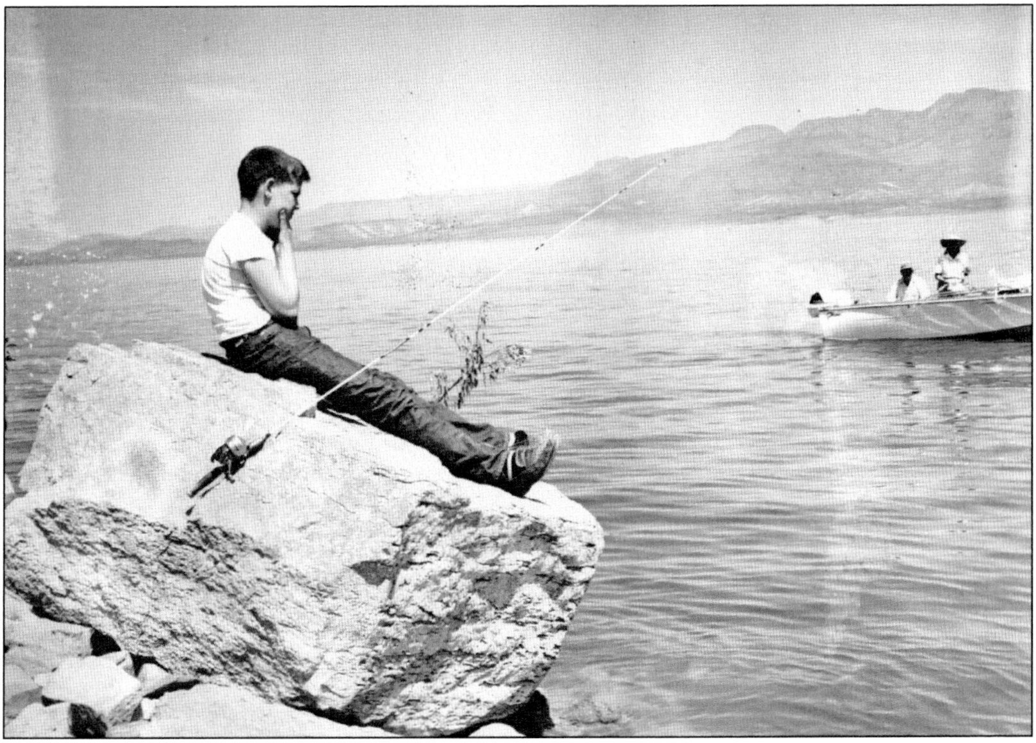

Fishing has long been a favorite pastime for people of all ages. The young fisherman at Roosevelt Lake (above) is waiting for a nibble, as a pair of anglers passes by in a rowboat. Fishing was also a part of the enjoyable activities of local Boy Scout troops (below).

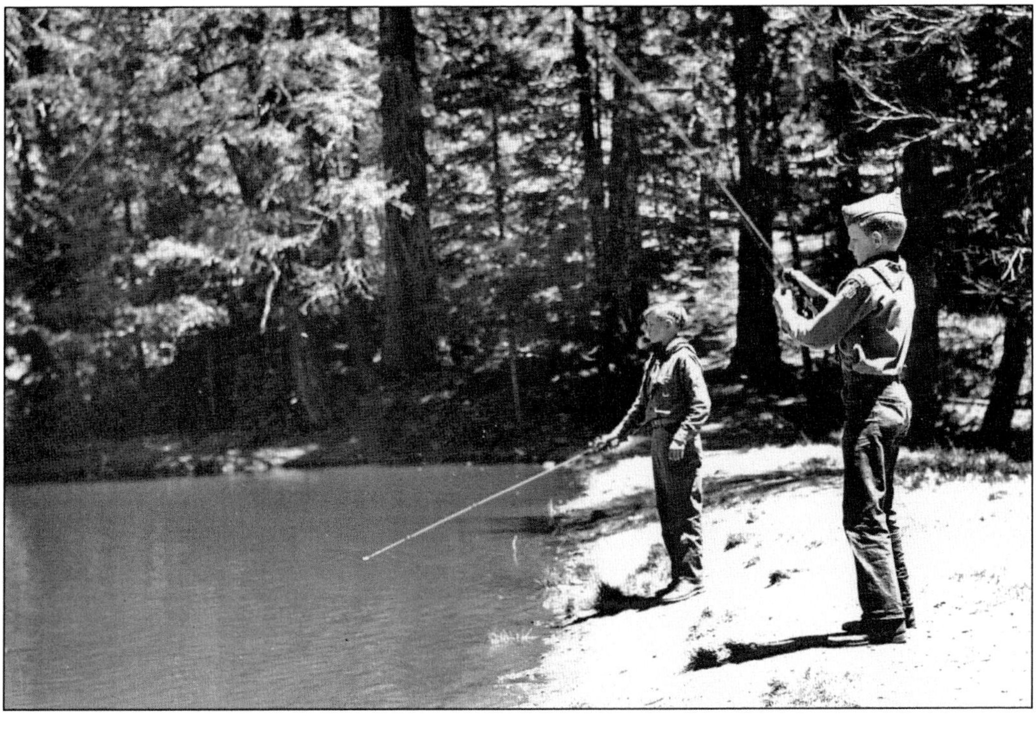

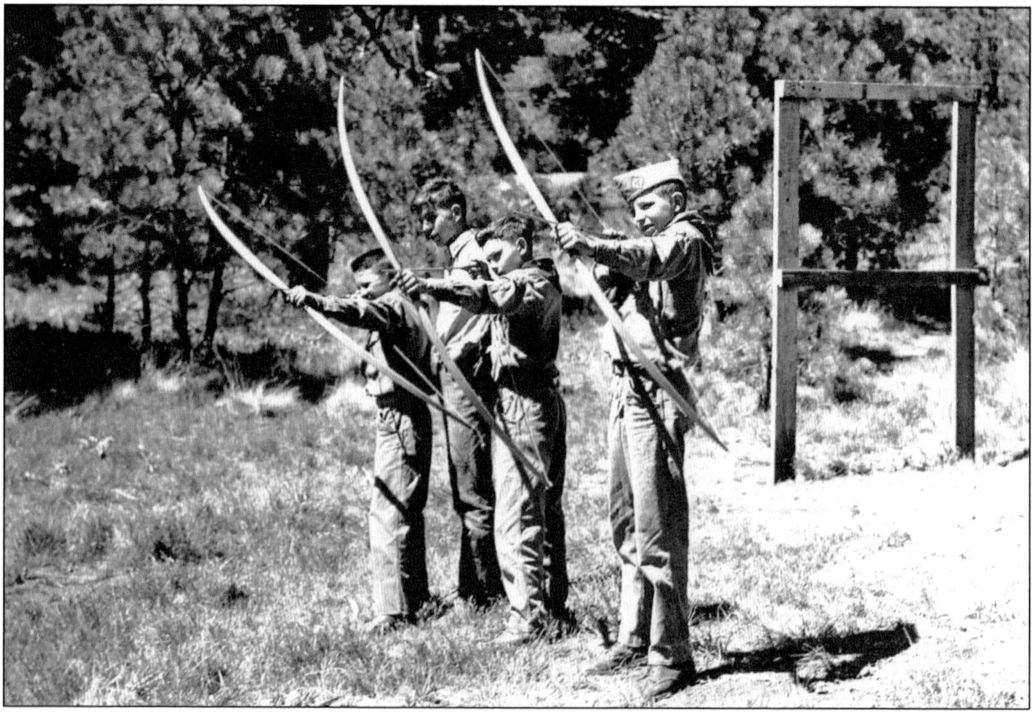

Archery was one skill taught to local Boy Scouts. Here an instructor watches as the three Scouts aim for the center of the target.

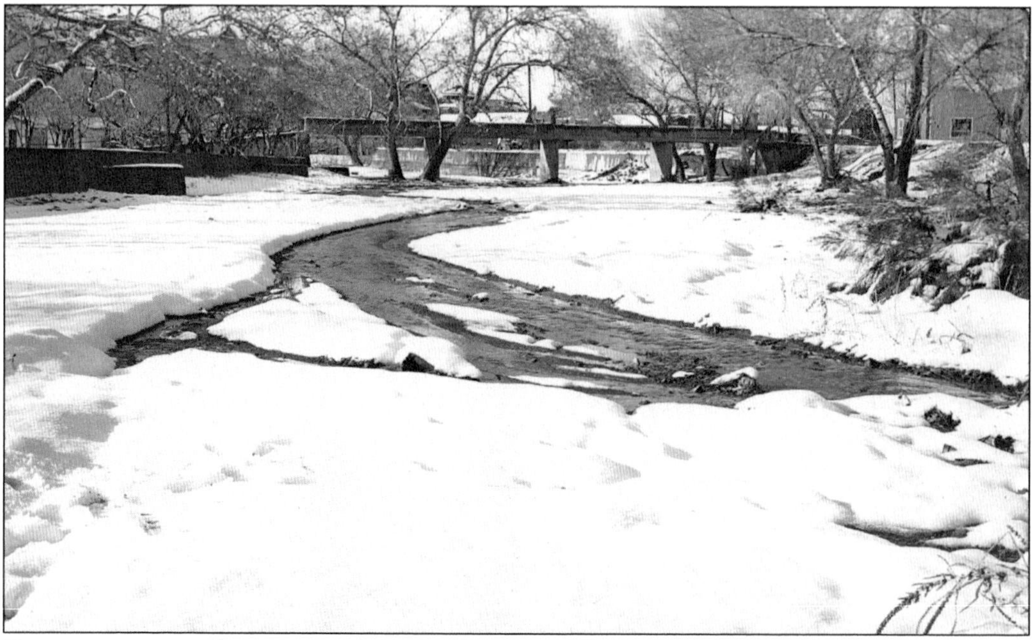

On rare occasions, there is enough snow at Kinney Park to attract kids of all ages. This morning scene will soon be filled with children having a snowball fight or making snow angels.

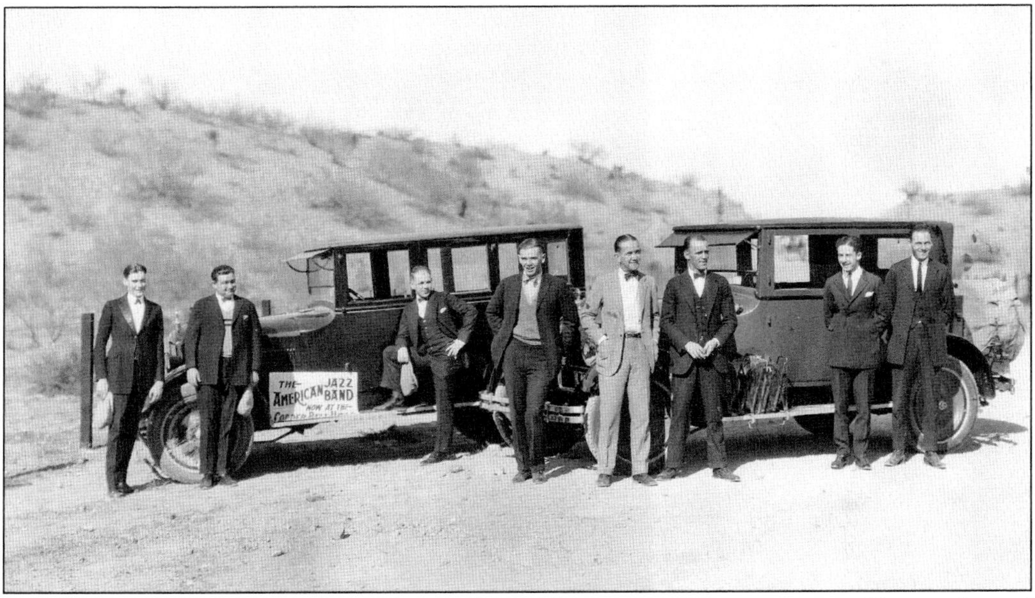

The well-dressed American Jazz Band arrived in Globe in two 1920s touring cars. They performed at the Copper Belt Hall (in Miami) and at the Royal Gardens (in Globe).

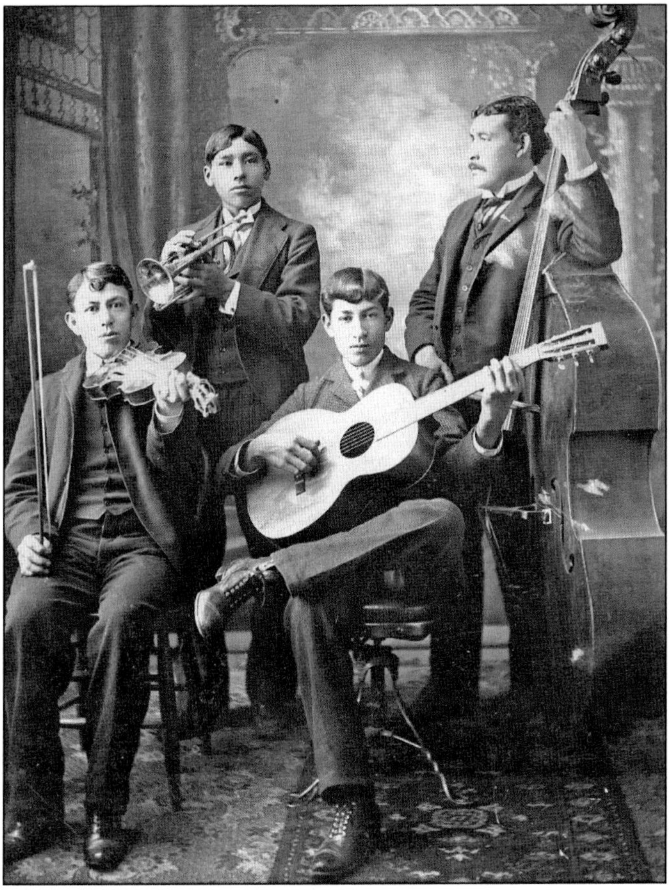

This 1905 photograph shows a four-man mariachi band. They played south-of-the-border music at fandangos, fiestas, and other gala occasions.

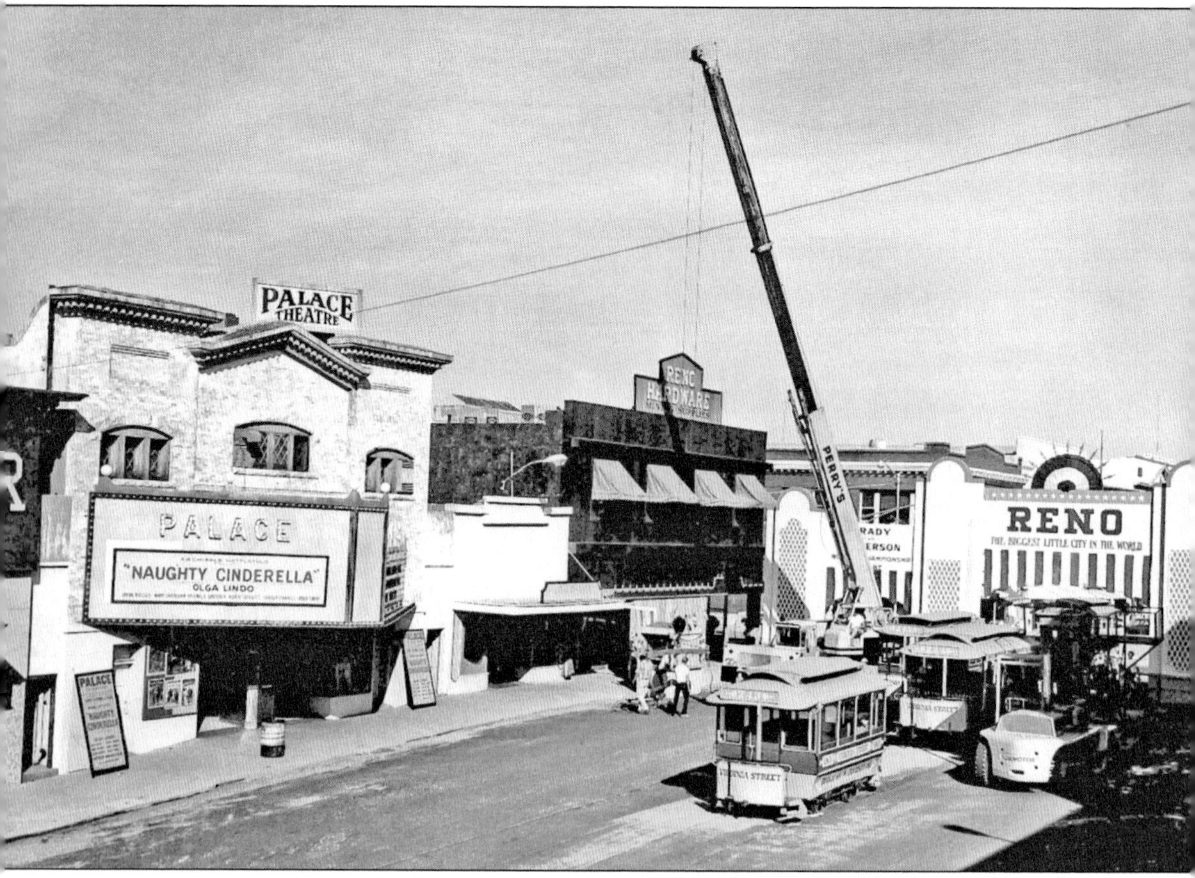

Twentieth Century Fox Studios came to Globe in the fall of 1969. Globe was selected as the venue for filming of the movie *Great White Hope*. James Earl Jones and Jane Alexander played the leading roles and nearly 1,500 local people were used as extras. Several blocks in downtown Globe were made to look like Reno, Nevada, in 1910. An outdoor boxing arena was erected adjacent to the railroad depot, the facade of a saloon stood across the street, and buildings were modified and given Reno names. Iron rails and these trolley cars were brought in to complete the scene. The filming took the Fox crews nine days to complete. The Globe scenes lasted only 11 minutes on the big screen.

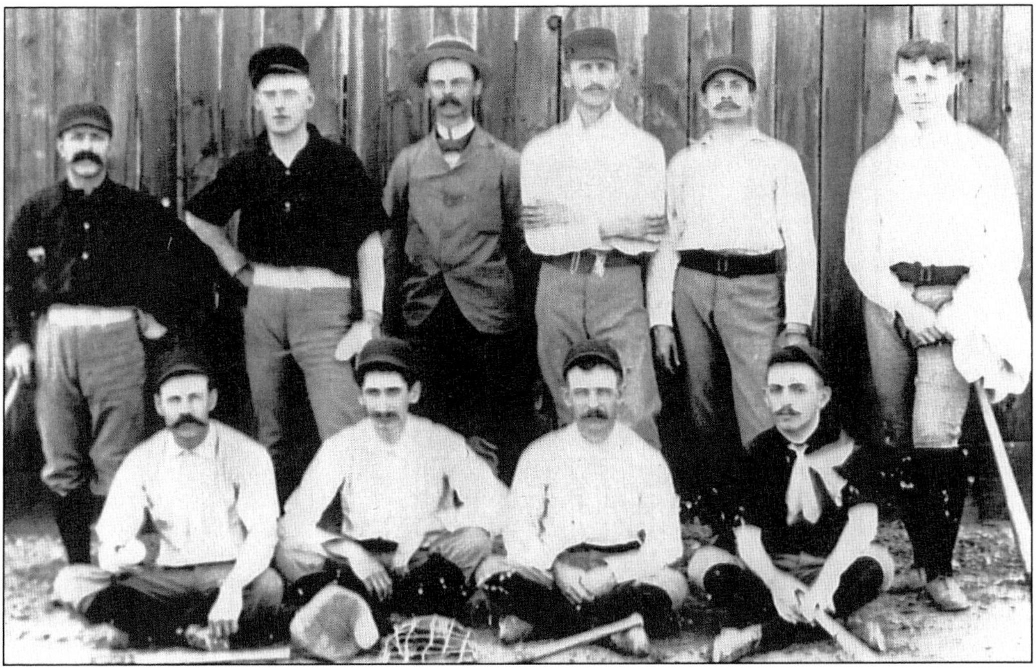

Baseball was a favorite sport for both participants and spectators as early as the 1890s. Teams included the Old Dominion team (above), the Stars (below), and the Miners and Scrubs from neighboring Miami. After 1900, the teams traveled many miles by train to enjoy the sport.

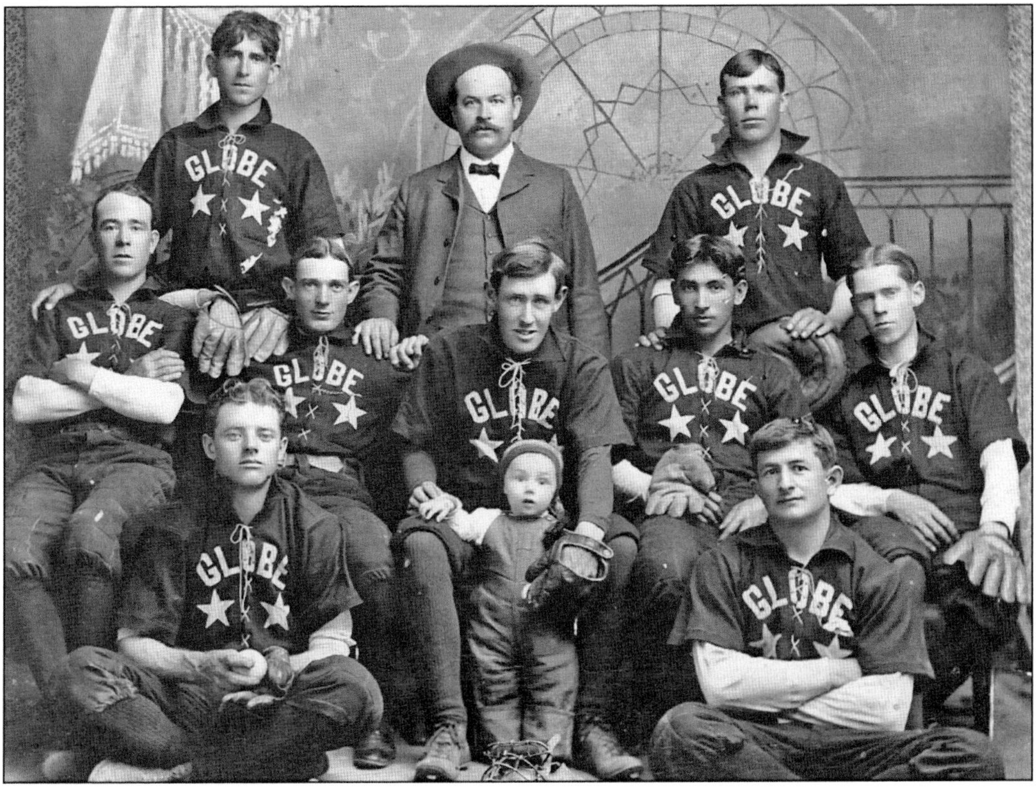

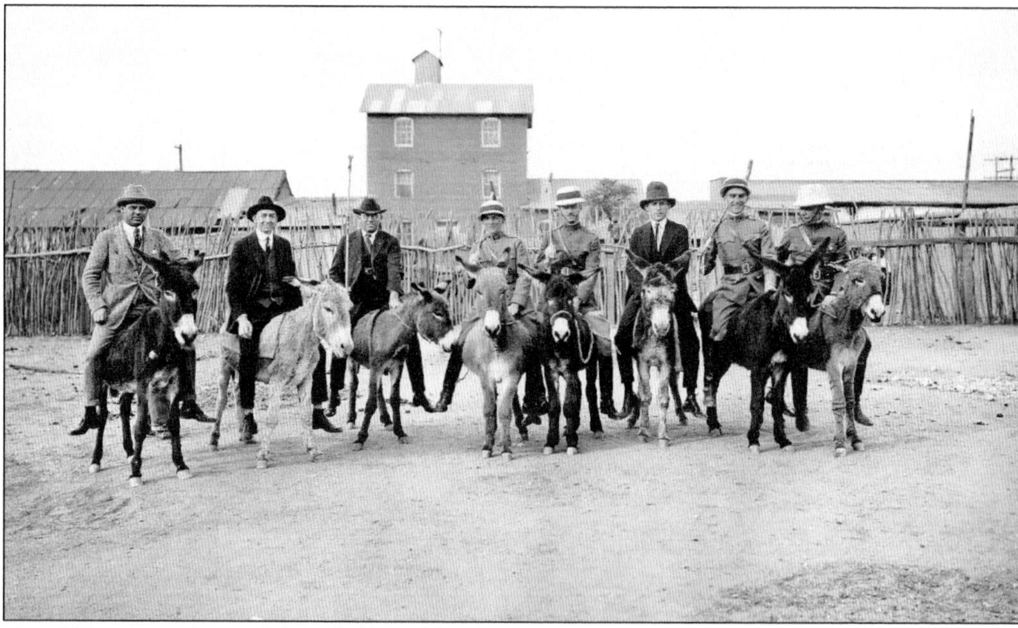

Creed Troutman (second from left) and his unidentified teammates, with long mallets in hand, look ready for a game of "burro polo."

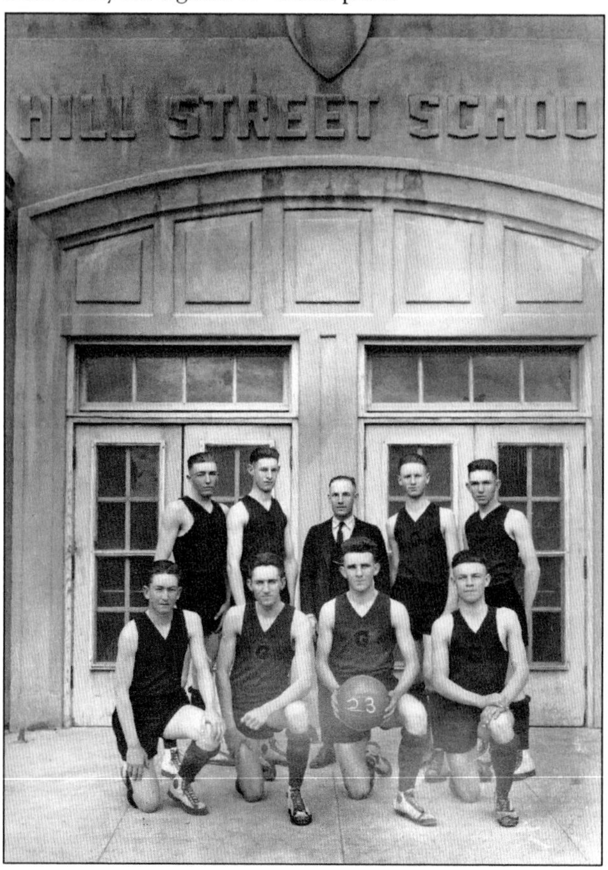

The tall, athletic Globe High School basketball team poses for this team photograph in 1923. Park E. Vickrey was the basketball coach for most of the 1920s.

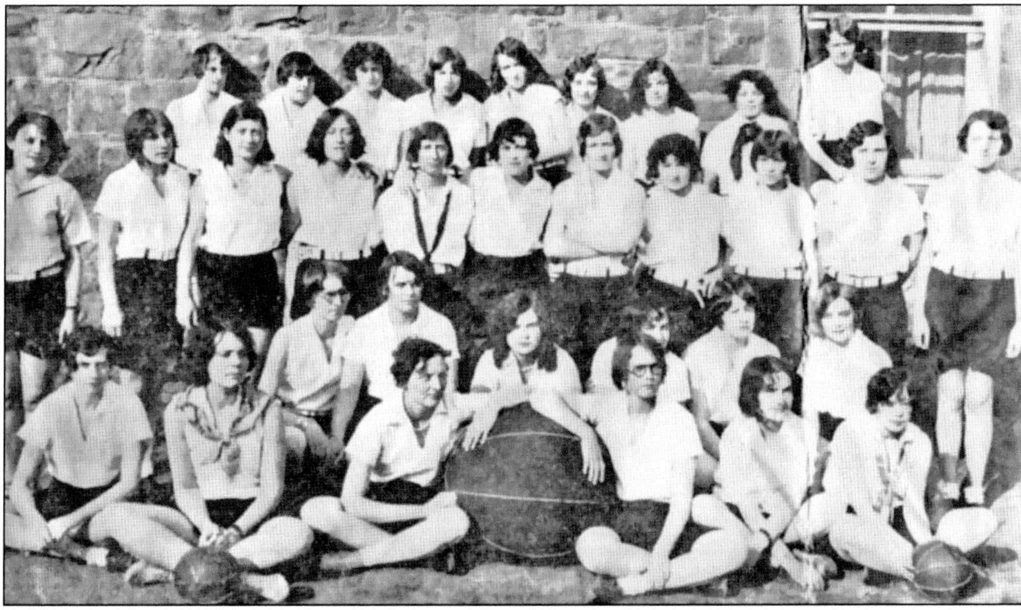

The girls' basketball team at Globe High School came up one game short of winning the state tournament in 1921. After the early 1920s, there was no girls basketball team until 1973. Marie Hachtel is the coach of this group of players.

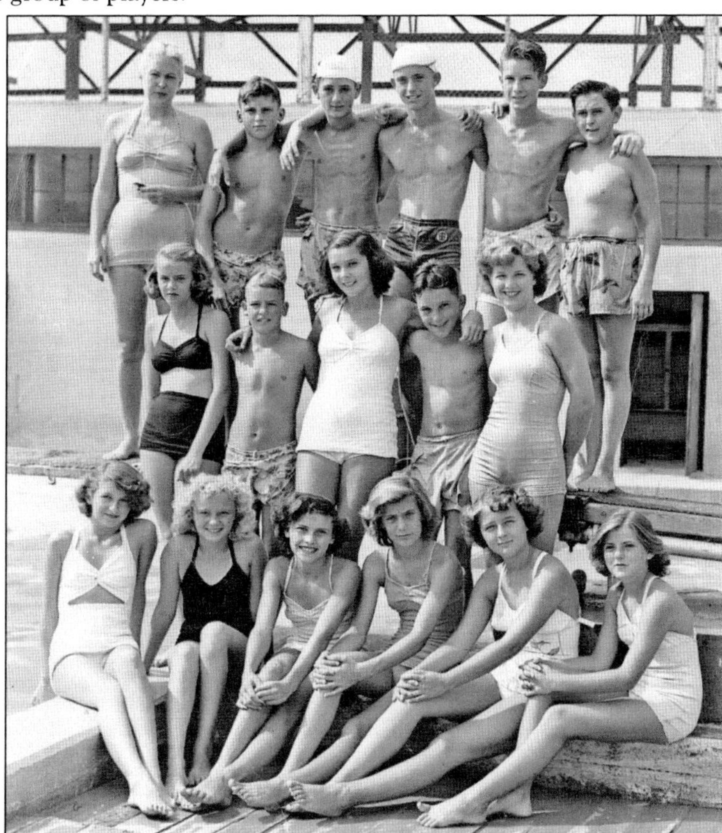

Swimmers pose poolside with their instructor in the 1930s. A competitive swim team known as the Piranhas now represents Globe in swim meets around the state.

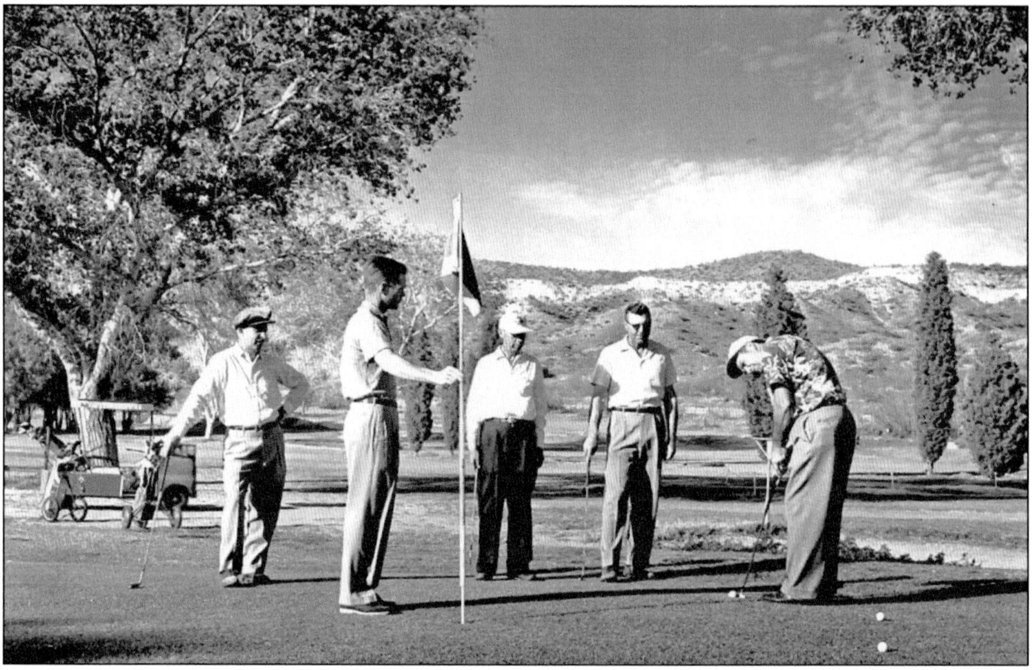

The Cobre Valley Country Club's golf course was laid out on mining company property in 1933. These five golfers are improving their skill on the putting green.

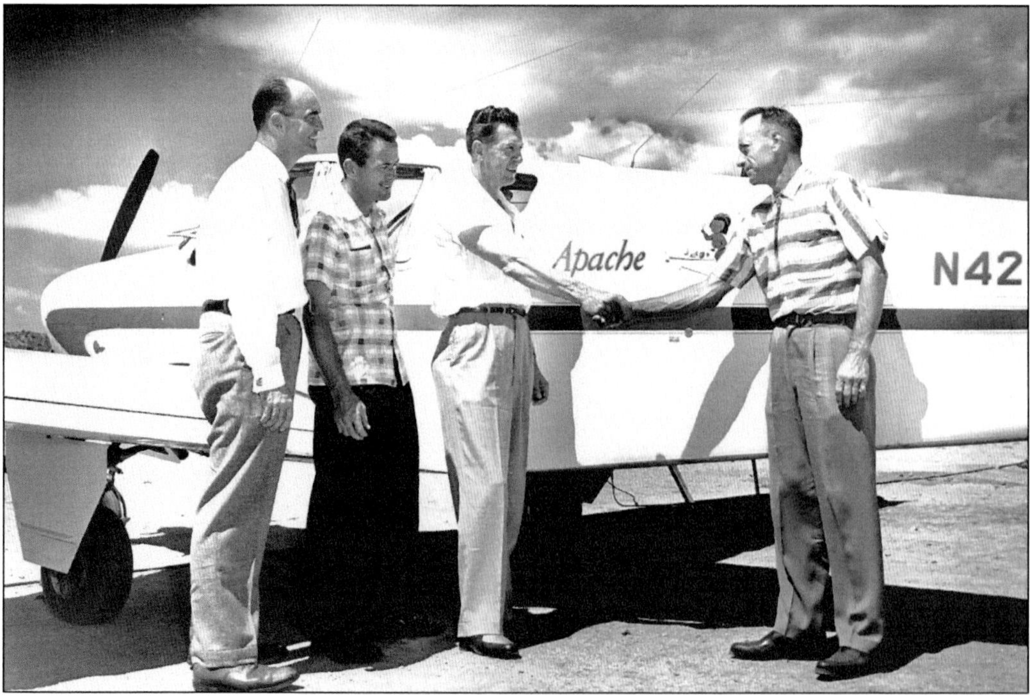

Lt. K. G. Vaughn barnstormed in Globe in the 1920s. Within a few years, Midland City Airport provided air transportation and recreational flying for the people of the Globe area. This 1958 photograph shows Globe's A. V. Hardt (right) with aviation officials at the new Cutter Airport.

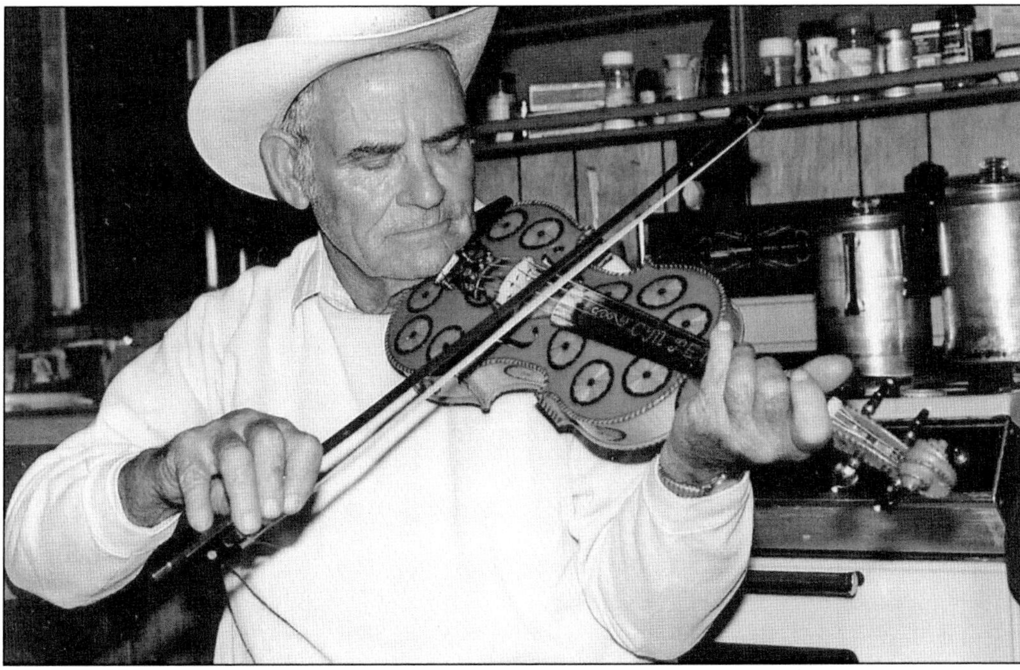

For over 60 years, C. M. Petty has been playing the fiddle at dances, rodeos, trail rides, benefits, weddings, and funerals. In this photograph he is playing a delicately crafted fiddle made by his friend Bob Wallace of Claypool, Arizona.

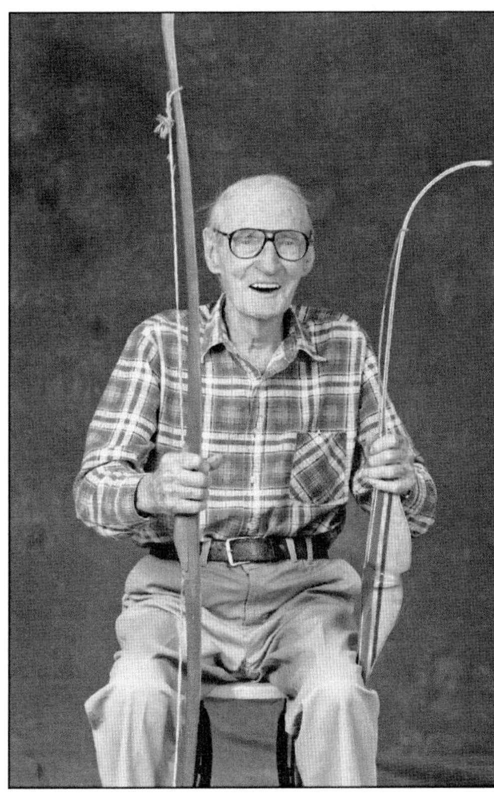

John C. "Red" McLachlan was a champion bow hunter. He won many archery events in Arizona and competed with the best at the national level. McLachlan, a gifted craftsman, made his own bows and arrows. He also taught Boy Scouts and others the arts of archery and bow hunting. (Photograph by Michael Colette Studios, Globe.)

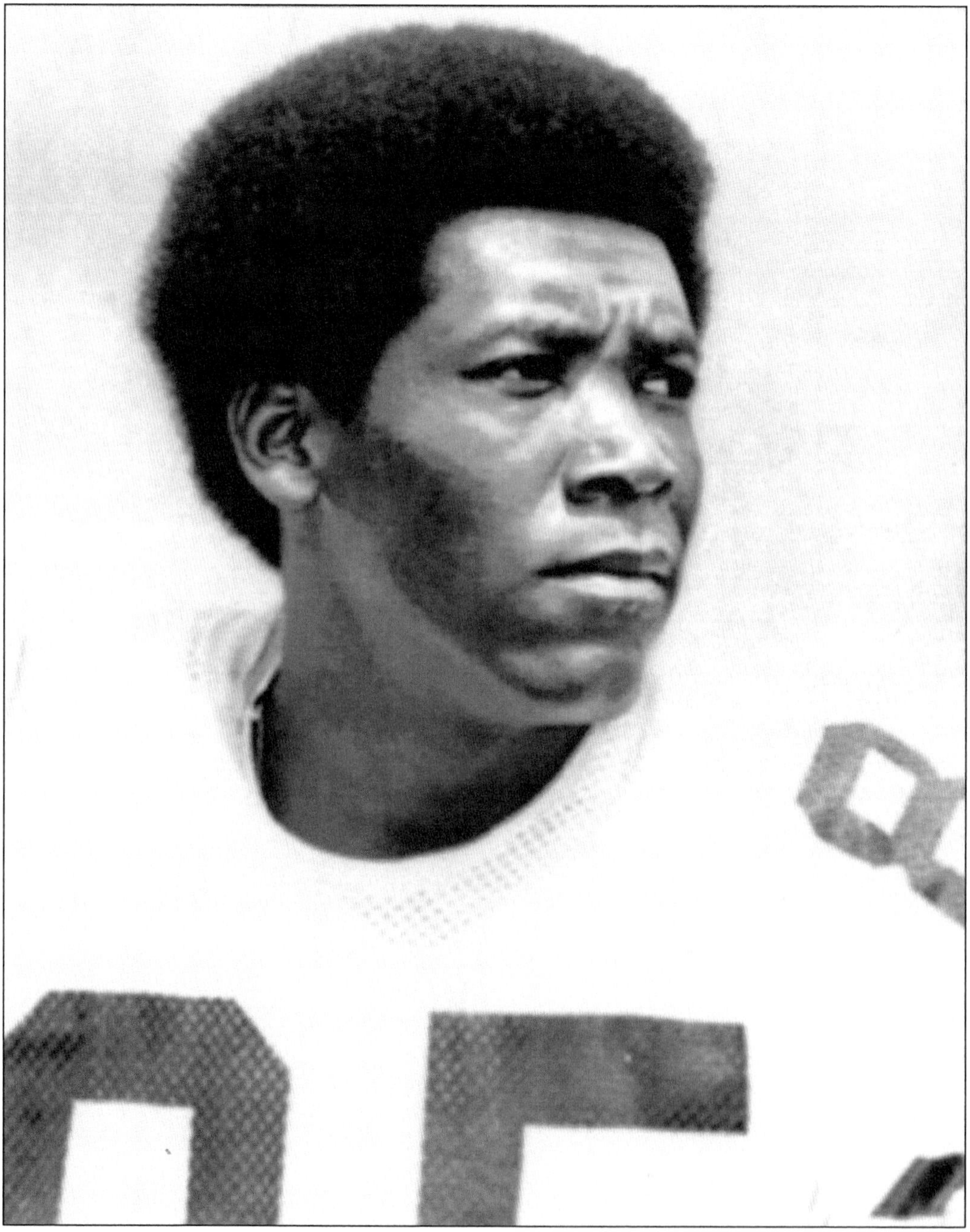

Cephus Weatherspoon attended Globe High School where he lettered in three sports—basketball, football, and track. He graduated in 1967. He attended Mesa Community College in Arizona and Fort Lewis College in Colorado. At Mesa, he was an all-conference basketball player and a two-time All-American in the 440-yard run. He graduated from Fort Lewis College with a bachelor of arts in physical education. Weatherspoon was drafted into the National Football League in 1972 and played for four years on the New Orleans Saints and the Denver Broncos football teams. His business career included pharmaceutical sales, a cleaning service with his brother, and as regional sales representative with Ben and Jerry's.

Seven

The People of Globe

A young and capable miner came to Globe in 1883 seeking employment at the Old Dominion Mine. He spoke little English and could not spell his Polish name, so they called him John Newman and hired him to shovel ore. His fellow workers called him Blackjack. He worked at the mine for awhile and then started prospecting and mining on his own. He became a wealthy man when he discovered, and then sold, several copper claims west of Globe. With his profits, he invested in Globe real estate and made another fortune.

Joseph Cubitto was an Italian jeweler who settled in Globe in 1904. With an $80 tool set, he began a prosperous jewelry business. The Cubitto Jewelry Company remained in the family for over 90 years.

Madam Jenny Scott and her girls were very popular with some of Globe's male population. She was severely criticized by the "better" citizens and occasionally arrested by the sheriff. Madam Jenny's brothel remained in business for well over 30 years.

These representative individuals are just a few of the people who came to Globe from many nations and ethnic groups. One large neighborhood was made up of Cornish families. The men had been tin miners in Cornwall, England, and adapted well to mining copper in Globe. The Cornish families lived on Pascoe Hill and Noftsger Hill in northern Globe and were a stabilizing influence in a sometimes rough town. At one point in time, over half of the workers at the Old Dominion Mine were Cornish men.

Italian stonecutters came to the area to help build Roosevelt Dam. Later they came to Globe and became builders, merchants, grocers, railroad men, and professionals. Joseph Cubitto's friends probably included Domenic Zucco, Angelo Martimbianco, Constantine Giacoma, and the Rabogliatti brothers.

Globe's Chinatown was located behind the stores and shops of North Broad Street. In an area no larger than a couple of square blocks, there were stores, laundries, an opium den, the Chinese Masonic Lodge, and some 200 Chinese people. Most of Globe's Chinese citizens lived and worked there. An exception was Gin Foo Dea, who opened the Sang Tai Restaurant on Broad Street. This fine eatery was operated by Dea and his son George until 1960.

There were more groups—French, Irishmen, Spaniards, Swedes, Slavs, Jews, Mexicans, Germans, and Lebanese—who came together to make up an Arizona community called Globe.

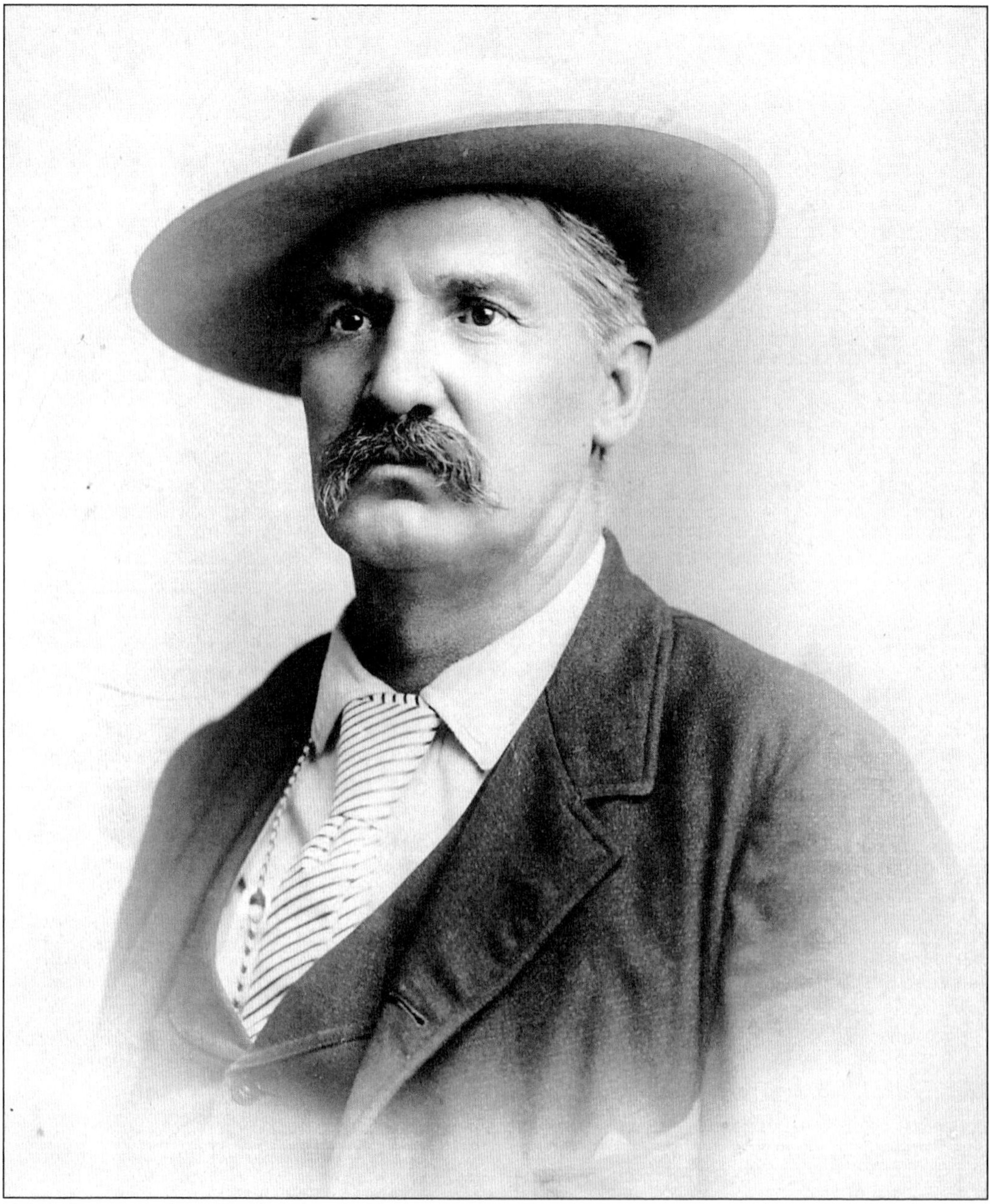

Al Sieber served as chief of the Apache scouts for 20 years. There were two things he liked to do on his time off: prospecting and visiting Globe. His favorite haunt in Globe was the Knox and McNelly's Champion Billiard Hall and Saloon. One cold and rainy night, Seiber led his scouts on an excursion near Globe, and he guided his men to the warm and dry environs of the Champion Saloon where he ordered a shot of whiskey. Lt. James Watson secured permission for them to spend the night in the saloon, and while the scouts bedded down, Watson provided each man with "a stiff drink to ward off the chills." Al Sieber was dismissed from his army contract in 1891, and Globe became his headquarters for the rest of his life. His last job was at Roosevelt where he supervised an Apache construction crew. He was killed there on February 19, 1907, by a falling boulder. His grave is in the Globe cemetery.

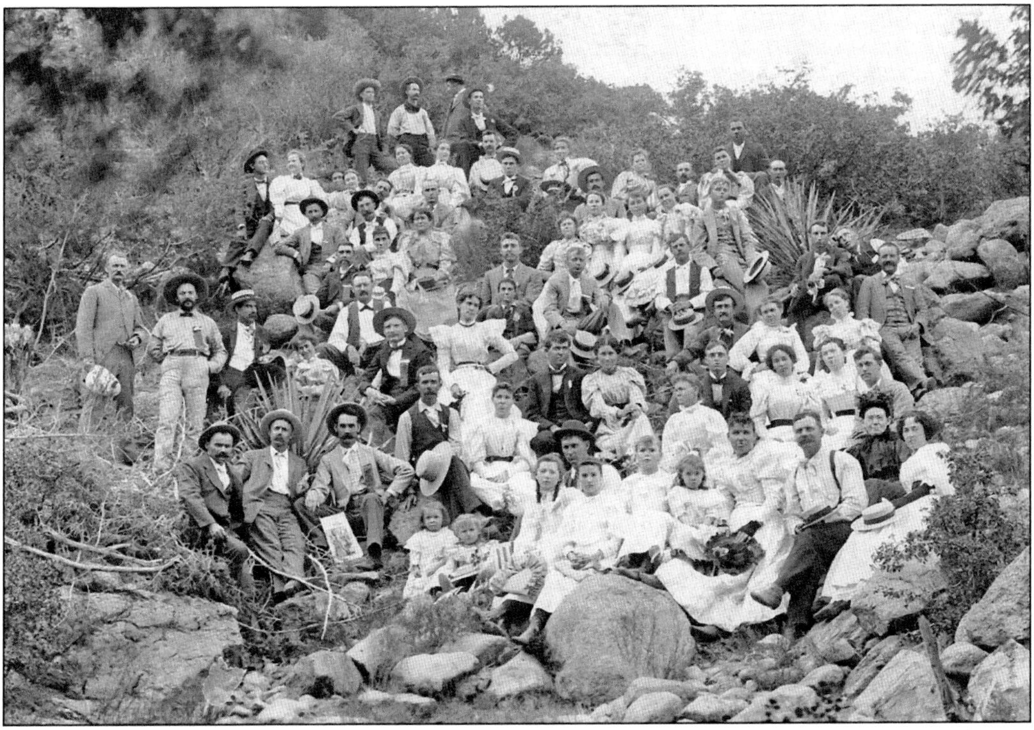

In the museum files this photograph is labeled "Old Timers Picnic." The suits and ties, elegant dresses, and hats suggest a more formal occasion. The ladies' hats are in their laps, and the men's hats are tipped back to show their faces in the photograph.

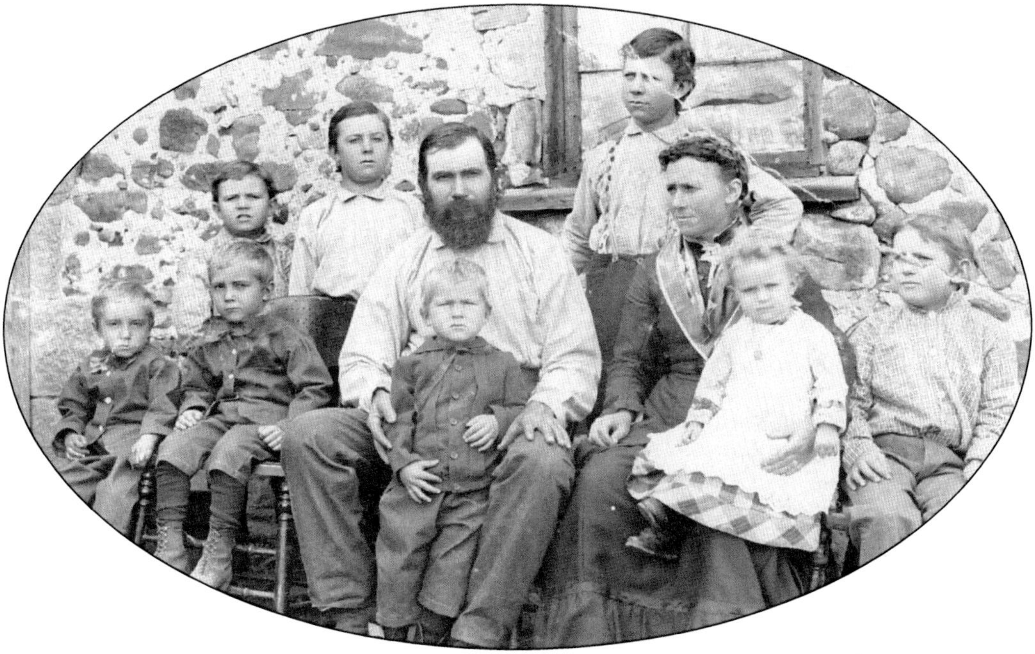

Andre Maurel came to Globe in 1884 driving a horse-drawn buggy. He was a trained stonemason and cut stone for several of Globe's historic buildings, including his own hotel, the Maurel Hotel.

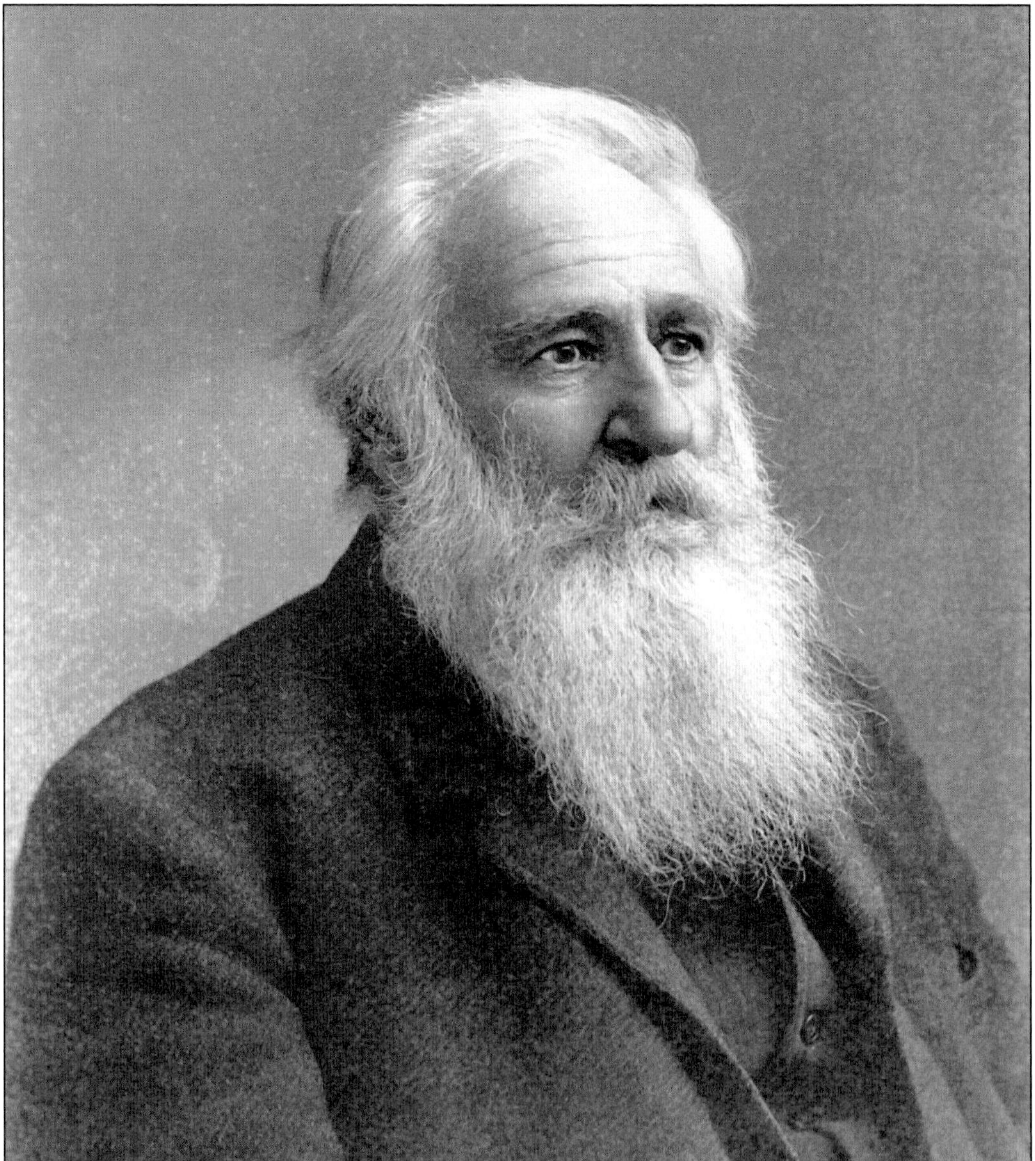

Judge Aaron Hackney received his title as a county commissioner, or judge, in the state of Missouri. He came to Globe with his printing press in 1878. The first issue of his newspaper, the *Arizona Silver Belt*, was issued in May of that year. Hackney wrote the news of the day in flowing, often witty prose promoting the young town and its people and businesses. He was much respected by local readers and newsmen around Arizona. James McClintock, editor of a competing newspaper, called him "a veritable father of the community." Seeing the first train arrive in Globe would have been Hackney's greatest delight, but he suffered a stroke and was unable to attend the historic event. Judge Hackney died on December 2, 1899. The newspaper remembered him for his "life of usefulness and honor."

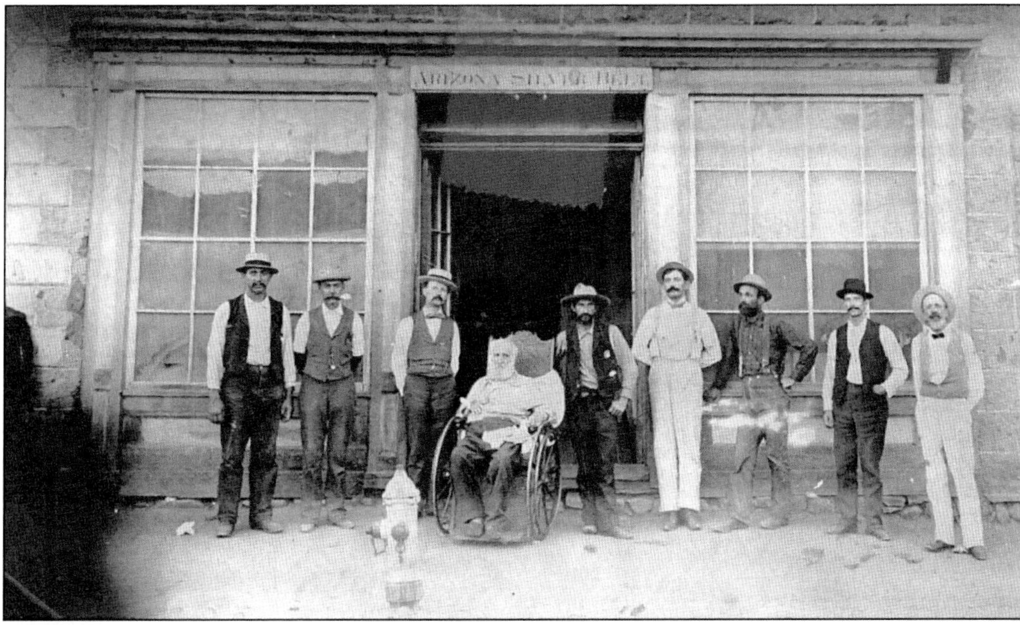

Aaron Hackney is pictured sitting in his "invalid" chair (above). Joseph Hamill stands to his right. Hamill joined his uncle Aaron at the *Arizona Silver Belt* in the early 1880s. He became owner and editor of the newspaper after his uncle's death in 1889. He retired and moved to San Diego in 1907. A few years later, he was back in Globe serving as editor of a new rival, the *Arizona Record*.

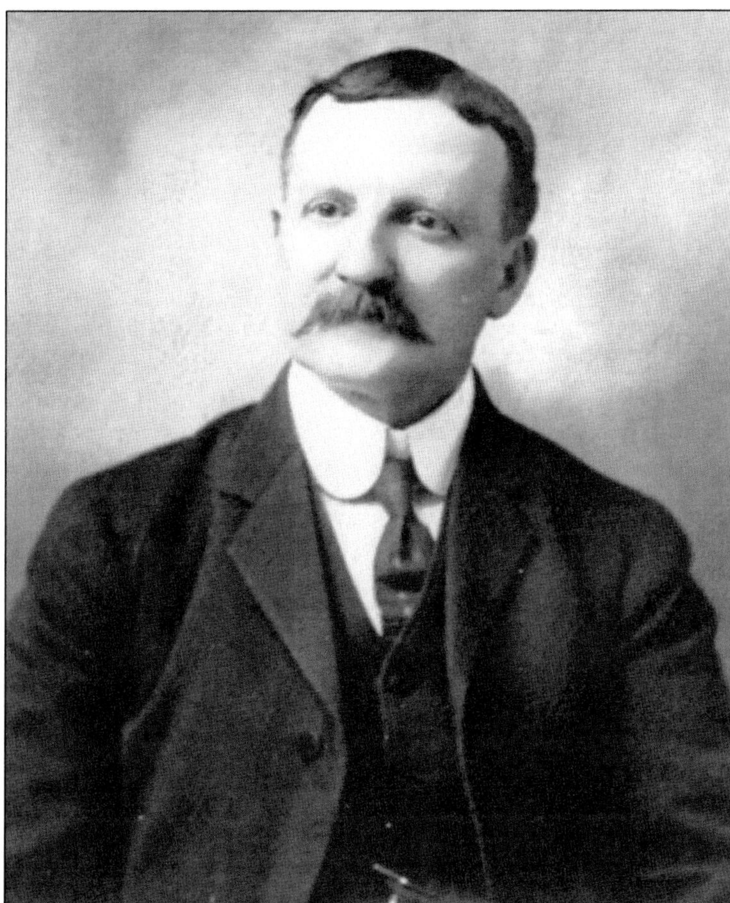

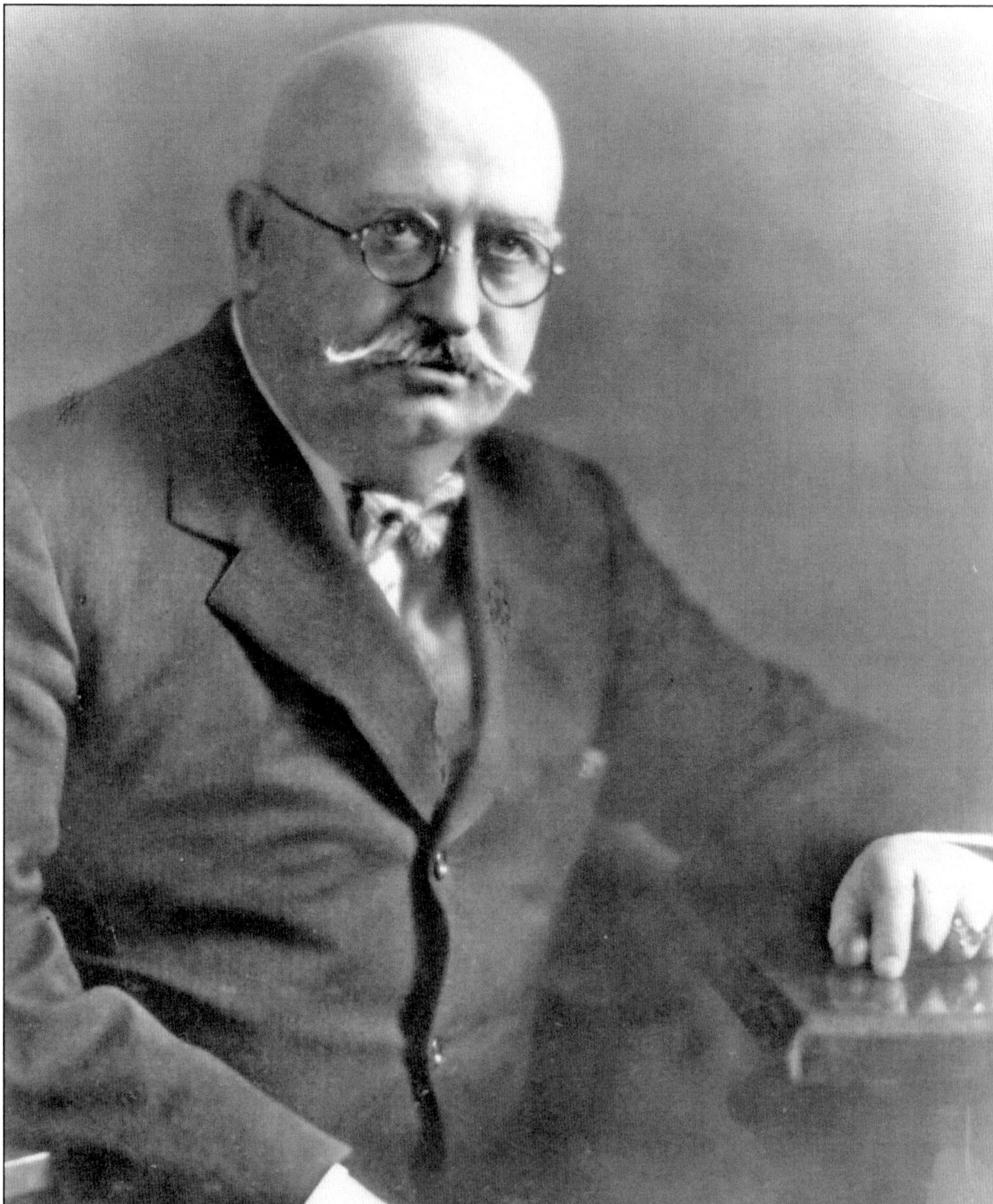

Less than 20 years after his 1881 arrival in Globe, George W. P. Hunt advanced from "slinging hash" at Pasco's Restaurant to the presidency of the Old Dominion Commercial Company. During this time, he became involved in politics. He served seven terms on the Arizona Territorial Legislature and was elected president of the Arizona Constitutional Convention in 1910. Two years later, he became the first governor of the State of Arizona. Hunt sold his Globe business and home and moved permanently to Phoenix, but his sentiments remained in his "beloved Globe." On trips around the state, he often managed to spend time in Globe, visiting old friends and renewing acquaintances, and his election campaigns usually ended in Globe. After some last-minute campaigning, he'd go to the polls to vote. He would then retire to the Kinney House to await the election returns. Hunt said, "It always makes me feel good to get into the old town again."

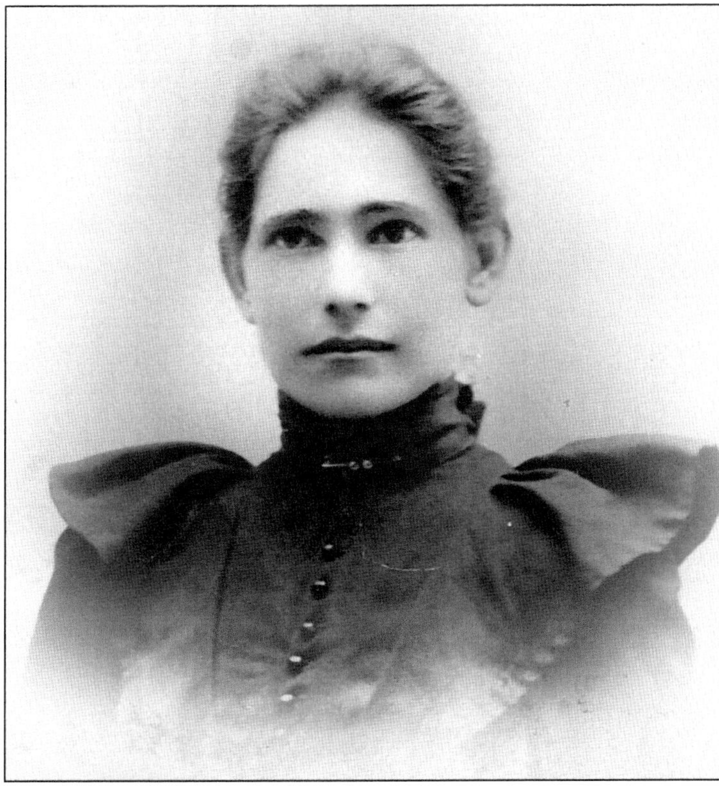

Helen Duett Ellison worked as a cowgirl on the family ranch in northern Gila County. She was just as good as her brothers at riding, roping, and hunting. In 1904, Duett married George W. P. Hunt. For the next 30 years, she lovingly and patiently stood by her husband's side through the sweeping changes in his political career.

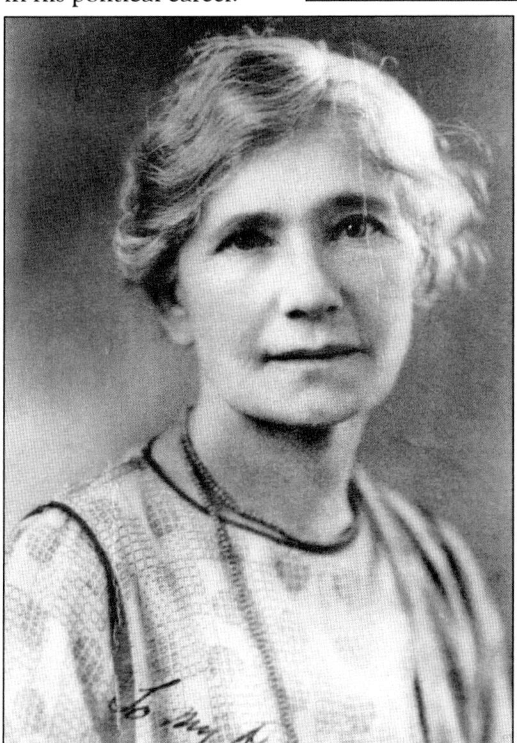

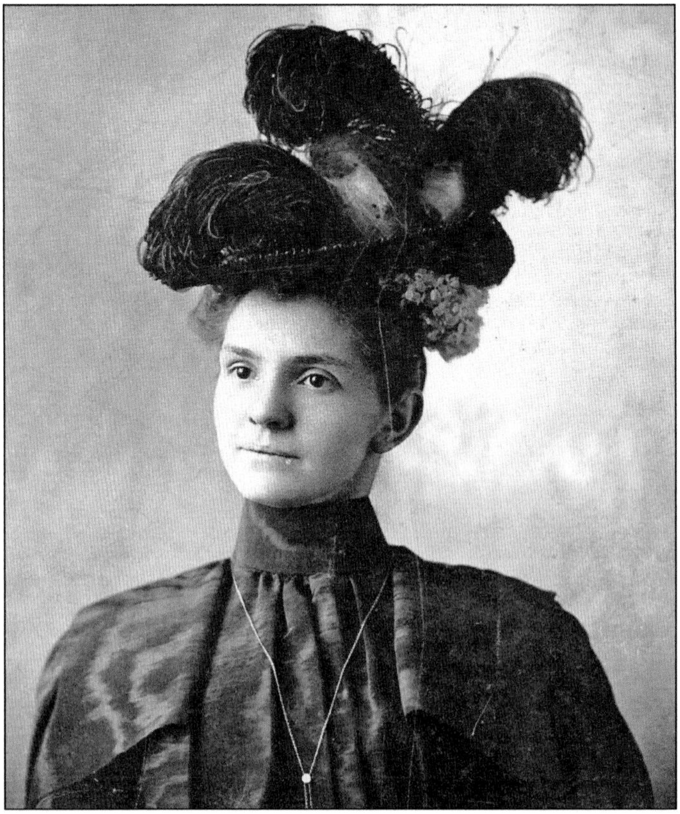

Ladies' hats were hot in Globe 100 years ago! Rose M. Naysmith was probably a good customer at milliners' shops named Whelan, Brown, and Fout.

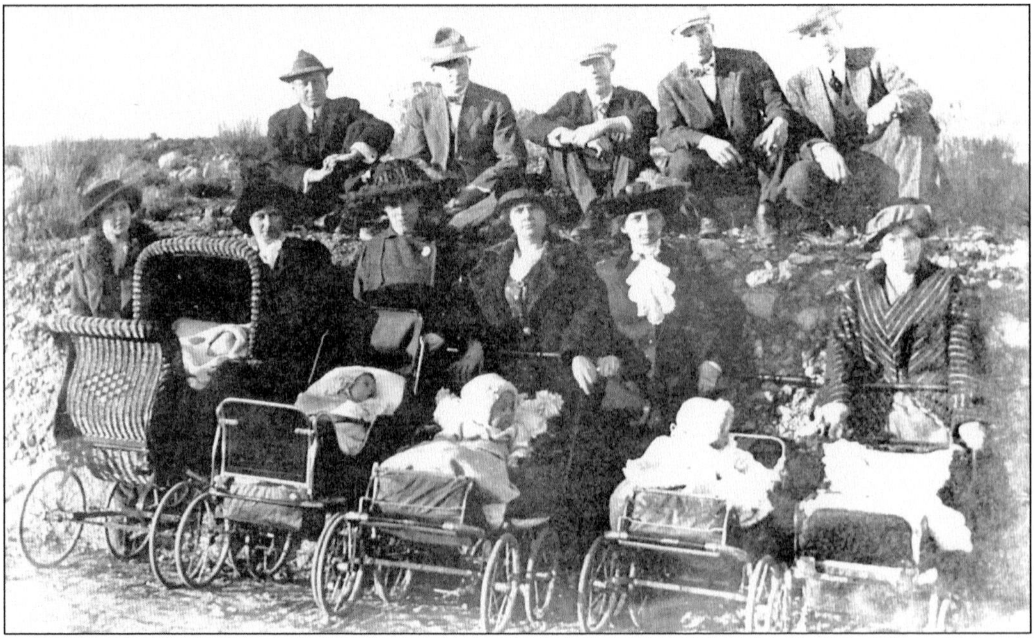

This is a photograph of five Miami Copper Company engineers with their wives and young babies. Only their last names are known: Peyton, Wetmer, Navarro, Scott, and Biggs, in no particular order.

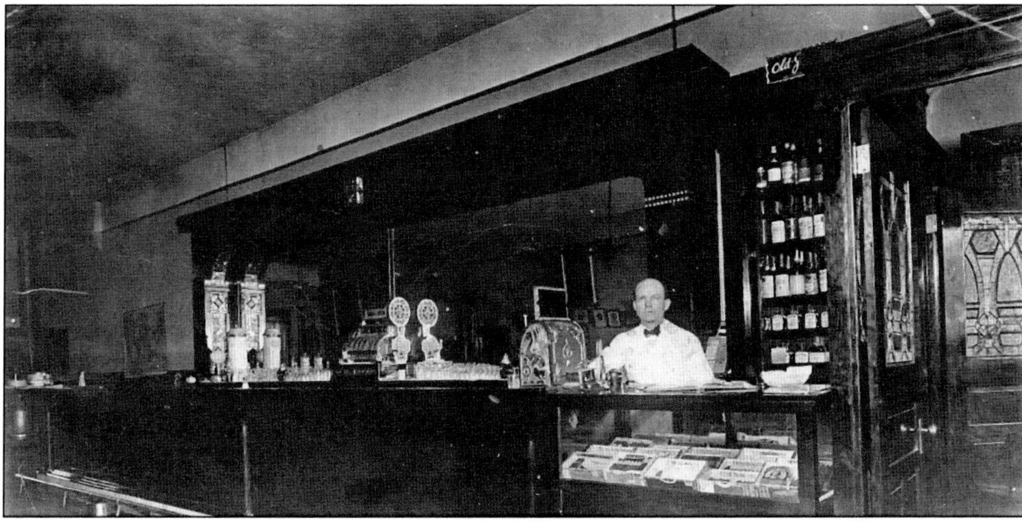

Tending bar at the Van Slyke and Meyers Saloon is co-owner Sol Meyers. The St. Elmo Saloon was next door in the same building. Both had a thriving business.

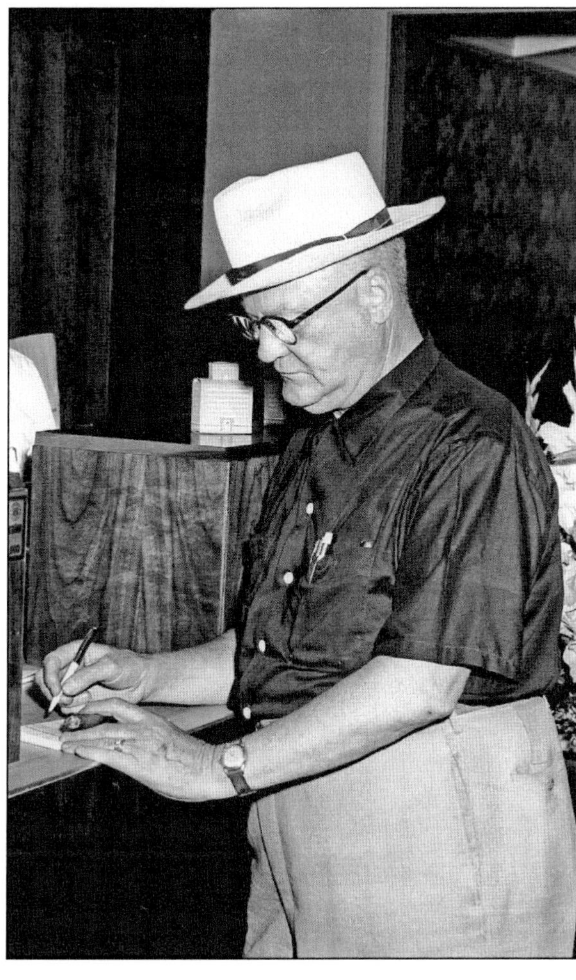

Everyone called him "Sully." William A. Sullivan operated the Mine Supply and Hardware for 48 years and was very active in community projects. As mayor of Globe from 1934 to 1941, he is credited with helping the citizens of Globe get through the years of the Great Depression.

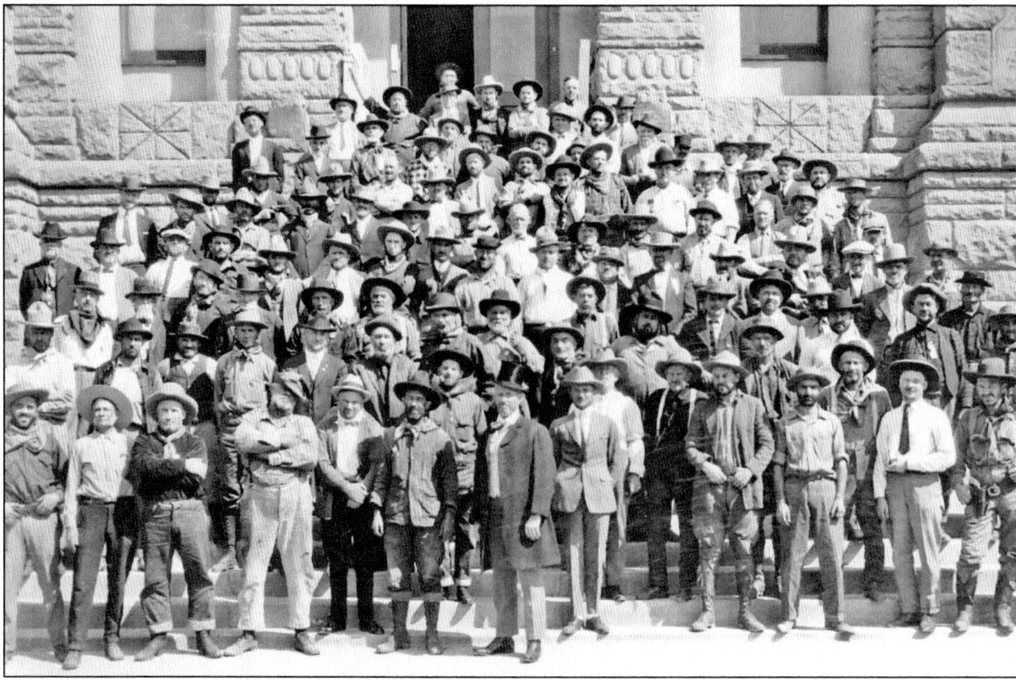

The "49ers" celebration in October 1924 featured a number of special events. The bearded and mustached men were entrants in the "Whiskerino" contest. The rowdy-looking bunch is dressed in 1870s attire, as are the ladies in the photograph below. The lady in the center of the third row took honors for outrageous hats.

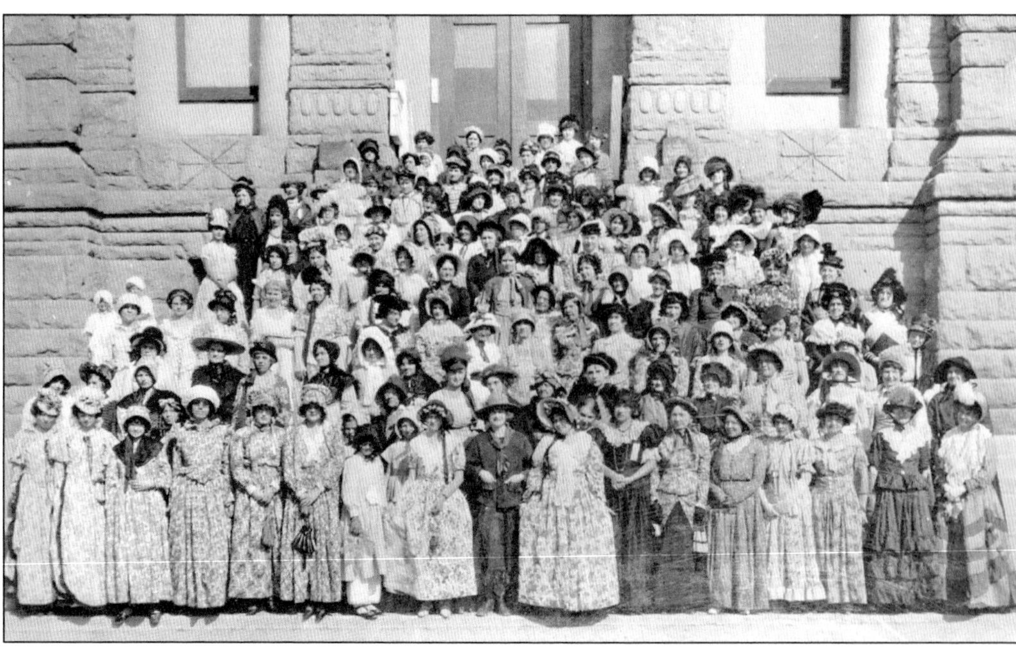

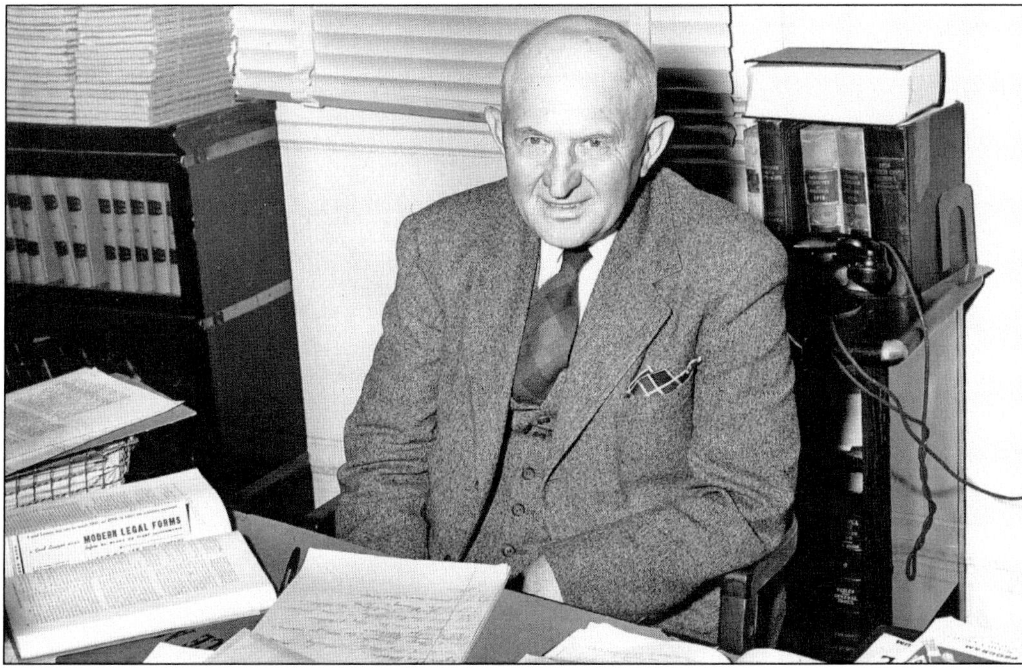

Clifford C. Faires was a private lawyer, an Arizona legislator, the assistant Gila County attorney, and the Globe city attorney before he was elected judge of the Gila County Superior Court in 1923. He was known as a stern but fair judge. Faires retired in 1953 and concentrated on his other interests: fishing, hunting, and golf.

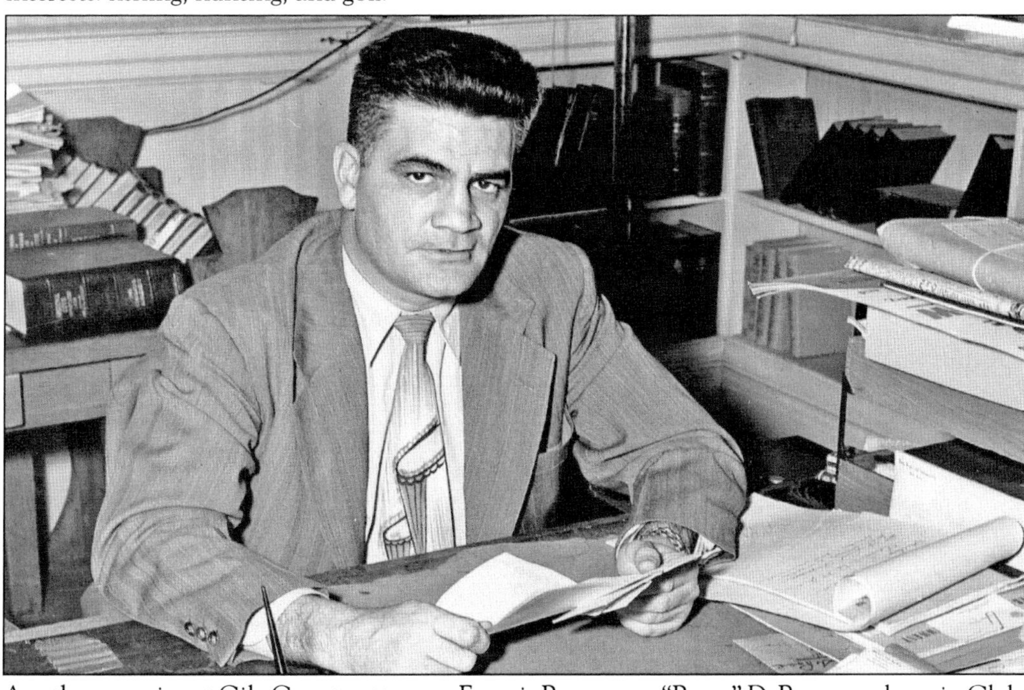

Another prominent Gila County attorney, Francis Barrymore "Barry" DeRose, was born in Globe in 1919. Voters elected him to three terms as county attorney. From 1975 through 1987, he served as judge of the Superior Court of Gila County.

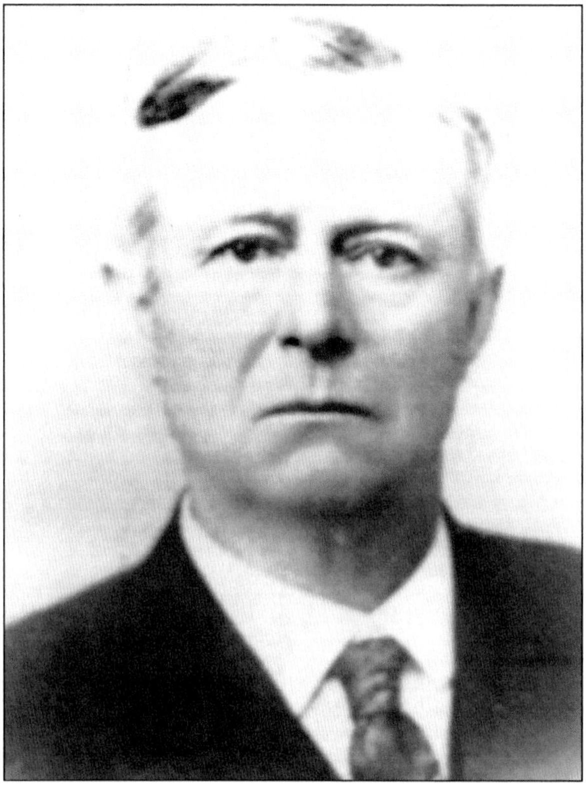

While John W. Wentworth was justice of the peace in Globe, he fined three men $17.50 each for disturbing the peace. Years later one of the men inquired about the 50¢ amount of the fine. Wentworth told him, "It was a fancy assessment to buy drinks for me and the constable." He later spent 35 years as clerk of the Superior Court.

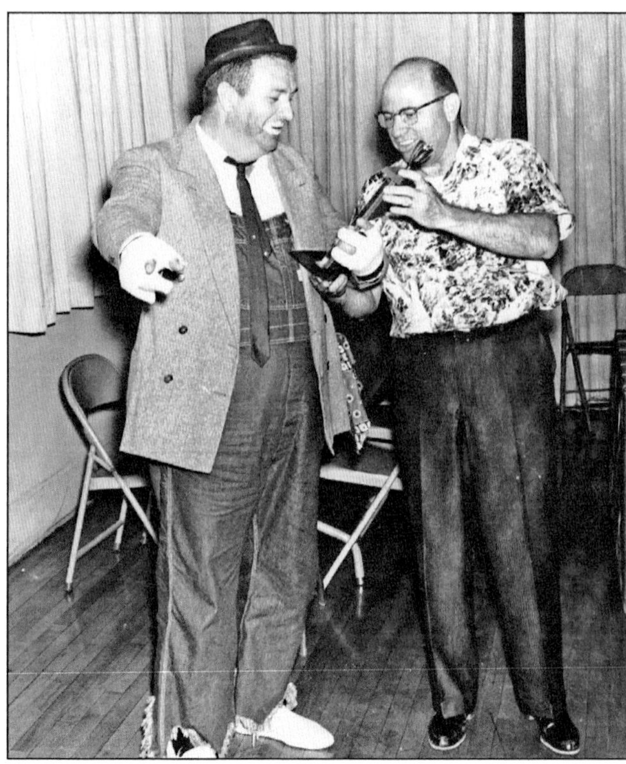

Eugene Rabogliatti presents a trophy to an unidentified clown for an unknown achievement. Rabogliatti, the son of Globe pioneers, was a popular local dentist who served as mayor of Globe for three terms.

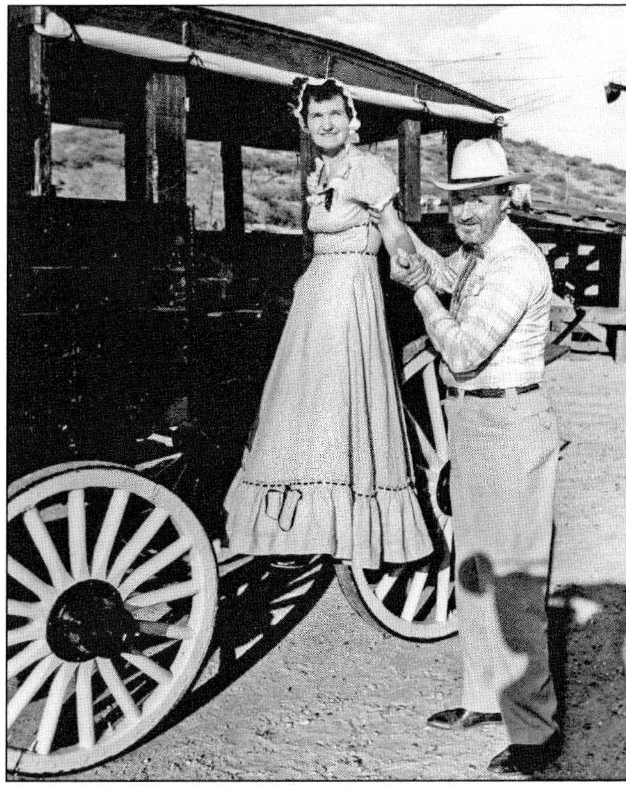

Jess and Stella Hayes pose beside a stagecoach during a Globe celebration. Jess Hayes was a teacher and the Gila County superintendent of schools for most of his 40-year career. He authored three books on Gila County history.

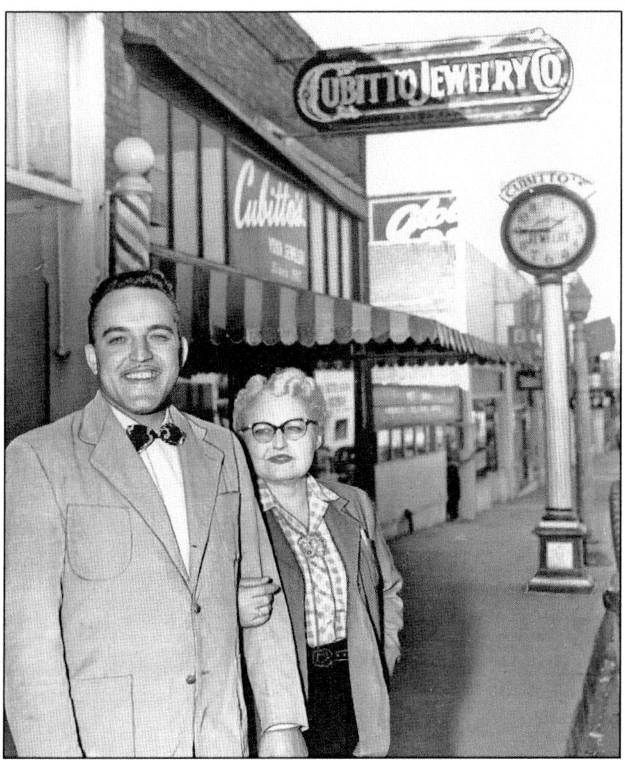

After Joseph Cubitto died in 1946, his wife, Marie; their son Claude D.; and granddaughter Claudia managed the Cubitto Jewelry Company until it went out of business in 1995. Pictured are Claude D. Cubitto and his mother, Marie.

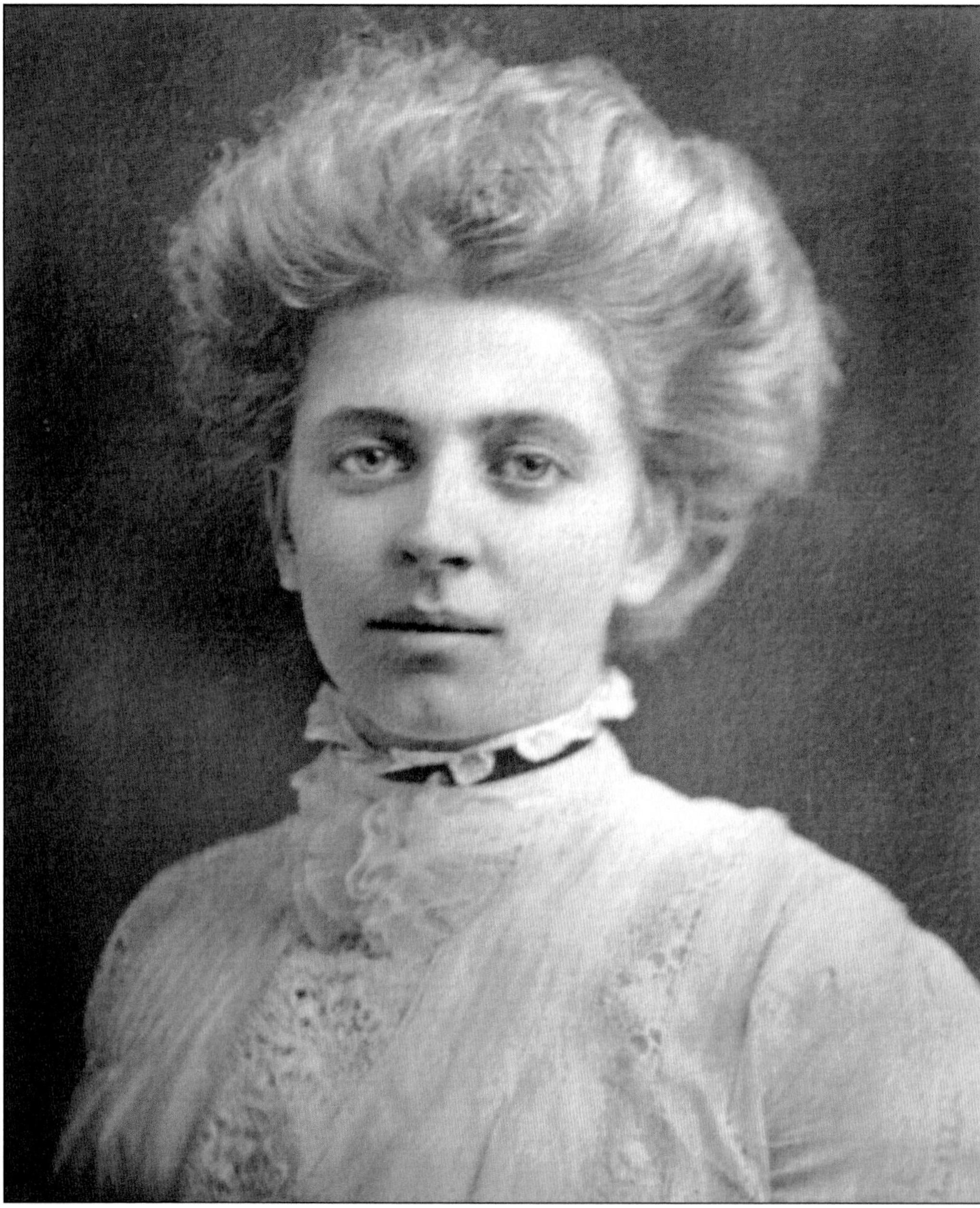

Local historian Clara T. Woody was born in Kansas in 1885. Soon after she came to Globe in 1917, she became interested in Arizona's pioneer history. She gathered historical data from newspapers, records on file at the Gila County Courthouse, and personal interviews. She was instrumental in the founding of the Gila County Archeology and Historical Society and its museum, which was dedicated to her. For many years, she was a member of the board of directors of the Arizona Historical Society. Woody wrote numerous articles for Globe newspapers, and her book *Globe Arizona*, written with Milton Schwartz, was published in 1977. Clara T. Woody's son John, daughter Jean Stiles, and granddaughter Diane Stewart have carried on her interest in local history. All three have been active members and volunteers of the Gila County Historical Society. (Courtesy of Jean Stiles.)

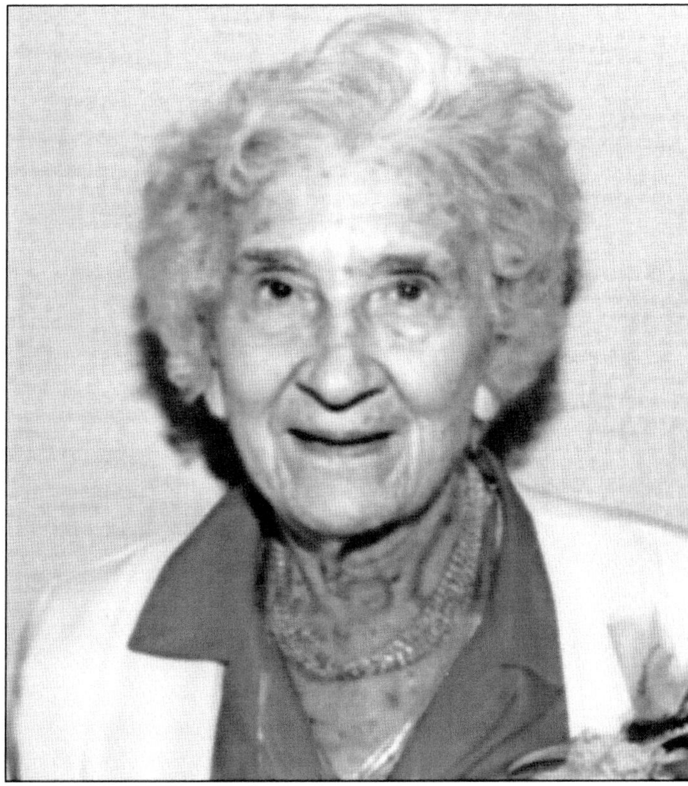

Polly Rosenbaum lived an entire century plus parts of two more. She was born in 1899 and died in 2003. In 1946, she was appointed to fill the term of her late husband in the Arizona House of Representatives. She won every succeeding election until 1994. This photograph was taken for her 100th birthday.

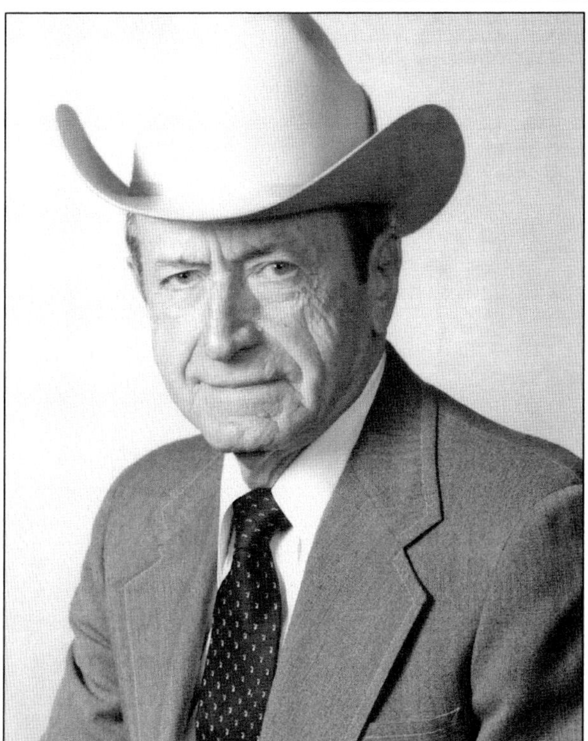

August V. "Bill" Hardt came to Arizona from Texas in 1933. In Globe, he operated a pool hall and a sporting goods store. He served six years as Globe mayor. He was then elected to the Arizona Legislature, where he served two years in the House of Representatives and 28 years in the Senate.

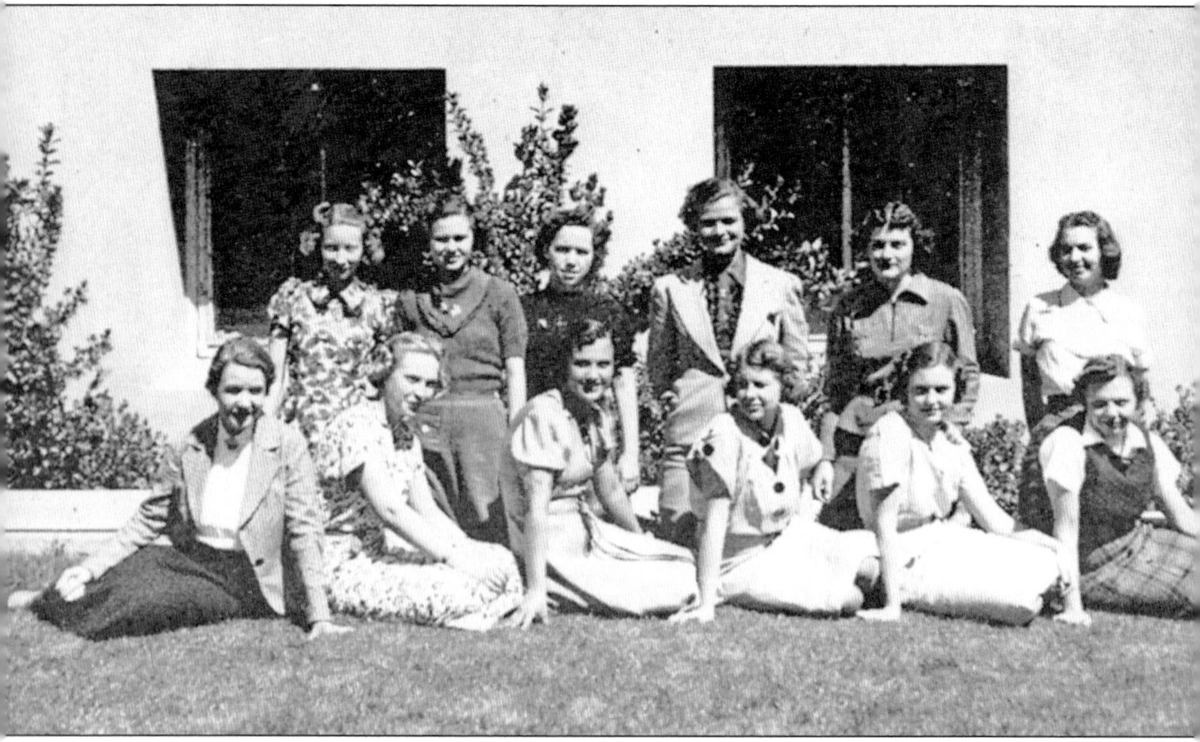

Rose Perica (third from the right, second row) was an all "A" student at Globe High School. She was class president, student body president, and class valedictorian. She excelled in basketball, softball, and tennis. After graduation she played softball with the Cantaloupe Queens, who won a national championship. Perica went to work for the State of Arizona in Phoenix where she eventually became Arizona's secretary of state. During this time, she met and married T. H. Mofford. As secretary of state, Rose Mofford was first in line to succeed the governor. When Gov. Evan Mecham was impeached, Mofford completed his unfinished term of office. Rose Mofford, from Globe, was Arizona's first lady governor.

Eight

Law and Disorder

Someone once wrote that, from a law and order standpoint, Globe was a relatively quiet western town. It is true there was no shoot-out at Globe's O.K. Corral. There was no Black Jack Ketchum, Buckskin Frank Leslie, or Soapy Smith, but there surely were thugs and crimes in Globe. In some respects the town is better remembered for its timely administration of justice.

Some of the most notorious criminal acts occurred some distance from Globe. A pack train was robbed in the Pinal Mountains in 1882, and Globe's beloved Dr. Vail and the Wells Fargo messenger were killed. Zach Booth killed two shepherds at faraway Gisela in 1903. On New Years Day 1907, William Baldwin was arrested near Roosevelt for murdering a mother and her young daughter. William Stewart and John B. Goodwin were convicted of killing two Globe hunters at Tuttle Station on the San Carlos Reservation in 1910. Each of these crimes occurred in Gila County. The sheriff, the jail, the courts, and the gallows were all in Globe.

There were six hangings in Globe; four of them legal. The sheriff directed the hanging of Nah-diz-az, who shot and killed Lt. Seward Mott at San Carlos in 1889. A sheriff also directed the hangings of Zach Booth, William Stewart, and John B. Goodwin. During the night, Sheriff John Henry Thompson and nine of his deputies quietly and quickly shuttled William Baldwin out of town on a railroad handcar to prevent his lynching by an angry crowd. Baldwin was tried, convicted, and hanged in Solomonville.

Many of Globe's adult males were present at the lynching of Lafayette Grime and Curtis Hawley, the men who had signed confessions for the 1882 robbery and murders in the Pinal Mountains. Conspicuously absent was Sheriff William Lowther.

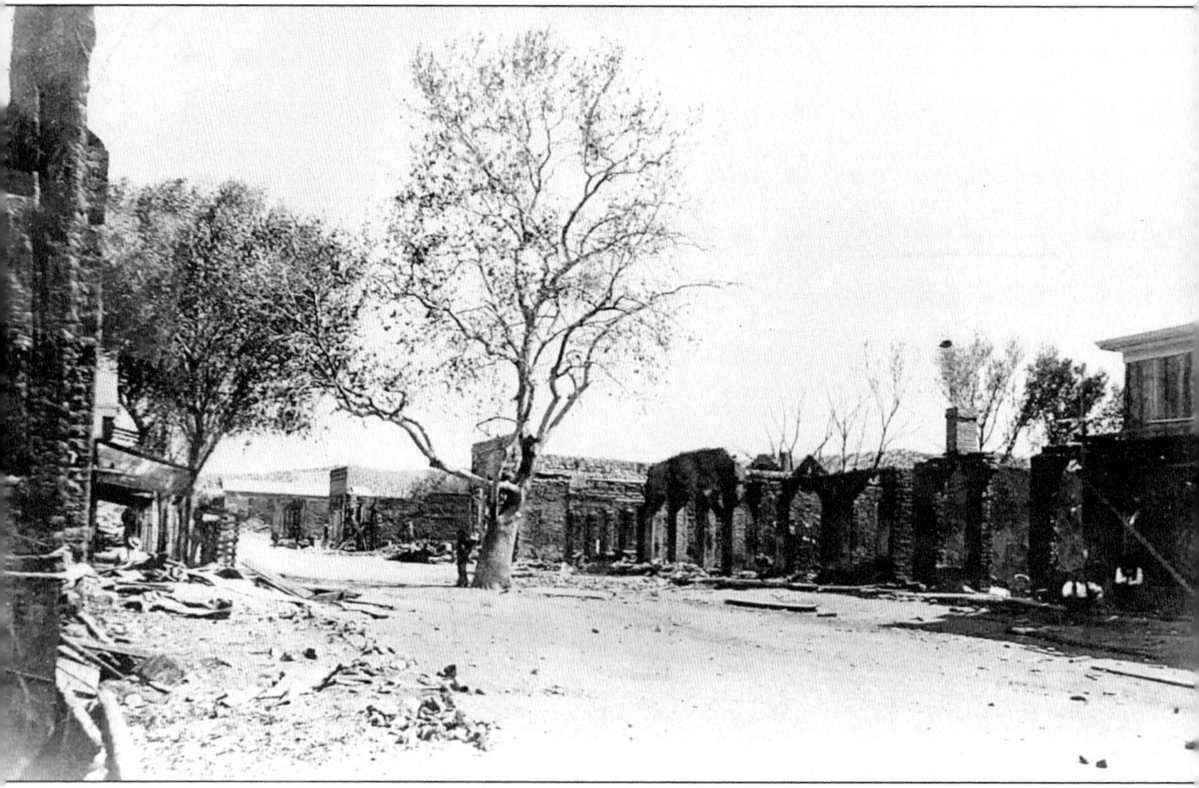

Lafayette Grime and Curtis Hawley were put in the one-room adobe jail to await trial and sentencing for the murders of Dr. Vail and Andy Hall, a Wells Fargo messenger. The people of Globe, however, were eager to expedite the proceedings, and Sheriff William M. Lowther reluctantly turned the suspects over to Judge Allen. A hearing was held at T. C. Stallo's Hall, where the two men signed confessions. Judge Allen then turned them over to the citizens of Globe. The hangings took place on a sycamore tree that stood in the middle of Broad Street. A fire in 1899 destroyed many buildings on North Broad Street as well as the hanging tree, and it was soon cut down. This photograph was taken soon after the fire had burned itself out.

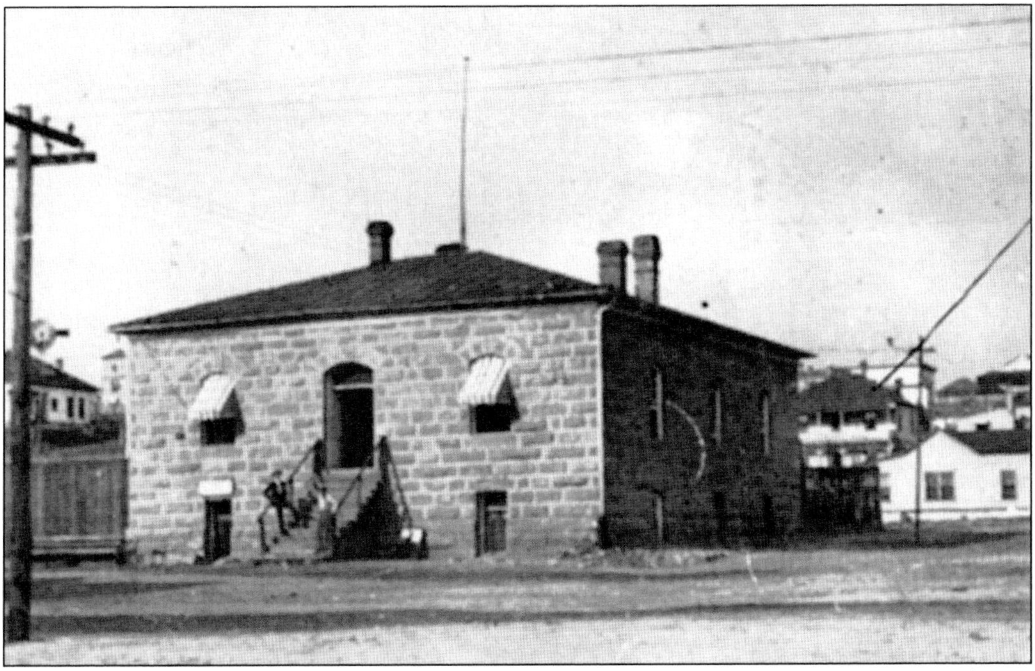

After working out of temporary adobe structures for several years, Gila County built a courthouse in 1888. The sheriff kept his prisoners in basement cells. On four occasions, temporary gallows were put up in the fenced exercise yard.

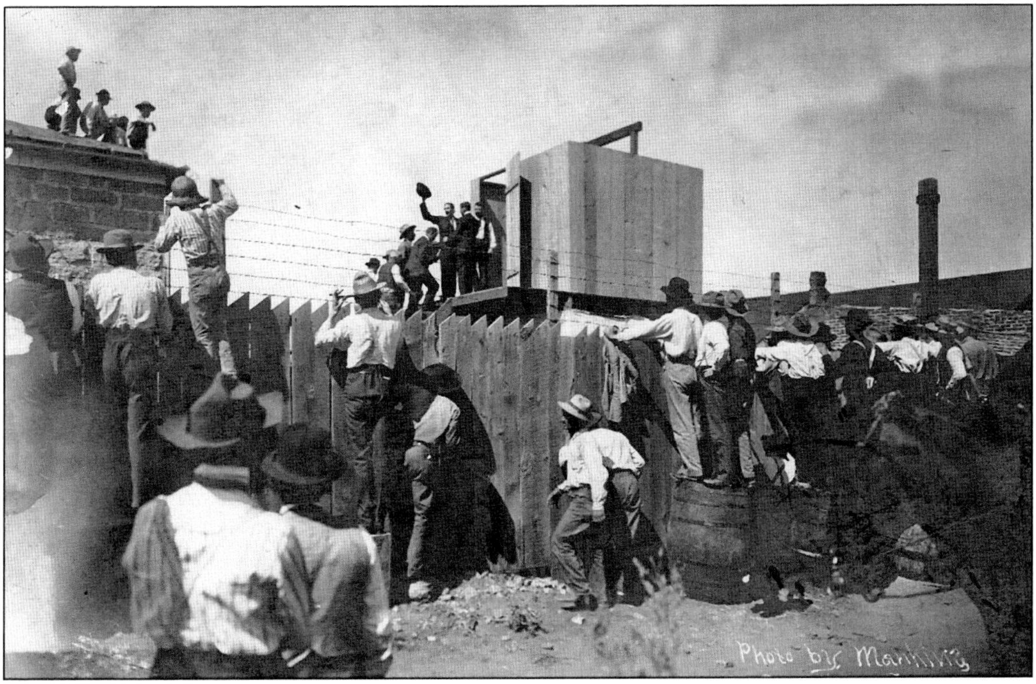

Zach Booth was sentenced to hang for the murder of two shepherds. On September 15, 1905, just before the noose is lowered, Booth waves nonchalantly at the curious crowd of onlookers.

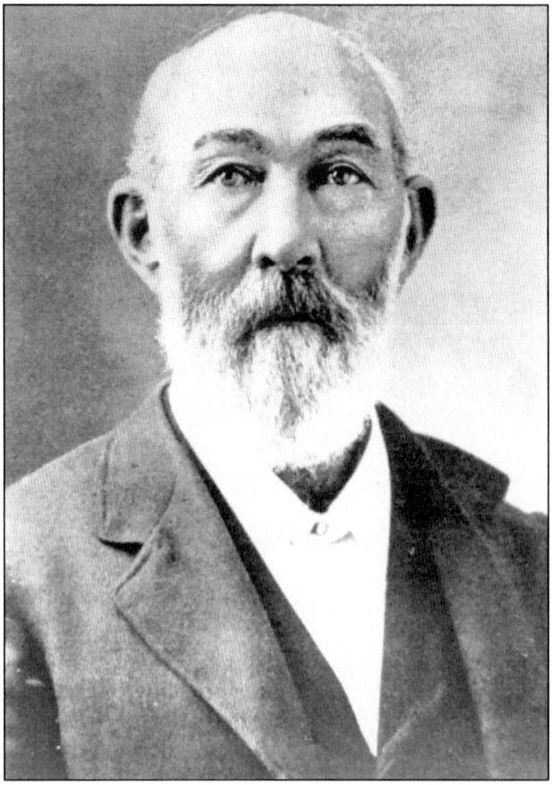

In 1883, several prisoners escaped from the jail by digging under the adobe walls. One of them left Sheriff Ben Pascoe a note, which said, in part, "Thank you for all the kindness and favors. I regret to have to go away but liberty is sweet. We all join in wishing you success in the future."

John Henry Thompson first became sheriff of Gila County in 1890. The voters of Gila County loved that Thompson was tough and persistent and elected him to seven more nonconsecutive terms in office. In 1912, while drinking in a local saloon, Thompson was involved in an altercation during which the bartender was shot and killed. The Gila County Board of Supervisors asked for his resignation. Thompson was acquitted in a jury trial.

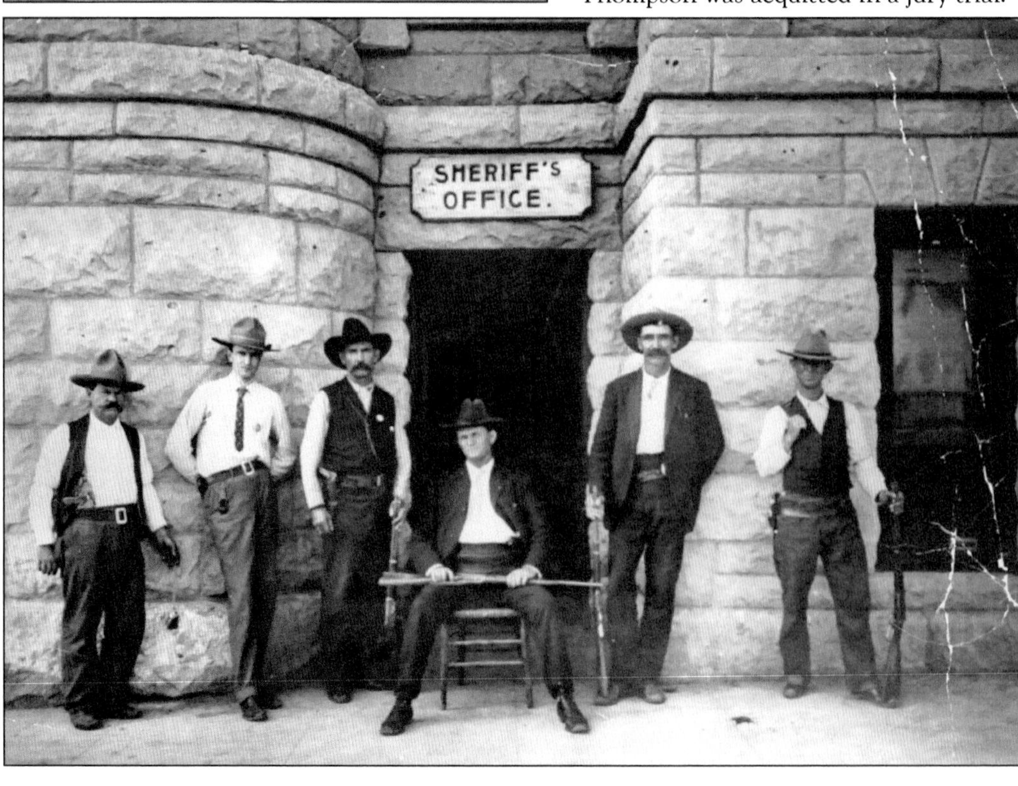

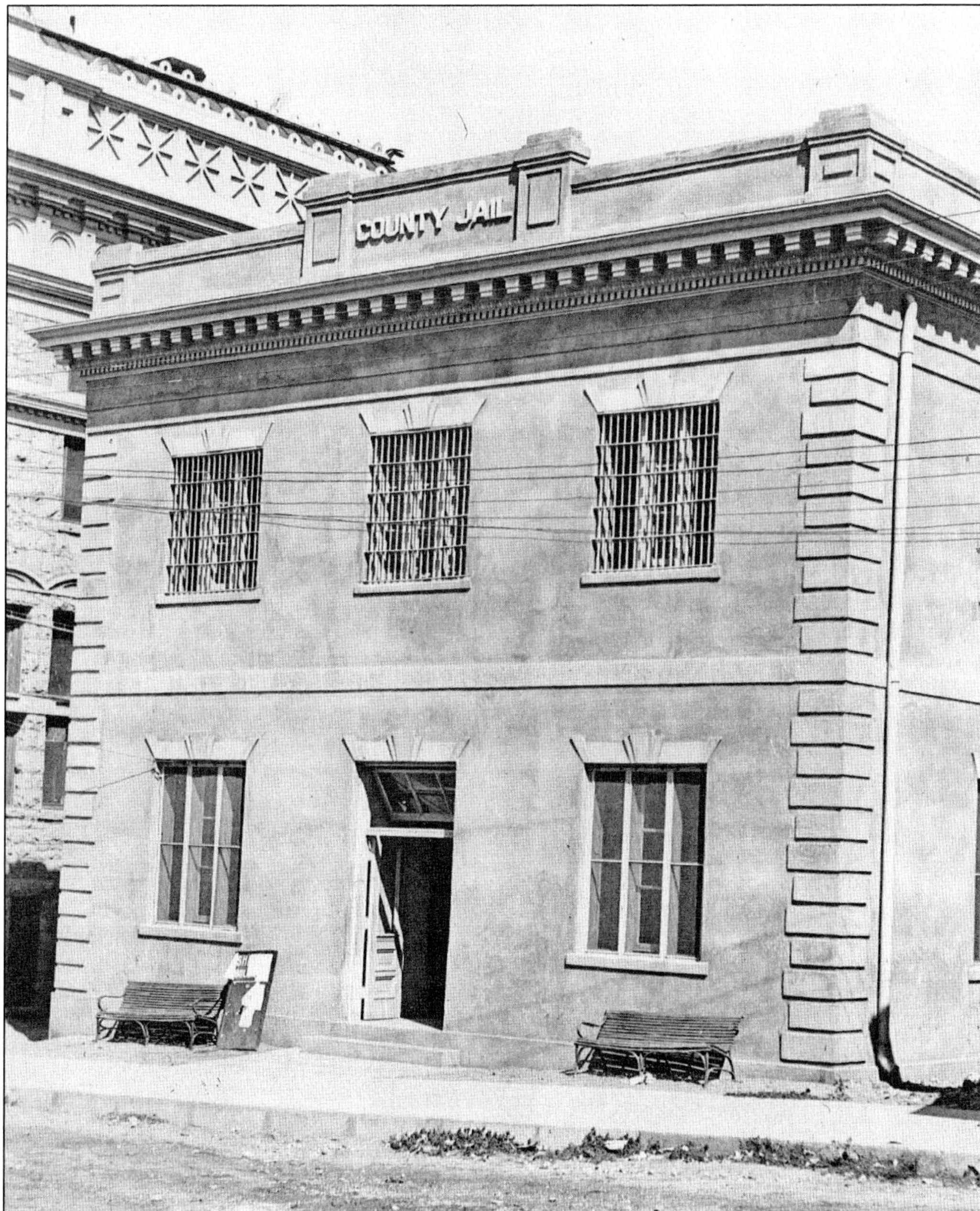

The jail in the new courthouse was too small from the beginning. In 1909, a new county jail was built adjacent to the courthouse. It was constructed of poured concrete, had sturdy barred windows, and was equipped with recycled cells from the Territorial Prison in Yuma. Jails are meant to protect the public from the criminals; sometimes they may also protect the criminals from the public. In June 1910, this system failed though. Kingsley Olds was in jail, having been found responsible for the drowning of two young girls. His cell faced the alley and courthouse next door. During the night, a gunman made his way into the courthouse to the judge's chambers on the third floor. From that window, there was a direct line of sight into Olds's cell. A shot rang out, and Olds died immediately. The gunman was never apprehended.

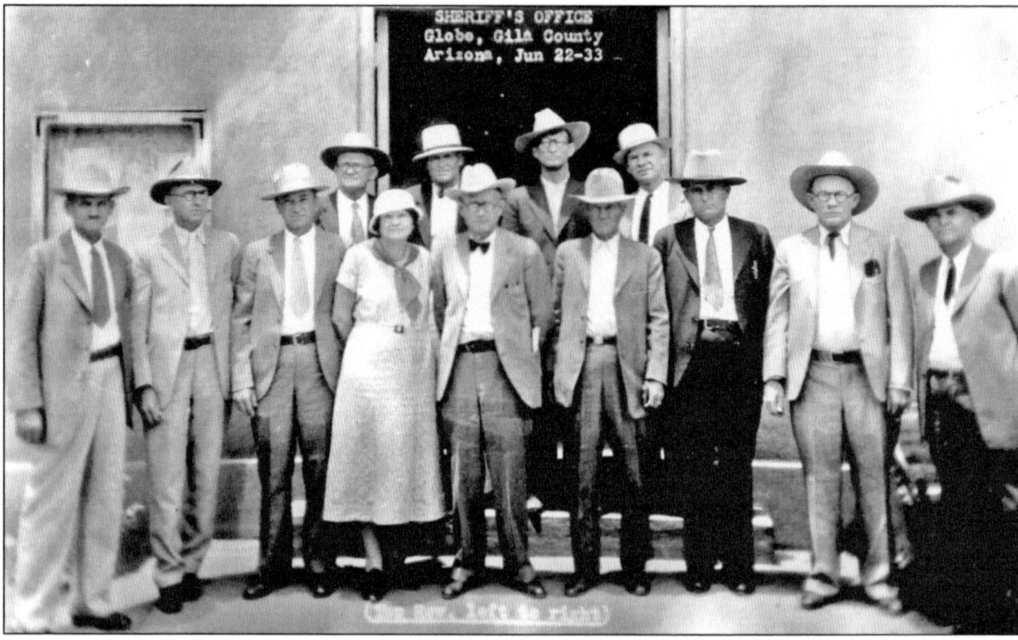

This is the Gila County sheriff's office in 1934. The lady in the front row is Lena Hubbel, the jail matron; to her right is Charles Byrne, sheriff; and in the second row (left) is former sheriff Alf Edwards.

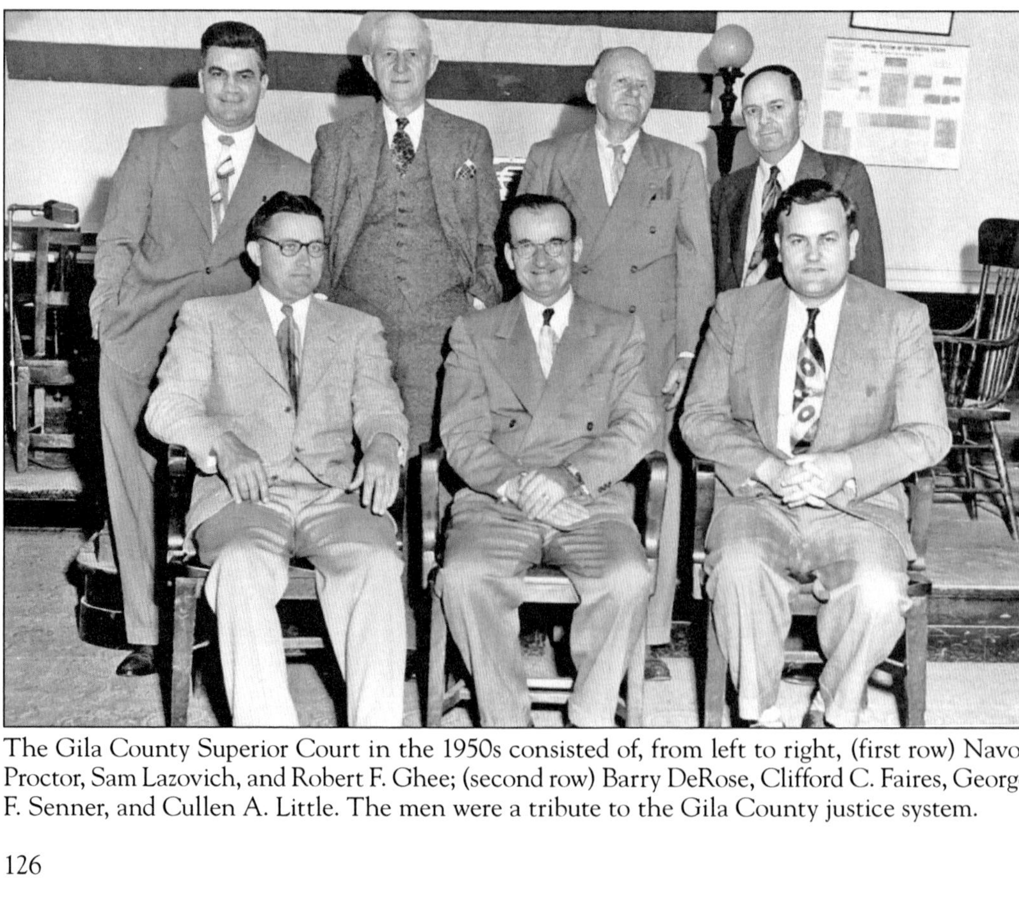

The Gila County Superior Court in the 1950s consisted of, from left to right, (first row) Navor Proctor, Sam Lazovich, and Robert F. Ghee; (second row) Barry DeRose, Clifford C. Faires, George F. Senner, and Cullen A. Little. The men were a tribute to the Gila County justice system.

SELECTED BIBLIOGRAPHY

Anderson, Donna L. *History of Globe, Arizona*. Seattle, WA: Classic Day Publishing, 2007.

———. *Honor the Past—Mold the Future*. Globe, AZ: Gila Centennials, Inc. 1975.

Arizona Silver Belt: Special Mining Edition. Globe: 1910.

Bigando, Robert. *Globe, Arizona: The Life and Times of a Western Mining Town 1864–1917*. Globe, AZ: Mountain Spirit Press, 1989.

Globe Central District Historic Resource Survey. Arizona Historic Preservation Office, 1986.

Haak, Wilbur A. *Globes Historic Buildings*. Globe, AZ: Gila County Historical Society, 1990

———. *Pioneers and Other Characters of Gila County*. Unpublished typescript.

Myrick, David F. *Railroads of Arizona, Volume II*. Berkley, CA: Howell-North Books, 1980.

The Border. Globe, Arizona, Special Edition. Tucson: 1909.

Woody, Clara T., and Milton L. Schwartz. *Globe, Arizona*. Tucson, AZ: Arizona Historical Society, 1977.

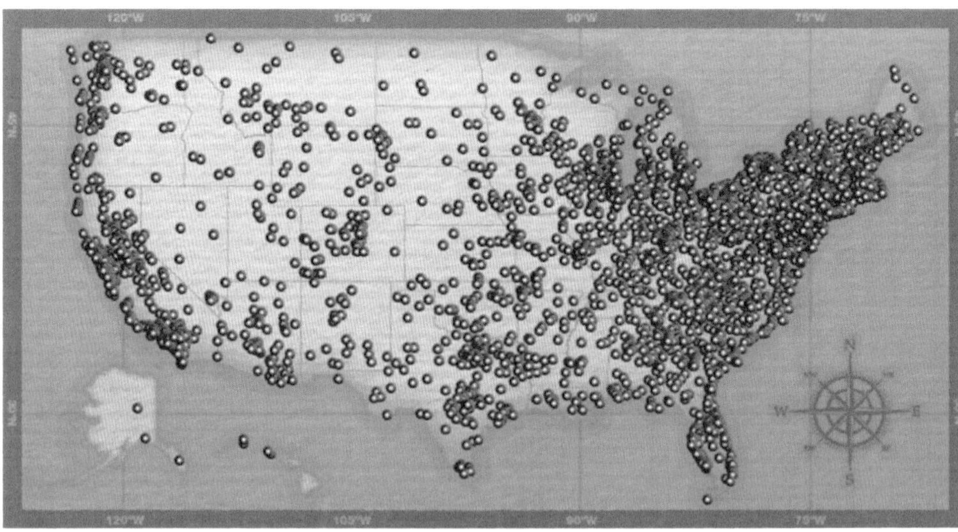

Consistent with our mission to preserve history on a local level, this book was printed in South Carolina on American-made paper and manufactured entirely in the United States. Products carrying the accredited Forest Stewardship Council (FSC) label are printed on 100 percent FSC-certified paper.